SCOTTISH WOMEN'S GOTHIC AND FANTASTIC WRITING

To Liliana and Ludovico, my parents,

With love and gratitude

SCOTTISH WOMEN'S GOTHIC AND FANTASTIC WRITING

FICTION SINCE 1978

Monica Germanà

EDINBURGH UNIVERSITY PRESS

© Monica Germanà, 2010

Edinburgh University Press Ltd
22 George Square, Edinburgh

www.euppublishing.com

Typeset in Sabon and Gill Sans
by Servis Filmsetting Ltd, Stockport, Cheshire, and
printed and bound in Great Britain by
CPI Antony Rowe, Chippenham and Eastbourne

A CIP record for this book is available from the British Library

ISBN 978 0 7486 3764 5 (hardback)

The right of Monica Germanà
to be identified as author of this work
has been asserted in accordance with
the Copyright, Designs and Patents Act 1988.

CONTENTS

ABBREVIATIONS

The following abbreviations will be used in the main text and endnotes after first references:

CK Sian Hayton, *Cells of Knowledge*
HD Sian Hayton, *Hidden Daughters*
TLF Sian Hayton, *The Last Flight*
SE Sigmund Freud, *Standard Edition*

ACKNOWLEDGEMENTS

Although the ideas contained in this book emerge partly from my doctoral thesis 'Re-Working the Magic' (University of Glasgow, 2004), the book would have taken longer to come to life, had it not received the support of numerous colleagues and friends I was lucky to meet at the three institutions that I have worked at. At Roehampton University I would like to thank Laura Peters for the support shown towards my research and career development, Mark Knight, Jane Kingsley-Smith and Clare McManus, without whose encouragement the proposal would not have made it past my desk, and Simon Edwards for the support and interest shown in the early days of my lecturing career. I should also say thank you to Sam Kasule and Anne Wales at the Faculty of Arts, Design and Technology and Paul Bridges, Head of Research at the University of Derby, for the financial support and teaching relief granted to complete two of the chapters included in this volume.

In my current position, at the University of Westminster, I am extremely grateful to Alex Warwick and the Research Committee of the Department of English, Linguistics and Cultural Studies for supporting the progress of this and other research projects. I also wish to thank Simon Avery, Michael Nath, Emily Horton and Anne Witchard, for reading my work, suggesting further resources to underpin its arguments and general good advice; thanks also to Sas Mays, who invited me to deliver a paper at the AHRC seminar on Spiritualism and Technology, and Leigh Wilson, whose contribution at the same seminar proved very useful for the development of my own reading of spectrality.

I am also grateful to Arnot Macdonald and Margaret MacKay at the School of Scottish Studies of the University of Edinburgh, Gary West for recommending its library and archive, and to the authors Margaret Elphinstone, Alison Fell, Sian Hayton, Ali Smith and Alice Thompson, for the interviews that helped the development of my doctoral thesis. Thanks also to the commissioning editor at Edinburgh University Press, Jackie Jones, for her supportive enthusiasm and tolerant patience.

Last, but certainly not least, I am most grateful to Liam Murray, for giving life to Usbathaden's family tree, and his ongoing support throughout the book's lengthy gestation.

Chapter 1

MEET THE OTHERS: AN INTRODUCTION TO NATION, GENDER AND GENRE

For most of our history, [. . .] our narrative tastes have been for the epic
adventure, the romantic quest, the fantastic voyage, the magical mystery.[1]

Veronica Hollinger

We live in Gothic times.[2]

Angela Carter

FOREWORD

The last two decades of the twentieth century were significantly regarded as
a regenerative phase for literature produced in Scotland: the 'New Scottish
Renaissance' was marked by the establishment of key authors such as Alasdair
Gray, Edwin Morgan and James Kelman, and the rise of a literary avant-garde
including Iain Banks, Irvine Welsh and Alan Warner. The last twenty years
of the century also witnessed the development of Scottish studies as a new
academic field pioneered by the critical works of Cairns Craig, Ian Duncan,
Douglas Gifford and Murray Pittock, accompanied by an increased interest
in Scottish women's writing explored thoroughly for the first time by Douglas
Gifford and Dorothy McMillan's *A History of Scottish Women's Writing*
(1997); parallel to the scholarly effort to unveil an existing women's literary
tradition, Scotland witnessed the consolidation and establishment of literary
figures such as Liz Lochhead, Kathleen Jamie, Janice Galloway and, more

recently, the emergence of important writers such as Ali Smith, A. L. Kennedy, Louise Welsh and Denise Mina, whose voices have already achieved national and international recognition.

This climate of rejuvenation has been a fertile ground for the re-born fascination with the supernatural, identified as one of the prominent trends in the literary production of the late twentieth century: 'major changes took place throughout the 1980s', when the Scottish literary production showed, 'a new kind of imaginative relationship [. . .] which refused to accept a simple realism of generally bleak and economically deprived urban character'.[3] Although fantasy has virtually never been absent from the Scottish canon, the last twenty years of the twentieth century registered a manifest 'return' to a genre temporarily overshadowed by the Scottish realism of the 1960s and 1970s, launching a new phase marked by the publication of Gray's *Lanark* (1981).

In this context, this book proposes an earlier date for the 'fantastic revival', and begins its investigation in 1978, the publication date of Emma Tennant's *The Bad Sister*. As the first critical work to bring together contemporary women's writing and the Scottish fantasy tradition, this study pioneers an in-depth investigation of largely neglected texts – Ali Smith's *Hotel World* (2001), Alice Thompson's *Pandora's Box* (1998), Alison's Fell's *The Mistress of Lilliput* (1999) – as well as offering new readings of critically acclaimed texts such as Tennant's *Two Women of London: The Strange Case of Ms Jekyll and Mrs Hyde* (1989), A. L. Kennedy's *So I Am Glad* (1995), and Kate Atkinson's *Behind the Scenes at the Museum* (1995). Underlying the broad scope of this project are the links – both explicit and implicit – established between the examined texts and the Scottish fantasy canon. Firstly, evident bonds with the Scottish tradition emerge in those texts that engage in an overt dialogue with literary precedents, in the forms of rewriting, parody or extensive transtextuality, as exemplified by Tennant's rewritings of James Hogg's *The Private Memoirs and Confessions of a Justified Sinner* (1824) and Robert Louis Stevenson's *Strange Case of Dr Jekyll and Mr Hyde* (1886) in *The Bad Sister* and *Two Women of London*. Secondly, the representative strategies discussed in relation to the four thematic areas (quests and other worlds, witches, doubles and ghosts) in the following chapters point to a distinctively Scottish blend of supernatural and psychological elements: 'Scots fantasy is inward-looking', Colin Manlove reminds us, 'concerned to discover something within'.[4] The Scottish supernatural does not belong in a transcendent other world, but challenges the stable boundaries of seen and unseen, real and imagined, same and other; overarching the selected texts is the deployment of four supernatural motifs as manifestations of 'otherness', pointing to the uncanny coalescence of the unfamiliar within the familiar, as theorised by Sigmund Freud in his seminal essay on 'The Uncanny' (1919). The articulation of repressed secrets and desire emerges crucially in works such as Smith's *The Accidental* (2005) and Atkinson's *Behind the Scenes at the Museum* (1995).

Having established a connection with a distinctively Scottish context, the selected texts simultaneously break from the past tradition and reveal points of departure through their engagement with feminist and postmodernist discourses. In relation to gender, many of the texts, including Fell's *The Bad Box* and Hayton's trilogy, articulate feminist preoccupations with the patriarchal social/symbolic order; the constraints of heteronormativity are satirically exposed in Ellen Galford's *The Fires of Bride* (1986) and *Queendom Come* (1990), while texts such as Thompson's *Pandora's Box* radically address gender definitions. The deconstructive approach extends to broader ontological categories, unveiling a postmodernist engagement with a critical interrogation of the real: the self-reflexive spectrality of texts such as Kennedy's *So I Am Glad* and Smith's *Hotel World* marries the conventional forms and genres of Gothic fantasy with eminently postmodernist narrative strategies and preoccupations.

The transposition of traditional *topoi* to accommodate the interrogation of categorical structures underpins the overarching argument of this study; the deployment of a range of narrative, thematic and stylistic structures derived from non-realist literary precedents propels the investigation into the contentious boundaries that separate the self, the seen and familiar from the other, the invisible and unknown.

THE OTHER NATION

Dramatic political changes from the first referendum in 1979 to the achievement of devolution in 1997 accompanied the awakening of a 'second' cultural Renaissance in Scotland: 'the profusion and eclecticism of creative talent across all genres and all three of the nation's languages has led some to speak not simply of revival', Gavin Wallace and Randall Stevenson commented in 1993, 'but of a new – perhaps even more real – Scottish Renaissance'.[5] Scottish devolution emerged in the context of centrifugal tensions and insurgences of nationalism across Europe and the world: the Balkan wars, the fragmentation and fall of the former Soviet Union and the rise of nationalist parties throughout Europe still represent the most visible symptoms of this political trend. In 1979 Julia Kristeva commented on the twilight of the nineteenth-century concept of nation after the Second World War, suggesting that the idea of nation had evolved from a nineteenth-century 'dream and reality' shaped by 'economic homogeneity', 'historical tradition' and 'linguistic unity' to a post-war unstable entity based on a globalised economic system, shared histories and multilingualism.[6] Kristeva's emphasis on the loss of 'homogeneity' and coherence in the late twentieth-century notion of 'nation' suggested the deployment of different parameters of identity and belonging, based on otherness and heterogeneity, issues which Homi K. Bhabha later supported in his deconstructive discussion of national cultures: 'the very concept of homogenous national cultures, the consensual or contiguous transmission of historical traditions, "organic" ethnic communities [. . .] are in a profound process of redefinition'.[7] Bhabha openly criticised Benedict Anderson's theoretical reading of national identities based on mutual feelings of 'sameness' and 'belonging' to an 'imagined community', 'imagined because the members of even the smallest of nation will never know most of their fellow members, meet them, or even hear of them, yet in the minds of each lives the image of their communion'.[8] Against Anderson's view that behind the birth of national identity is 'the search [. . .] for a new way of linking fraternity, power and time meaningfully together',[9] Bhabha drew attention to the fluctuating, unstable and dynamic boundaries of late-twentieth century cultural consciousness: 'In the *fin de siècle*, we find ourselves in the moment of transit where space and time cross to produce complex figures of difference and identity, past and present, inside and outside, inclusion and exclusion'.[10] The focal shift from the centre – the representative nucleus of a hegemonic culture – to the periphery – the marginal communities and oppressed minorities of a larger entity – is reflective of the wider deconstructive drives of post-structuralist thought and the fall of grand narratives of postmodernist cultures. The subversion of political hierarchies and de-centring of authority has had two important effects on nation discourse: firstly, the marginal 'other' – be it the colonised subject or the smaller nation under the hegemonic power of a larger one – became the centre of investigative work on (national) identity; secondly, the interrogation of nineteenth-century 'homogenous' foundations of identity has led to a deeper investigation of the heterogeneous components of identity, integrating 'other' parameters of identity such as hybridity, migrancy and creolisation.

Deconstructive approaches to nation and the renewed focus on cultural minorities became visible in several studies on nation and theories of national identity in Scotland in the last decade of the twentieth century. In 1935 Edwin Muir had, however, already expressed his deep concerns about the state of Scottish culture, divided at its core since the Union Treaty of 1707, a notion exemplified by the inner divisions of its national languages: 'Scotsmen feel in one language and think in another; [. . .] their emotions turn to the Scottish tongue [. . .]; and their minds to a standard English which for them is almost bare of associations other than those of the classroom'.[11] A schizoid reading of Scotland persisted throughout the twentieth century, with Scottish identity frequently theorised in terms of 'otherness' in relation to English hegemony: 'Englishness undoubtedly plays that role in relation to Scottishness', Jonathan Hearn wrote in 2000, 'a role arising out of a long and complex history of rivalry and interdependence'.[12] It has been argued, too, that such preoccupations about national identity in Scotland vanished after devolution: 'Since the mid-1990s, there has been an increasing lack of need for us to talk about Scottish identity' Joy Hendry claimed, 'There is less and less the need to talk about it, because we can *be* it, and, more importantly, *do* it'.[13] Arguably, rather than relaxing anxieties about national identity, the advent of devolution and achievement of political autonomy in 1997 seemingly has shifted the emphasis from the binary Scottish/English opposition to the intrinsically heterogeneous and problematic diversity *within* Scottish culture, as remarked by Hearn: 'Scottish national identity hangs in a constellation of over-lapping and interpenetrating identities – British, Celtic, European, Western, working class, to name just a few'.[14]

Gender is one such factor of differentiation that threatens the foundations of national identity categories artificially and anachronistically constructed on essentialist notions of traditional 'authenticity'. In 1996 Aileen Christianson criticised Anderson's male-centred theories of nation and national identity, as she discussed the problematic position of women within such constructions of Scottish identity. Being both 'female' and 'Scottish', Christianson argued, Scottish women are inevitably relegated to the margins of a hegemonic English, male, heterosexual cultural discourse:

> The question for us here is whether there are particular conjunctions and disjunctions for women in marginal societies between the marginality of our femaleness and of our nation. And whether these multi-dimensional perspectives of nation, region, gender, class and sexuality are in a perpetual state of flux, with oppositions and alliances in constantly shifting relationships within ourselves and with others.[15]

The question of gender shifts the emphasis on the effects that double marginalisation would have on the concept of nation: if women are to be accounted for within the centre of 'national' culture, their inclusion would simultaneously challenge the patriarchal foundations of Scottish identity. Christianson's suggestion of the need for the re-definition of Scottish national identity is crucial to the scope of this book: the works this study is concerned with point to complex issues of 'inclusion' and identity arising from the diverse geography of birth, upbringing and residence of their authors. Their partial 'belonging' to England via birth, upbringing or residence, raises more questions about nationality and marginality. Can a heterogeneous group of writers be easily described as Scottish? In what ways is 'Scottish' juxtaposed to 'English' in the context of devolution? The altering of conventional national boundaries may be a necessary step if English-born authors such as Atkinson, Elphinstone and Hayton or Scottish 'exiles' such as Fell, Smith, Spark and Tennant should be included in any discussion of Scottish writing. In 1997 Flora Alexander defined Fell and Tennant as 'Anglo-Scot' writers, suggesting that: 'Some contemporary Scottish women writers of fiction are living in England, and in several cases they have also been educated in England so that their Scottishness may not be immediately apparent'.[16] When interviewed, Tennant and Fell both claimed their right to be uncompromisingly included within the Scottish literary context; while Tennant emphasised the relevance of her Scottish background to her work,[17] Fell's concern with nation-labels – including the hybrid 'Anglo-Scot' – reflected anxiety about categorical parameters of identity: 'The term Anglo-Scot is completely foreign [. . .]. The imagination knows no country'.[18] The authors' responses to questions of national identity highlight the intricate and contradictory aspects of the debate on national identity in and beyond Scotland: while outwardly retaining an ideological – if loosely based – opposition to a hegemonic English culture, inwardly, such understanding of Scottish otherness is further complicated by a growing awareness of the heterogeneity of Scottish culture. Moreover, the feelings of utopian nostalgia for a mythical, independent, self-enclosed Caledonia conceal the double-edged risks of inward parochialism and outward intolerance, as argued by Christopher Whyte:

> The dangers of such a stance are that it is committed to the restoration, not only of Scotland as it was, but of relations between genders, classes, racial groups and differing sexual orientations that would be unacceptably oppressive in a modern context.[19]

As Whyte stipulated the necessity to discuss the two paradigms together in an analysis of contemporary Scottish culture, so have Aileen Christianson and Alison Lumsden drawn attention to the need to re-frame the paradigms of nation and gender jointly, arguing that 'there is a sense in which both denote a degree of "marginality", an exclusion from the dominant discourse of white male "Britishness"', as well as emphasising the heterogeneous culture of Scotland:[20] 'Now that a greater degree of autonomy has been achieved in Scotland and what many would regard as the common political goal attained, what begins to emerge is a sense, or a reminder, of Scotland's lack of homogeneity'.[21] If 'nation' is no longer represented by a central majority, but a growing entity spread across a number of diverse, marginal, centrifugal communities, is there such a thing as a distinctive national tradition? The deconstruction of centralised notions of 'nation', Bhabha argues, implicates the subversive redefinition of 'tradition':

> The right to signify from the periphery of authorised power and privilege does not depend on the persistence of tradition; it is resourced by the power of tradition to be reinscribed through the conditions of contingency and contradictoriness that attend upon the lives of those who are 'in the minority'.[22]

Within the Scottish context, Bhabha's paradigm of diversification of tradition supports a reading of tradition as the dialogue of opposing voices proposed by

Craig: 'traditions are not the unitary voice of an organic whole but the dialectic engagement between opposing value systems which define each other precisely by their intertwined oppositions'.[23] Only through this organically dynamic interpretation of tradition can modern Scotland be theorised: if it is accepted that tradition is not a static corpus but an organic body, then the fluctuating borders of national identity will be open to the heterogeneous contributions of gender, sexual orientation, race and ethnicity.

The texts examined in the following chapters reflect a dynamic and variable engagement with Scottish and non-Scottish traditions and a critical position towards universal notions of belonging, roots, homeland and, more specifically, Scotland. Elphinstone's early novels, for instance, overtly establish thematic links with Scottish ballads, while *Islanders* and *The Sea Road* derive from the author's experiences in Shetland,[24] the crossing point of Scandinavian and Celtic worlds. To the nomadic characters of Elphinstone's fiction, however, (national) boundaries remain in a state of flux, as does the problematic home/away dichotomy. The direct influence of Celtic/Welsh traditions is also evident in Hayton's trilogy and *The Governors*, though her novels expose challenging issues of origin, thus undermining a monologic understanding of tradition and identity. Questions of belonging and self are also articulated, in different ways, by Atkinson's *Behind the Scenes at the Museum*, which interrogates notions of home(land) throughout its subversive family saga. Inspired by Sade's work and Greek mythology respectively, Thompson's *Justine* and *Pandora's Box* are also indebted to the psychological investigation typical of Scottish fantasy, and of Hogg's and Stevenson's texts in particular. The influence of Hogg and Stevenson is overtly played out in Tennant's rewritings, *The Bad Sister* and *Two Women of London*, though both novels expose the contradictory essence of Scottish identity, which Fell's *The Bad Box* also draws attention to through close references to popular Scottish tales. *The Bad Box* presents a Scotland that is both split and other: something similar happens in Kennedy's *So I Am Glad*, whose disaffected character and schizoid/fantastic projections, may be read as a statement about postmodern, post-capitalist Scottish culture. In Spark's *Symposium*, modern Scotland is distinctly 'other', its historical associations with witchcraft still haunting the metropolitan centre of London from the shadowy margins of the other nation at the end of the twentieth century; the tidal topography of the fictional island of Jacob's Rock is possessed, too, in Thompson's *Pharos*, by the knowledge of its past history of corruption, violence and death. While spectrality invests the relationship between feminine subjectivity and landscape in Barker's *O Caledonia*, it is the Scottish 'other' woman who disrupts dysfunctional middle-class English lives in Smith's *The Accidental*. Other women return to repossess modern Scotland – and expose the unauthentic foundations of national identity – in Galford's satirical novels, *The Fires of Bride* and *Queendom Come*.

What the novels examined in this book contest, in different ways, is a monolithic reading of Scotland and its national culture, past and present. Lucie Armitt suggests that 'boundaries, borders and thresholds are always key concepts for any reading of the fantastic, linking together concepts of nation and the otherworldly, bodies and the grotesque, housing and hauntings'.[25] As notions of (otherworldly) displacement become crucial to critical readings of identity and belonging, the function played by generic conventions will be discussed more in detail in the last section of this introduction. By drawing attention to supernatural thematic areas largely associated with the Scottish canon, these narratives simultaneously travel beyond the conventional, accepted, boundaries of set traditions to articulate deconstructive patterns of same/other differentiation in relation to gender and the real.

THE OTHER GENDER

The critical investigation of the foundations of gender and the exploration of feminine subjectivity become of paramount importance in this critical revision of traditional motifs. The female 'other' and the consequent subordination of women in the patriarchal structures of Western thought has been the subject of much feminist theoretical work, captured by Simone de Beauvoir's claim that 'she is the incidental, the inessential as opposed to the essential',[26] a theoretical position foreshadowed in early feminist works such as Mary Wollstonecraft's *A Vindication of the Rights of Woman* (1792) and Virginia Woolf's *A Room of One's Own* (1929) and *Three Guineas* (1938). The secondary position occupied by the female sex in the binary opposition that opposes woman to man is part of a larger set of hierarchies, which constitutes the backbone of Western civilization, 'Everywhere (where) ordering intervenes', as noted by Hélène Cixous in *The Newly Born Woman* (1976), 'where a law organizes what is thinkable by oppositions (dual, irreconcilable; or sublatable, dialectical)'.[27] Such binary patterns have led to a reading of the female sex as body (as opposed to mind), and madness (as opposed to reason). The aesthetic responses to the female form in Western art and culture reflect the pervasive dynamics of the controlling male gaze and the object of its voyeuristic and pleasure-driven addresses, the female body; in John Berger's words, 'Men Act and Women Appear'.[28] As Laura Mulvey pointed out in her crucial study of the male gaze in classic cinematography, the function of the gaze is dual: on one level, it produces pleasure; on the other, it asserts masculinity in portraying the female body as fragmented and exposed in its sole role of supporting the male hero's controlling authority: 'In their traditional exhibitionist role women are simultaneously looked at and displayed, with their appearance coded for strong visual and erotic impact so that they can be said to connote *to-be-looked-at-ness*'.[29] The capitalist ethos of the late twentieth-century exacerbated the commodification of women's bodies and their consequent subjection to constant surveillance, not only by the male gaze, but also, as Susie Orbach remarked in 1988, women's own scrutinising surveillance: 'To get a man, a woman must learn to regard herself as an item, a commodity, a sex object. Much of her experience and identity depends on how she and others see her'.[30]

Problematically as the outer shell of the female body may present itself in relation to the aesthetic and cultural responses produced by Western art and culture, theories of its interior anatomy move discourse from production to reproduction. Limited to its biological essence by traditional medical and classic psychoanalytical discourse, the female body is paradoxically reduced to the reproductive function her organism accommodates, while its sexuality is, at the best of times, relegated to a vacuum. Notions about female sexuality (or lack of it) in Victorian Britain were exemplified by William Acton, who, in 1857 wrote that 'The majority of women (happily for them) are not very much troubled by sexual feeling of any kind. What men are habitually, women are only exceptionally'.[31] In his manual Acton also advised that 'Literary women are not likely to be much sought after in marriage', adding that 'great accomplishments so seldom survive the first year of married life, that ordinary men are too sensible to prefer them to a pleasant manner, a sweet temper, and a cheerful disposition':[32] with regard to a man's appropriate choice of a wife, Acton, a member of the medical profession, seemed to share the views expressed in Coventry Patmore's lines, 'Her disposition is devout, / Her countenance angelical', in his famous poem *Angel in the House* (1854).[33] A specific kind of scopophilic discourse is attached to Patmore's celebration, one that is picked up by the anonymous 'clever unmarried woman' who, in an appendix to Acton's work, suggests that 'comeliness of form and beauty of feature ought not to be despised', though 'It is more a kind of pleasure conveyed to *the mind of the beholder* than any special personal attraction of form or figure' (my emphases).[34] The commentator's remarks echo Wollstonecraft's argument that 'Taught from their infancy that beauty is woman's sceptre, the mind shapes itself to the body, and, roaming round its gilt cage, only seeks to adore its prison',[35] and build the foundations of later feminist thought aimed to expose the patriarchal basis of ideals of feminine beauty.

Late twentieth-century feminists such as Angela Carter and Germaine Greer became perhaps the most vocal critics of views of womanhood as the synthesis of angelic femininity and reproductive fertility: 'the womb is', Carter argued in *The Sadeian Woman*, 'an organ like any other organ, more useful than the appendix, less useful than the colon but not much use to you at all if you do not wish to utilise its sole function, that of bearing children'.[36] In comparing the two Sadeian women, Justine ('the holy virgin') and Juliette ('the profane whore'), Carter advocated the 'secularisation' of woman through the implicit 'death of the goddess'. In her polemical work *The Female Eunuch* (1970) Greer had reached similar conclusions, when she discussed the fallacy of biological essentialism in gender constructs: 'of forty-eight chromosomes only one is different: on this difference we base a complete separation of male and female, pretending as it were that all forty-eight were different'.[37]

Second-wave feminism has produced, however, other readings of female body and sexuality as site/methodology of subversive resistance to Western phallologocentrism. In *This Sex Which is Not One* (1977) Luce Irigaray articulated a critique of previous readings of female sexuality in terms of passivity and 'lack', as theorised by Sigmund Freud's famous lecture on 'Some psychical consequences of the anatomical distinction between the sexes' (1925),[38] arguing for a more comprehensive understanding of the complex bisexuality that the female body presents. The re-appropriation of the female body, and, in particular, the maternal space, became central to the work of Julia Kristeva, who placed the maternal back in the centre of linguistic discourse, establishing a link between the semiotic level of language, which roughly corresponds to Jacques Lacan's 'imaginary' stage and precedes the symbolic order, and the notion of '*chora*', 'a non-expressive totality formed by the drives and their stases in a motility that is as full of movement as it is regulated'.[39] The chora's 'rhythmic space' between the maternal and the infant's body is, as Marilyn Edelstein emphasises, 'womb-like', and, simultaneously, exceeding the feminine/masculine dichotomy, referring instead to a pre-Oedipal state of undifferentiated sex.[40] Kristeva's theory of language draws attention to the disruptive subversiveness of semiotic linguistic patterns that emerge in poetic language and are reminiscent of that pre-symbolic stage; 'more archaic' and 'unconsciously driven', as Noëlle McAfee explains, the semiotic is a 'ravenous mode of signifying': 'When it seeps out in signification, as it does in avant-garde poetry, it disrupts the more orderly, symbolic effort of communication'.[41] In her reworking of binary oppositions, Kristeva reached conclusions which, while exposing woman's intrinsic otherness in a patriarchal system of signification, also replaced old categories with new ones: 'Femininity is exactly this lunar form, in the way that the moon is the inverse of the sun of our identity'; woman's role is, according to Kristeva, the embodiment of 'strangeness', but also 'to be on guard and contestatory'.[42]

In the first half of the twentieth century Woolf had already interrogated the difficult affiliations between women and patriarchal language, suggesting:

> it is still true that before a woman can write exactly as she wishes to write, she has many difficulties to face. To begin with, there is the technical difficulty – so simple, apparently; in reality, so baffling – that the very form of the sentence does not fit her. It is a sentence made by men; it is too loose, too heavy, too pompous for a woman's use.[43]

The notion of women's otherness implies the inadequacy of normative language to accommodate feminine writing and subjectivity. Cixous's notion of *écriture féminine* emerges from this awareness of the outcast position of women in relation to the symbolic; turned on its head, this produces a subversive effect: feminine subjectivity must adopt a language that deviates from patriarchal systems of signification, as Cixous argued in 'The Laugh of the Medusa' (1976), a literary/political manifesto on sexual difference and the impossibility of theorising women's writing:

> It is impossible to define a feminine practice of writing, and this is an impossibility that will remain, for this practice can never be theorised, enclosed, coded – which doesn't mean that it doesn't exist. But it will always surpass the discourse that regulates the phallocentric system; it does and will take place in areas other than those subordinated to philosophico-theoretical domination.[44]

Juxtaposed to the masculine model, the type of writing Cixous endorses as 'feminine' resists coherence and regular structures of signification: 'woman unthinks [sic] the unifying, regulating history that homogenizes and channels forces, herding contradictions into a single battlefield'.[45] While Cixous proposed ways of 'un-thinking' sexual difference, her work still relied on binary male/female, masculine/feminine oppositions. Launching her investigation from the discourse of sexuality – rather than biological sex – the work of queer theorist Judith Butler moved away from such models, introducing the notion of performativity, defined in *Gender Trouble* (1990) as a metaleptic effect 'in which the anticipation of a gendered essence produces that which is outside itself', but also as a repetition and a ritual, 'which achieves its effect through its naturalization in the context of a body'.[46] As she clarified in *Bodies That Matter* (1993), performativity undermines both the notion of 'constructed' and 'determined' sexualities, arguing that such mutually exclusive approaches fail to accommodate the complexity of sexual identities that simultaneously react to and are sustained by cultural norms; performative theory, therefore, proposes a strategy to overcome binary oppositions in relation to gender: 'If we call into question the fixity of the structuralist law that divides and bounds the "sexes" by virtue of their dyadic differentiation within the heterosexual matrix', Butler argued in *Bodies That Matter*, '[. . .] it will constitute the disruptive return of the excluded from within the very logic of the heterosexual symbolic'.[47]

In the chapters that follow, gender preoccupations take different routes. In some of the earlier texts, including Tennant's *The Bad Sister* and *Two Women of London*, concerns with patriarchal oppression also display the intrinsic sectarianism within different kinds of feminisms; elsewhere, a critique of heteronormative structures is a prominent motif in Galford's *The Fires of Bride* and *Queendom Come*, while more emphatic references to notions of performativity and the slippages that may exist between gender – as projected fantasy

– and sex emerge strongly in Thompson's *Justine* and *Pandora's Box* especially. Butler's position, which draws from a Foucauldian reading of sexuality in relation to power structures, exposes the ideological ways in which bodies are 'given' sexes within the normative context of a given society. In her famous 'A Cyborg Manifesto' (1991), Donna Haraway proposed to rethink the body as 'code' and gender identities in the context of the technology-driven economy and culture of the late twentieth century. The man–machine hybrid of science fiction, the cyborg, becomes a model and a metaphor for the meltdown of man/woman, nature/culture categorical divisions of Western philosophy.[48] Simultaneously 'utopian' and 'subversive', the cyborg self, which Haraway celebrates, confuses hierarchical distinctions making them, effectively, redundant in the new, genderless world the cyborg will inhabit.

Within the heterogeneous discourse that various strands of feminisms and queer theory collectively contribute to, what emerges as a shared pattern is the crucial link between gender and the linguistic systems – broadly understood to incorporate a plurality of speech, text, but also fashion, science and any other relevant code – that represent it. Haraway's study draws attention to the literary discourse of a specific kind, implicating an important factor to be addressed in relation to the representation of gender: genre. As Mary Eagleton has argued, the relationship between gender and the choice of non-realist genres is not coincidental: 'To query the truth, coherence and resolution of realism is to undermine the symbolic order. Non-realist forms permit the woman writer to express the contradictions, fantasies or desires that the demands of realism silence'.[49] The ways in which gender is approached in the texts examined in this volume are closely interlinked to the codes of various generic conventions that, moving away from the conventions of realism, may be, in one way or another, described as 'fantasy'.

THE OTHER GENRE(S)

Fantasy, intended in the broadest sense and not as one specific kind of formulaic genre fiction, allows for the world, as we know it, and its logic, as we understand it, to be violated and transformed. Resistant to rational certainties and defiant of social conventions, fantasy challenges political, social and ontological assumptions. The sense of 'hesitation' generated by the insurgence of unexplained supernatural – though not transcendent – phenomena within the boundaries of the known world was theorised by Tzvetan Todorov as the essence of the fantastic, in the earliest influential study of fantasy writing: 'In a world which is indeed our world, the one we know, a world without devils, sylphides, or vampires, there occurs an event which cannot be explained by the laws of this same familiar world'.[50] Henry James's *The Turn of the Screw* (1898), Todorov suggested, is the perfect example of the sustained narrative ambiguity that qualifies the fantastic as a mode. In its structuralist approach,

Todorov's study concentrated on the mechanics of the fantastic, drawing attention to the subversive language of its form, rather than content and contexts. Identified by the 'hesitation' typically shared by character and reader in relation to the supernatural, the fantastic was distinguished by Todorov from two categories in which the supernatural is accepted as part of the world of the story (marvellous), or rationally explained as an illusion, dream, or drug-induced hallucination (uncanny).

As well as a 'phantom' or a 'hallucination', the word fantasy refers to, as the *Oxford English Dictionary* entry confirms, simultaneously the 'imagination', and the 'image' projected by it. Derived from the ancient Greek verb *fantázein*, 'to make visible', and *faínein*, 'to show', the etymology of the word reinforces fantasy's archetypal bond with the realm of representation. As the philosopher Ludwig Wittgenstein asserted, 'It is obvious that an imagined world, however different it may be from the real one, must have something – a form – in common with it'.[51] With realism, therefore, fantasy has an ambivalent relationship, particularly, as Rosemary Jackson proposed, with regard to its mimetic function: 'Fantastic narratives confound elements of both the marvellous and the mimetic',[52] deliberately undermining the foundations of realism while borrowing its stylistic strategies; rather than the opposite side of realism, fantasy embodies its 'other' side: 'The fantastic gives utterance to precisely those elements which are known only through their absence within a dominant 'realistic' order';[53] it follows, too, that the closer a fantastic narrative sits to realistic situations, the more subversive is its violation of the real.

As fantasy exposes the weaknesses and contradictions of the known world, the psychological consistency of its human characters is progressively lost, and the disintegration of self is the primary feature of the narrative world: 'partial and dismembered selves break a 'realistic' signifying practice which represents the ego as an indivisible unity'.[54] The Gothic, as a descendant of the archetypal romance that fantasy stems from, exposes the loss of self-unity and identity most overtly, as David Punter claims, in 'the taboo quality of many of the themes to which Gothic addresses itself – incest, rape, various kinds of transgression of the boundaries between the natural and the human, the human and the divine'.[55] Typically resisting definition, the Gothic is a self-conscious discourse that evokes a certain kind of response – fear, horror, repulsion – from the recipient of its cultural products, through its relentless re-fashioning of archetypal taboos, which may include, as it has been noted, anything from incest to necrophilia. The overarching narrative, which, in its recurrent state, underpins the Gothic overall, Robert Miles argues, is the notion of 'the subject in a state of deracination, of the self finding itself dispossessed in its own house, in a condition of rupture, disjunction, fragmentation'.[56]

What both Gothic and fantastic share is their focus on liminal borderlands and conditions: life/death, animate/inanimate, man/woman, kin/lover; the Gothic/fantastic texts of Anne Radcliffe, Edgar Allan Poe, Mary Shelley, Stevenson and Bram Stoker all point to those interstitial spaces that, as emphasised by T. E. Apter in *Fantasy Literature: An Approach to Reality* (1982), are designed to unsettle its reader: 'All reassurance or reprieve is illusory in face of the anxiety arising from the knowledge that the familiar can take on, and tends to take on, strange or threatening forms'.[57] Apter's discussion of the 'familiar' is based on Freud's study 'The Uncanny' (1919), a pivotal text in the development of the critical discourse of fantastic texts, particularly those of the Gothic kind. The closeness of the uncanny to the familiar is crucially associated with the repressed memories of the unconscious, as remarked by Freud: 'this uncanny is in reality nothing new or alien, but something which is familiar and old-established in the mind and which has become alienated from it only through the process of repression'.[58] The uncanny, therefore, offers a range of reading strategies that point to the haunting nature of individual and collective past histories in relation to the Gothic; fantasies of the Gothic kind are closer to Todorov's model of narrative/ontological ambiguity, where, as Lucie Armitt notes, 'Structured around the discourse of the uncanny, [. . .] this world has invaded our own space to fracture and disrupt the reassuring presence of inner worlds'.[59]

But fear, and its repression, is not the only key to a psychoanalytical reading of Gothic/fantastic writing: 'A fantastic text tells of an indomitable desire, a longing for that which does not exist', Jackson argues, 'or which has not been allowed to exist'.[60] The relevance of desire belongs, as Northrop Frye suggested, to the archetype of romance, the 'nearest of all literary forms to the wish-fulfilment dream',[61] though, as Fred Botting notes, 'In contrast to romance's ascendant quest, [. . .], Gothic romances manifest a descent into anxiety and nightmare, into realms of shadowy doubles'.[62] That desire and the fulfilment of pleasure drives are strongly linked to Gothic/fantastic narratives emerges clearly in, though it is not limited to, the eroticisation and self-splitting function of desire in texts such as Oscar Wilde's *The Picture of Dorian Gray* (1890) and Bram Stoker's *Dracula* (1897). Desire is in fact the principal drive of fantasy or phantasy, which, in Freudian terms, is crucial to the development of the ego. Jacques Lacan developed the notion further, placing fantasy as desire between the subject and the real: 'the real supports the fantasy, the fantasy protects the real'.[63] The subject can never achieve knowlege of the real, though she longs for it: it is the longing that sustains their relationship, but also, as Botting explains, controls it: 'fantasy serves as a frame in which subjectivity can continue desiring'.[64] Lacan's notion of the *objet petit a* captures the unfulfillable and unknowable essence of desire, or, in Botting's words, 'the missing part of oneself'.[65] As Slavoj Žižek stressed, in order for the subject to exist, fantasy should remain unfulfilled:

The point is that subjectivity fades if the fantasy is realised, for being a subject depends on the split between its fantasmatic support and its Symbolic/Imaginary identifications. If the balance is disturbed, the subject loses either stake in the Real or its identifications in the Symbolic.[66]

Elsewhere Žižek revised his theory of fantasy in relation to the virtual reality of cyberspace, suggesting that, through its promotion of inter-passivity and the blurring of boundaries between simulacrum and appearance,

cyberspace opens up the domain of shifting multiple sexual and social identities, at least potentially liberating us from the hold of the patri-archal Law; it [. . .] realizes in our everyday practical experience the 'deconstruction' of old metaphysical binaries ('real Self' versus 'artificial mask', etc.).[67]

Žižek's argument builds on Jean Baudrillard's *Simulacra and Simulation* (1981), which claimed the disappearance of the real in the culture of postmoder-nity. With its emphatic stress on mediated information, postmodernist culture only gives access to simulated images (simulacra) of the otherwise inaccessible (and unknowable) real: Disneyland becomes, paradoxically, real, in staging a fantastic other world that is in fact more authentic than the real America, a world long lost and utterly inaccessible in the capitalist culture of the late twen-tieth century: 'The impossibility of rediscovering an absolute level of the real is of the same order as the impossibility of staging illusion. Illusion is no longer possible, because the real is no longer possible'.[68] Postmodernism's disenchant-ment with the real is reflected in the insurgence of various strands of fictions that, while eroding previously accepted high/low cultural barriers, interrogate the foundations of the real. As Brian McHale rightly remarked, the dominant of postmodernist fiction is ontological, articulating questions such as 'What is a world? What kinds of worlds are there, how are they constituted, and how do they differ? [. . .] How is a projected world structured?'[69] The collapse of the grand narratives of Western civilisation culminates with the dismantling of the most fundamental of categories, producing, as a result, aesthetic responses to accommodate the ideological crisis: in different ways, the works of Thomas Pynchon, Paul Auster and Kurt Vonnegut in America and John Fowles, Angela Carter and Salman Rushdie in Britain contributed to the clusters of literature gathered under the most untheorisable of critical labels, postmodernism.

Along with the laws and ideology of realism, postmodernism refutes the conventions of fantasy writing that borrow from realism their mimetic strate-gies. Since the real is unknowable, so do all coherent strategies of narration that attempt its representation become redundant. The fragmented psyche of modernist literature gives way to the textual, self-reflexive dimension of post-modern subjectivity: 'the worlds summed up by literary texts are grounded simply in their own textual mechanisms', Steven Connor remarks, 'subjectivity gives way to textuality'.[70] In doing so postmodernism inherits some of the strategies of modernist fiction – temporal discontinuities, the loss of coherent subjectivity, formal experimentalism – but replaces the emphasis of modernist formal preoccupations with a range of contradictory strategies: the deeper investigation into the nature and boundaries of the real is accompanied by the playful approach to the boundaries that may exist between fantasy and reality; the erosion of hierarchical divisions, including the 'sacred' barriers that separate author and reader and/or character, may, as Roland Barthes would have it, have caused 'the death of the author', though this results in a highly self-reflective discourse of authorship intruding within the boundaries of the fictional text, exemplified by Fowles's *The French Lieutenant's Woman* (1969) and Auster's *New York Trilogy*. Similar metafictional strategies emerge, it will be seen, in the works of Atkinson, Kennedy, Smith and Thompson.

With its self-obsessive replication of its own stock motifs on one hand, and its half-way engagement with the marvellous, the Gothic, arguably, presents characteristics that make it akin to postmodernism: self-conscious of its own strategies and reverberating echoes from historical, literary and personal pasts, it also articulates a postmodern ontological interrogation, as 'Gothic fictions generally play with and oscillate between the earthly laws of conventional reality and the possibilities of the supernatural'.[71] Hogg's *Justified Sinner* does just this, as it sustains the possibility of at least two interpretations – either Gil-Martin *is* the devil or Wringhim's schizoid other – in the palimpsest of its 'postmodern' narrative structure. Indeed, if we look at Scottish fantasy, the supernatural is rarely devoid of psychological nuances, producing, in turn, unsettling readings of the real: 'In Scottish fantasy the fantastic experience and the world from which it emanates are very close to ours – into which they can come at any time'.[72] Manlove suggests that such 'continuity' works on two levels: from a canonical point of view, the continuum of the supernatural tradition throughout Scottish literature makes it a very distinctive trait of its literary production; on a discursive level, the contiguity of supernatural and real implies that 'in Scots fantasy personal identity is often without boundaries'.[73] Adopting a post-structuralist view, Elphinstone challenges Manlove's statement, taking his argument further:

> [Gregory] Smith and Manlove both draw attention to the way that Scottish fantasy locates the supernatural in the heart of contemporary realism. The implication is that fantasy subverts the assumptions of that world. I think it does more: in a poststructuralist world, it destabilises contemporary notions of what is real, drawing upon past traditions, dreams, subconscious hopes and fears about the supernatural and giving them a validity which is at least equal to, and often stronger than, the rational laws that supposedly govern the external world.[74]

In destabilising the laws of this world, the texts explored in the following chapters find the narrative strategies of fantasy and the Gothic, as stated at the beginning of this section, appropriate for ontological interrogations and the exploration of feminine subjectivity. Questioning the foundations of gender, other kinds of identity, dictated by notions of homeland, nationality and belonging, come to the foreground of the investigation into the other, where the stability of boundaries and the stubbornness of roots are replaced with visions of vanishing lands and dislocated selves.

CHAPTER OUTLINE

Underpinned by the three discourses of otherness elucidated in this introduction, the following chapters are arranged around four broad thematic areas, which overlap on many levels, particularly when certain themes coexist within the same text. A theoretical section at the beginning of each chapter is followed by in-depth analyses of selected texts.

Chapter 2 launches this thematic investigation with an analysis of quests and other worlds. By definition, (magical) journeys embody the metaphor of border crossing, the overcoming of familiar thresholds to explore the 'other' (world) beyond the safety of the known. An in-depth discussion of Elphinstone's *The Incomer* (1987), *A Sparrow's Flight* (1989) and *The Sea Road*, Hayton's trilogy and Fell's *The Mistress of Lilliput* highlights the deconstructive function the journey and the other world perform in relation to stable notions of identity and ontology.

Chapter 3 concentrates on the witch, as simultaneous embodiment of female marginalisation and feminist subversion. The recurrent presence of the elusive dangerous woman in the examined texts loads the narratives with questions about gender and power: far from reinstating any essentialist binary gender hierarchies, in the examined texts, which include Galford's *Queendom Come* and *The Fires of Bride*, Spark's *Symposium*, Thompson's *Pandora's Box* and Smith's *The Accidental*, the dangerous woman challenges binary oppositions between gender and the established hierarchical order, pointing, simultaneously, to the fragility of all categorical thinking.

Chapter 4 explores the double motif, a thematic area deployed to express the self/other dichotomy, and, simultaneously, the interrogation of binary oppositions. In the examined texts – Fell's *The Bad Box*, Hayton's *The Governors*, Atkinson's *Behind the Scenes at the Museum*, Tennant's *The Bad Sister* and *Two Women of London* and Thompson's *Justine* – the doppelgänger prompts the interrogation of gender categories while exposing the schizoid divisions within the female psyche.

Chapter 5 considers the revenant motif; as the paradoxical site of theoretical discourses about corporeality and ethereality, life and death, seen and unseen, in the late twentieth century the ghost crucially signifies the overcoming of structuralist dualism. In the light of post-structuralist thought, the chapter discusses the haunted narratives of Barker's *O Caledonia*, Kennedy's *So I Am Glad*, Thompson's *Pharos* and Smith's *Hotel World*.

Finally, in 'The Death of the Other?' concluding remarks about the notions of three kinds of otherness explored in the book raise further questions about the future of the 'others' and the aftermath of postmodernism in a post-feminist, globalised twenty-first century.

NOTES

1. Veronica Hollinger, 'Preface', in Patrick R. Burger, *The Political Unconscious of the Fantasy Sub-genre of Romance* (Lewiston: Edwin Mellen Press, 2001), pp. iii–vii (p. iv).
2. Angela Carter, 'Afterword to *Fireworks*' [1974], in *Collected Short Stories* (London: Vintage, 1996), p. 460.
3. Douglas Gifford, 'Imagining Scotlands: The Return to Mythology in Modern Scottish Fiction', in Susanne Hageman (ed.), *Studies in Scottish Fiction: 1945 to the Present* (Frankfurt am Main: Peter Lang, 1996), pp. 17–49 (p. 17).
4. Colin Manlove, *Scottish Fantasy Literature: A Critical Survey* (Edinburgh: Canongate Academic, 1994), p. 11.
5. Gavin Wallace and Randall Stevenson (eds), *The Scottish Novel Since The Seventies* (Edinburgh: Edinburgh University Press, 1993), p. 1.
6. Julia Kristeva, 'Women's Time' (1979), in *The Kristeva Reader*, ed. Toril Moi (Oxford: Blackwell, 1986), pp. 187–213 (p. 188).
7. Homi K. Bhabha, *The Location of Culture* (London and New York: Routledge, 1994), p. 7.
8. Benedict Anderson, *Imagined Communities: Reflections on the Origin and Spread of Nationalism* [1983] (London: Verso, 1991), p. 6.
9. Anderson, *Imagined Communities*, p. 36.
10. Bhabha, *Location of Culture*, p. 1.
11. Edwin Muir, *Scott and Scotland: The Predicament of the Scottish Writer* (London: Routledge, 1936), p. 21.
12. Jonathan Hearn, *Claiming Scotland: National Identity and Liberal Culture* (Edinburgh: Polygon, 2000), p. 11.
13. Joy Hendry, quoted in Tom Devine and Paddy Logue (eds), *Being Scottish: Personal Reflections on Scottish Identity Today* (Edinburgh: Polygon, 2002), p. 99.
14. Hearn, *Claiming Scotland*, p. 11.
15. Aileen Christianson, 'Imagined corners to debatable land: passable boundaries', *Scottish Affairs*, 17 (1996), pp. 120–34 (p. 121).
16. Flora Alexander, 'Contemporary Fiction III: The Anglo-Scots', in Douglas Gifford and Dorothy McMillan (eds), *A History of Scottish Women's Writing* (Edinburgh: Edinburgh University Press, 1997), pp. 630–40 (p. 630).
17. Emma Tennant, 'Intrinsically Scottish', *Times Literary Supplement*, August 2001, p. 15.
18. Monica Germanà, unpublished interview with Alison Fell, in 'Re-working the Magic: A Parallel Study of Six Scottish Women Writers of the Late Twentieth-Century', unpublished doctoral thesis, University of Glasgow, 2004, pp. 341–52 (pp. 343–4).
19. Christopher Whyte (ed.), *Gendering The Nation: Studies in Modern Scottish Literature* (Edinburgh: Edinburgh University Press, 1995), p. xii.
20. Aileen Christianson and Alison Lumsden (eds), *Contemporary Scottish Women Writers* (Edinburgh: Edinburgh University Press, 2000), p. 2.

21. Christianson and Lumsden, *Contemporary Scottish Women Writers*, p. 3; see also Christie L. March, *Rewriting Scotland: Welsh, McLean, Warner, Banks, Galloway and Kennedy* (Manchester: Manchester University Press, 2002), pp. 1–9.
22. Bhabha, *Location of Culture*, p. 2.
23. Cairns Craig, *The Modern Scottish Novel: Narrative and The National Imagination* (Edinburgh: Edinburgh University Press, 1999), pp. 32–3.
24. Germanà, unpublished interview with Margaret Elphinstone, in 'Re-working the Magic', pp. 322–40 (p. 332).
25. Lucie Armitt, *Contemporary Women's Fiction and the Fantastic* (Basingstoke: Palgrave, 2000), p. 1.
26. Simone de Beauvoir, *The Second Sex* [1949], trans. H. M. Parshley (Harmondsworth: Penguin, 1972), p. 16.
27. Hélène Cixous, 'Sorties', in Hélène Cixous and Catherine Clément, *The Newly Born Woman* [1975] (London: I. B. Tauris, 1996), p. 64.
28. John Berger, *Ways of Seeing* (London: Viking, 1972), p. 47.
29. Laura Mulvey, 'Visual Pleasure and Narrative Cinema', *Screen* 16: 3 (Autumn 1975), pp. 6–18 (p. 11).
30. Susie Orbach, *Fat is a Feminist Issue* (London: Arrow, 1988), p. 22.
31. William Acton, *The Functions and Disorders of the Reproductive Organs* [1857] (Philadelphia: Lindsay and Blakiston, 1867), p. 133.
32 Acton, *Functions and Disorders*, p. 107.
33. Coventry Patmore, Prelude, 'The Rose of the World', *Angel in the House* [1854] (London and Cambridge: Macmillan, 1863), canto IV, lines 11–12.
34. Acton, *Functions and Disorders*, pp. 108 and 256.
35. Mary Wollstonecraft, *A Vindication of the Rights of Woman* [1792] (London: Penguin, 1992), p. 132.
36. Angela Carter, *The Sadeian Woman: An Exercise in Cultural History* [1979] (London: Virago, 1982), p. 109.
37. Germaine Greer, *The Female Eunuch* [1970] (London: Flamingo, 1993), pp. 33–4.
38. See Sigmund Freud, 'Some Psychical Consequences of the Anatomical Distinction Between the Sexes' [1925], *The Standard Edition of the Complete Psychological Works of Sigmund Freud*, trans. James Strachey, 24 vols (London: Hogarth Press, 1953–74), vol. 19, pp. 248–58. (The Standard Edition is abbreviated elsewhere in the text as *SE*.)
39. Julia Kristeva, *Revolution in Poetic Language* [1974], trans. Leon S. Roudiez (New York: Columbia University Press, 1984), p. 25.
40. Marilyn Edelstein, 'Metaphor, Meta-narrative and Mater-narrative in Kristeva's 'Stabat Mater', in David Crownfield (ed.), *Body/Text in Julia Kristeva: Religion: Women and Psychoanalysis* (Albany: State University of New York Press, 1992), pp. 27–52 (p. 44).
41. Noëlle McAfee, *Julia Kristeva* (New York and London: Routledge, 2004), p. 39.
42. Julia Kristeva, 'Interview with Suzanne Clark and Kathleen Hulley' [1989], in R. M. Guberman (ed.), *Julia Kristeva Interviews* (New York: Columbia University Press, 1996), pp. 35–58 (p. 45).
43. Virginia Woolf, 'Women and Fiction' [1929], in *Selected Essays*, ed. David Bradshaw (Oxford: Oxford University Press, 2008), pp. 132–9 (p. 136).
44. Hélène Cixous, 'The Laugh of the Medusa', trans. Keith Cohen and Paula Cohen, *Signs* 1: 4 (Summer 1976), pp. 875–93 (p. 883).
45. Cixous, 'Laugh of the Medusa', p. 882.
46. Judith Butler, *Gender Trouble* [1990] (London and New York: Routledge, 1999), pp. xiv–xv.

47. Judith Butler, *Bodies That Matter: On the Discursive Limits of Sex* (London and New York: Routledge, 1993), pp. 11–12.
48. Donna Haraway, *Simians, Cyborgs and Women: The Reinvention of Nature* (New York: Routledge, 1991), pp. 149–81.
49. Mary Eagleton, 'Genre and Gender', in David Duff (ed.), *Modern Genre Theory* (Harlow: Pearson Education, 2001), pp. 250–62 (p. 253).
50. Tzvetan Todorov, *The Fantastic: A Structural Approach* [1970] (Ithaca: Cornell University Press, 1975), p. 25.
51. Ludwig Wittgenstein, *Tractatus Logico-Philosophicus* [1921], trans. D. F. Pears and B. F. McGuiness (London: Routledge and Kegan Paul, 1977), p. 7.
52. Rosemary Jackson, *Fantasy: The Literature of Subversion* (London: Routledge, 1981), p. 34.
53. Jackson, *Fantasy*, p. 25.
54. Jackson, *Fantasy*, p. 90.
55. David Punter, *The Literature of Terror: A History of Gothic Fictions from 1765 to the Present Day*, 2 vols (London: Longman, 1980), vol. 1, p. 17.
56. Robert Miles, *Gothic Writing 1750–1820: A Genealogy* [1993], 2nd edn (Manchester: Manchester University Press, 2002), p. 3.
57. T. E. Apter, *Fantasy Literature. An Approach to Reality* (London: Macmillan, 1982), pp. 2–3.
58. Sigmund Freud, 'The Uncanny' [1919], *SE*, vol. 17, pp. 217–52 (p. 241).
59. Lucie Armitt, *Theorising the Fantastic* (London: Arnold, 1996), p. 7.
60. Jackson, *Fantasy*, p. 91.
61. Northrop Frye, *Anatomy of Criticism: Four Essays* (Princeton: Princeton University Press, 1957), p. 186.
62. Fred Botting, *Gothic Romanced: Consumption, Gender and Technology in Contemporary Fictions* (London and New York: Routledge, 2008), p. 9.
63. Jacques Lacan, *The Four Fundamental Concepts of Psychoanalysis*, trans. Alan Sheridan (London: Penguin, 1977), p. 41.
64. Botting, *Gothic Romanced*, p. 30.
65. Botting, *Gothic Romanced*, p. 29.
66. Slavoj Žižek, 'Fantasy as a Political Category: A Lacanian Approach' [originally published in the *Journal for The Psychoanalysis of Culture and Society* 1: 2 (Fall 1996), pp. 75–85], reprinted in *The Žižek Reader*, ed. Elizabeth Wright and Edmond Wright (Oxford: Blackwell, 1999), pp. 87–101 (p. 89).
67. Slavoj Žižek, 'Is it Possible to Traverse the Fantasy in Cyberspace?', in *Žižek Reader*, pp. 104–24 (p. 112).
68. Jean Baudrillard, *Simulacra and Simulation* [1981], trans. Sheila Faria Glaser (Ann Arbor: University of Michigan Press, 2006), p. 19.
69. Brian McHale, *Postmodernist Fiction* (London: Routledge, 1987), p. 10.
70. Steven Connor, *Postmodernist Culture*, 2nd edn (Oxford: Blackwell, 1997), p. 130.
71. Jerrold Hogle (ed.), *The Cambridge Companion to Gothic Fiction* (Cambridge: Cambridge University Press, 2002), p. 2. For a more extensive and focused discussion of Gothic/postmodernist convergences, see Maria Beville, *Gothic-Postmodernism: Voicing the Terrors of Postmodernity* (Amsterdam: Rodopi, 2009).
72. Manlove, *Scottish Fantasy Literature*, p. 13.
73. Manlove, *Scottish Fantasy Literature*, p. 14.
74. Margaret Elphinstone, 'Scottish Fantasy Today', *Ecloga*, 1 (2000–1), pp. 15–25 (p. 16).

Chapter 2

QUESTS AND OTHER WORLDS

Faerie cannot be caught in a net of words; for it is one of its qualities to be indescribable, though not imperceptible.[1]

J. R. R. Tolkien

Gothic remains ambivalent and heterotopic, reflecting the doubleness of the relationship between present and past.[2]

Fred Botting

English fantasy more often deals with the quest outwards, where Scots fantasy deals with the inward search.[3]

Colin Manlove

From Faerie to Heterotopias

Otherworldliness and magical quests form the quintessential landscape and narrative drive of the fantastic romance. A familiar motif in myth, fairy tale and (popular) literature across the world, from the *Arabian Nights* to Dante's *Divine Comedy*, the voyage beyond the boundaries of the known world has been a constant feature in archetypal narratives and belief-systems. In African cosmogony, for instance, the dynamic aspect of creation stresses the emphasis of journeying as part of initiatory rituals for mythological god-heroes.[4] In classical Greek and Roman literature, epic voyages feature prominently in

Homer's *Odyssey*, Apollonius Rhodius's *Argonautica* and Virgil's *Aeneid*.[5] Though different in other ways, with the other spaces of classical Greek and Roman mythology, the Celtic other world shares the permeable nature of its boundaries, which are mostly set in this world, as opposed to the transcendent notions of the Christian heaven. Faerie, an important part of the Celtic other world, is an immanent, liminal dimension, even though only heroes and chosen human beings are allowed to 'visit' the world of fairies.[6]

In literary terms, fictional other worlds both determine and derive from generic conventions; the specificity of setting is arguably one of the most prominent features of Gothic: revolving, with endless variations, around the claustrophobic spaces of sinister mansions haunted by their own past, Gothic fiction is, as Botting suggests, distinctly 'heterotopic'. As the Gothic castle signifies the heterotopia haunted by the spectre of a destabilised hierarchical order, so have other ideologically charged fantasies of other worlds constituted important channels of social and political propaganda, from the publication of Thomas More's *Utopia* (1516) to the prolific canon of twentieth-century dystopian fiction, including Aldous Huxley's *Brave New World* (1932), George Orwell's *Nineteen Eighty-Four* (1949) and Gray's *Lanark*. In the late twentieth century the convergence of postmodernism and science fiction pushes the interrogation of the boundaries of the real towards the boundless complexity of virtual spaces, first defined by William Gibson's cyberspace novel *Neuromancer* (1984), while exposing, as Baudrillard does, the simulacral structure of postmodern culture, whose sense of the real is replaced by the depthless surface of the hyperreal.

This chapter examines the complex trajectories traced by the most eminently fantastic texts discussed in this study; while in Elphinstone's *The Incomer* (1987) and *A Sparrow's Flight* (1989) quests within (dystopian) other worlds articulate environmental concerns, in *The Sea Road* (2000) the otherworldliness of Greenland is set against the orthodox Christianity of eleventh-century Europe; the Celtic roots of Hayton's trilogy (1989, 1992, 1993) prompt an investigation of origin and genealogy; Fell's sequel to Swift's *Gulliver's Travels* (1726), *The Mistress of Lilliput* (1999), tells the 'other' story, that of Mary Gulliver's own journey to the South Seas and Lilliput. What these texts share is an ambivalent relationship with the Scottish/Celtic literary and cultural canons: while retracing, in many ways, past journeys and familiar routes, the novels analysed in this chapter simultaneously move beyond set traditions, known histories and familiar geographies. As references to literary and mythological precedents manifestly emerge in Elphinstone's and Hayton's fictions, their textual palimpsests represent, nevertheless, a narrative frame for broader feminist preoccupations. Similarly, while retracing Swift's account of Gulliver's fantastic journey to Lilliput, Fell's pastiche subverts the patriarchal ideology underlying the original text in an oblique critique of (eighteenth-century) Presbyterian Scotland.

Other worlds and magical quests occupy a prominent position throughout Scottish fantasy from the frequent, albeit elusive, references to otherworldly places in ballads such as 'Thomas the Rhymer' and 'Tam Lin' to the postmodernist visions of Gray's *Lanark* and Banks's SF novels. As Elphinstone argues, 'place is paramount' throughout Scottish fantasy.[7] This is true of Hogg's *Kilmeny* (1813) as of George MacDonald's *Phantastes* (1858) and J. M. Barrie's Peter Pan stories. Three features consistently belong in such different renditions of fantastic other worlds: the permeability of the other world, interpretative ambivalence and the epistemological quest.

The first quality of Scottish fantasy refers to the problematic notion of borderlands, that is, the strong sense that the world of Faerie, much as the underground Institute of *Lanark*, appears to exist in seamless contiguity with the world of ordinary things. While notions of a pre-Christian Celtic other world can be contaminated with celestial visions of Christian heavens, in the ballad tradition of England and Scotland, other worlds generally retain their immanent locations in underground caves, in the secluded green of a forest or underwater;[8] Walter Scott also remarks the Scottish fairies' proclivity for 'the interior of green hills'.[9] In Barrie's work the topographic continuity between the human and other worlds is visually supported by the map of Kensington Gardens, which appears as a frontispiece to *Peter Pan in Kensington Gardens* (1906). Fairies, we are told, exist side by side with humans, particularly since fairies 'can't resist following the children';[10] moreover, even though the fairies' world subverts some of the conventions of the ordinary world – for instance, 'you can see their houses by dark, but you can't see them by day' (Barrie, *Peter Pan*, p. 32), and 'one of the great differences between the fairies and us is that they never do anything useful' (p. 32) – nevertheless, the degree of permeability and similarity between the two worlds is also signified by the fairies' ability to take on the appearance of flowers, 'putting on white when lilies are in and blue for bluebells, and so on' (p. 30). The geographical contiguity of Faerie is reinforced by the simple device of open windows, to allow Peter Pan to intrude into the domestic world of ordinary families and their children to fly away to Neverland in *Peter and Wendy* (1911). Faerie's apparent penetrability is, however, not hazard-free, as demonstrated by the ambiguous sexual subtext of the story and the ongoing menace of Captain Hook and his crew of pirates, or the more hidden threats concealed in the complex narrative of George MacDonald's *Phantastes*. The protagonist's name, Anodos, Greek for 'aimless' or 'wandering', is suggestive of, as Manlove notes, the emphasis placed on the character's quest for (self-) knowledge: the journey to the land of fairies is, after all, an introspective journey within one's psyche.[11] Anodos's journey begins – like Wendy's – within the familiar boundaries of his bedroom, a space that disturbingly turns into a magical world overnight. The transition between the two worlds signals the disruption of binary logic, as is Anodos's inability to define what differentiates the two dimensions: 'There was little to distinguish the woods to-day from those of my own land'.[12] Yet the world Anodos explores teems with creatures that, deceptively camouflaged within the natural features of Faerie, progressively disintegrate Anodos's ability to decode his own perceptions: 'Part of the impulse here is to erode our categorisations of things', Manlove rightly suggests, 'our desire to grasp and know reality'.[13] The question of boundaries between human imagination and the notion of other worlds is an old one, preoccupying, as Marina Warner reminds us,[14] neo-Platonist philosophers such as Robert Fludd, who in 1617 included 'the imaginative soul, or fantasy' in his 'Vision of the Triple Soul in the Body' in *Utriusque Cosmi* (*Of Both Worlds*); almost three hundred years later, Lewis Carroll similarly related of three states of the mind: (1) the 'ordinary state', when the mind is not aware of the world of fairies; (2) the 'eerie state', an in-between state that allows the mind to engage with the ordinary world simultaneously as the world of fairies; and (3) the 'trance', 'in which, while unconscious of actual surroundings, and apparently asleep, he (ie his immaterial essence) migrates to other scenes, in the actual world, or in Fairyland, and is conscious of the presence of Fairies'.[15]

A couple of decades after Carroll, Barrie also referred to the psychological dimension of fantastic imagination in his definition of Neverland, the centre of the mind's topography:

> I *don't know* whether you have ever seen a map of a person's mind. Doctors sometimes draw maps of other parts of you, and your own map can become intensely interesting, but catch them trying to draw a map of a child's mind, which is not only *confused*, but keeps going around all the time. There are zigzag lines on it, just like your temperature on a card, and these are *probably* roads in the island; for the neverland is always *more or less* an island [. . .]. (Barrie, *Peter Pan*, p. 73, my emphases)

Barrie's positioning of Neverland within the unstable boundaries of a child's imagination is suggestive of the ambivalent status of the fantastic other world, the definition of which, as in Fludd's theory, significantly draws from the language of scientific knowledge (cartography and medicine), while simultaneously exposing the limits of scientific discourse. Equally emphatic of the problematic issues of boundaries between this and the other world is Naomi Mitchison's novella *Beyond this Limit* (1935), a text which crosses boundaries at many levels, including those set by typographic conventions through the intrusion of Wyndham Lewis's illustrations within the main body of text. In content, Mitchison's story is also paradigmatic of the ambivalent relationship between the mundane world of ordinary things and Phoebe's surreal journey through the Paris underground system, an epic journey involving mythological and fantastic beings – including Persephone, Greek goddess of Hades, and an unfathomable bird-like 'creature' – which ominously ends with her descent in the lift of the 'Hotel Terminus'. As previously argued elsewhere, unlike Carroll's *Alice in Wonderland* (1865), with which *Beyond this Limit* shares the metamorphic motif and nonsensical plot, Mitchison's text remains emblematically open to more than one reading, including the possibility, which Todorov would classify as an example of the 'uncanny', that Phoebe may have hallucinated the whole journey into the underworld.[16]

As a result of such permeable boundaries between real and other worlds, in narrative terms, the second feature of Scottish fantasy refers to the sustained tension between psychological and supernatural readings of such journeys. The oscillation between two possible explanations – the uncanny and the marvellous, to use Todorov's terminology – runs through the haunted stories of Margaret Oliphant's 'The Open Door' (1881) and 'The Library Window' (1896) and Robert Louis Stevenson's 'The Beach of Falesa' (1892) and 'Thrawn Janet' (1881), though it is arguably Hogg's *Justified Sinner* (1824) that pushes the narrative ambivalence to embrace that notion of 'hesitation' that, in Todorov's system, truly identifies the fantastic. Though partially resolved in the end, the coexistence of two possible readings belongs firmly in MacDonald's *Phantastes* as in *Lanark*; both narratives frame their journeys into other worlds within the real worlds of the characters who undertake the journeys: in *Lanark*, such framing is subverted by the narrative and textual structure, whereby the fantastic story of Lanark (books 3 and 4) literally encloses the realist story of Thaw (books 1 and 2). Significantly, schizoid identity emerges as a recurrent motif of Scottish fantasy, epitomised by the classic doppelgänger narratives of Stevenson's *Jekyll and Hyde* and Hogg's *Justified Sinner* as more explicitly elucidated in Chapter 4 of this study, but persistently underlying most Scottish fantasy in various fashions: both Anodos and Peter Pan experience problematic issues with their 'shadows', Anodos acquiring an ominous shadow while journeying through Faerie, and Peter losing his to Nana, Wendy's dog-nurse. With the postmodernist works of Gray and Banks capitalising on such notions of split subjectivities in *Lanark* and *The Bridge*, it seems impossible not to agree with Elphinstone, when she claims that 'Supernatural agencies and other worlds become vehicles for the expression of a fragmented psychological state'.[17] Like Peter Pan, who is ultimately 'a Betwixt and Between' (Barrie, *Peter Pan*, p. 17), neither bird nor human, the quintessential condition in Scottish fantasy is that of a deconstructed, unstable borderline.[18] Though the journey may appear to take the subject to a world that is 'other', the engendered alienation reveals that the quest is in fact, as Manlove claims, inward-facing,[19] aiming to expose the otherness of the subject who is projecting the fantastic world.

The third feature of Scottish fantasy refers to its emphasis on the quest for knowledge and self-discovery. Literal borders and boundary crossings are of crucial importance in fantasy literature and, as Armitt proposes, 'If fantasy is about being absent from home [. . .], then the inhabitant of the fantastic is always the stranger'.[20] As processes of self-discovery, such journeys embody the metaphor of border crossing to signify the underlying interrogation of the familiar. When travellers begin to explore unknown territories, the journey epitomises the questioning process that underlies fantasy narratives, frequently resulting in what Todorov calls 'hesitation'. Such epistemological doubting emerges in many of the works examined in this chapter: both *The Incomer* and *A Sparrow's Flight* are framed by Naomi's search for knowledge of the past through music; secretive knowledge and deceit, both symbolically held within the walls of Usbathaden's fortress, pervade the three volumes of Hayton's trilogy; Mary Gulliver travels to the South Seas to discover her long-gone husband's fate (Fell, *The Mistress of Lilliput*) in a journey which progressively becomes a voyage of self-discovery. That Scottish fantasy appears centred around epistemological hesitation also emerges in the epiphanic deferral, the revelation of truth, which in some cases (Hogg's *Justified Sinner*) remains unfulfilled.

Fiction produced in the late twentieth century launches another level of questioning, which, McHale would argue, characterises the heterotopic space of postmodernist fantasy: 'in the context of postmodernism the fantastic has been co-opted as one of a number of strategies of an ontological poetics that pluralizes the real and thus "problematizes" representation'.[21] Postmodernism goes beyond the phase of epistemological questioning to embrace a more radical investigation of ontological concerns, and ultimately propose a notion of multiplicity and simultaneity that erases the boundaries between 'possible worlds': 'Space here is less constructed than deconstructed by the text, or rather constructed and *deconstructed* at the same time'.[22] The question therefore is not that of choice between which world to believe in, but of what type of dialogue exists between Kensington and Neverland, Glasgow and Unthank, the Scottish landscape and the 'elfland' Thomas the Rhymer is taken to, never to return. McHale borrows the notion of heterotopia from Michel Foucault's theorisation of 'other spaces'.[23] Heterotopias exist outside and beside the 'normal' spaces of everyday living; including the 'nowhere' (Neverland?) of a honeymoon trip, the suburban cemetery, the theatre, but also the retirement home and old-fashioned boarding school; what happens in these 'other spaces' somehow deviates from 'normal' living conditions. Heterotopias are, therefore, quintessentially 'other', deviant, but also intrinsically heterogeneous: 'The heterotopia is capable of juxtaposing in a single real place several spaces, several sites that are in themselves incompatible'.[24] Such inherent resistance to homogeneity is also linked to the notion of heterochrony, the simultaneous coexistence of multiple slices of time in places such as libraries and museums, but also in spaces which, by definition, expose the transitory quality of time (fairgrounds, vacation villages, etc.): 'Time as a theme has always been a focus for the science fiction writer', Armitt comments, 'with time travel and disrupted chronologies being a central preoccupation throughout the history of the form'.[25] The simultaneous coexistence of multiple spaces and times character-ises many postmodernist fictions, from the surreal world(s) of Pynchon's *The Crying of Lot 49* to the self-conscious anachronisms of Fowles's *The French Lieutenant's Woman*, prompting the incessant questioning of both spatial and chronological dimensions. The introverted character of Scottish fantasy allows for a blend of epistemological and ontological interrogations proposed by Foucault's heterotopias, a questioning that is frequently filtered through the category of gender, in women's fantastic texts of the late twentieth and early twenty-first centuries. Besides those considered in this chapter, the works of Kennedy – and particularly *So I Am Glad* – Tennant, Smith and Thompson, as seen in the following chapters, all interrogate the linear logic of time and space in their treatment of doubles, dangerous women and spectrality.

The juxtaposition of multiple other worlds, particularly those represented in the utopian/dystopian mode, which, as McHale has noted, has dominated the SF production of the late twentieth century, allows women writers to address gender definition within a patriarchal system: the utopian/dystopian fictions of Marge Piercy, Doris Lessing, Joanna Russ and Margaret Atwood, among others, constitute a coherent corpus of speculative feminist fantasy. Piercy's *Woman On The Edge Of Time* (1976) shares with Elphinstone's *The Incomer* and *A Sparrow's Flight* a concern with the intersections of gender and episte-mological and linguistic discourse. In Hayton's trilogy quests for knowledge are also indissolubly linked with gender preoccupations: the three giant's daughters, Marighal, Barve and Essullt, whose journeys the narratives follow, epitomise the desire for self-determination and freedom from the boundaries of paternal authority represented by the fortress. Likewise, in Fell's *The Mistress of Lilliput*, Mary's journey follows a double path of self-determination: hers is a quest for psychological and sensual fulfilment.

Mary Gulliver's journey to the South Seas is anticipated visually, at the threshold of the main text, with an illustration depicting 'A Map of the East Indies', inclusive of 'New Holland or Terra Australis Incognita', foreshadow-ing Mary's own journey into the unknown. Additionally, the graphic aspect of the multi-layered narrative of *The Mistress of Lilliput* is also rendered through the use of italicised typeface to identify passages from Mary's diary and cor-respondence. Other worlds can be seen, it has been remarked, as nothing but representations of the mind; in the case of fiction, the first level of such projections is given by the typographic signs on the page. The coexistence of heterogeneous worlds – be they literal or imagined – in the content of a story is reflected on such textual devices that add layers to the other world of textual representation: the paratext, which Genette defines as 'More than a boundary or a sealed border, [. . .] rather, a threshold, or [. . .] a "vestibule" that offers *the world at large* the possibility of either stepping *inside* or turning back' (my emphases).[26] The paratext is the textual dimension of Foucault's heterotopia, being, as Genette notes, 'an "undefined zone" between the inside and the outside, a zone without any hard and fast boundary on either the inward side (turned towards the text) or the outward side (turned toward the world's discourse about text)'.[27] Paratextual strategies (footnotes and typeface) support the representation of other worlds in Elphinstone's and Hayton's works.

Along with the paratext, transtextuality (to use Genette's broader definition)[28] constitutes a major narrative device supporting the heterotopic zone, as noted by McHale, of much postmodernist fantasy. The novels examined in this chapter all reveal 'an intertextual space', created, as McHale proposes, 'whenever we recognize the relations among two or more texts'.[29] Elphinstone's texts draw on several elements from the Scottish ballad and folk tradition, as well as from the Scandinavian sagas; the direct influence of Celtic folk tradition is also evident in Sian Hayton's trilogy; finally, though *The Mistress of Lilliput* does not establish a manifest link with a Scottish/Celtic precedent, its reliance on Swift's *Gulliver's Travels* lays the foundation for the subversive transtextual space of the sequel: moreover, Mary 's point of view discloses an implicit critique of her Scottish motherland.

Crossing the Boundaries: Margaret Elphinstone's Ghostly Dystopias and Other Worlds

From the post-apocalyptic communities of Clachanpluck and the empty lands in *The Incomer* and *A Sparrow's Flight* to the nineteenth-century North American context of *Voyageurs*, journeys and 'other' worlds are paramount throughout Elphinstone's fiction; even though the author has primarily turned to historical, rather than fantastic fiction, since the publication of *Islanders*, her historical narratives retain a degree of otherworldliness, as noted in a review of *The Gathering Night*: 'Novels about prehistoric life are kin to fantasy fiction: so little evidence has survived that any depiction is mainly surmise'.[30] Her characters are either wanderers or 'incomers'.[31] Significantly, Elphinstone's other worlds frequently exist between (fluctuating) boundaries, or as uncanny borderlands: both Clachanpluck and the empty lands lie on the Scottish/English borders; *Islanders* is set in the marginal Scottish gateway to the north of Europe; *The Sea Road* is partially set in the Green Land (*sic*), a territory still uncharted at the time in which the story takes place; *Hy Brasil* 'interrogates the relationship between real and imaginary islands'.[32] All of Elphinstone's fiction, since the publication of her first short-story collection *An Apple from a Tree*, exposes the dynamic relationship that exists between 'nomadic subjects' and changing other worlds, where the notion of roots is made obsolete by the multiplicity of directions journeys may take.[33] Much like Gilles Deleuze and Féliz Guattari's rhizome, the relationship that ties identity to homeland is based on 'principles of connection and heterogeneity'.[34] The problematic sense of belonging and the destabilised notion of 'roots' derive, at least in part, from Elphinstone's sense of her own displaced experience.[35]

Although not easily placed within the boundaries of SF or postmodernism, Elphinstone's earlier novels *The Incomer* and *A Sparrow's Flight* are emblematic of the heavy influence, noted by McHale, exercised by science fiction on fantasy produced in the last three decades of the twentieth century: 'On the whole', McHale proposes, 'postmodernist writing has preferred to adapt science fiction motifs of temporal displacement rather than its spatial galaxies';[36] as with other 'grim' dystopias of the late twentieth century, including Carter's *Heroes and Villains* (1969) and Pynchon's *Gravity's Rainbow* (1973), *The Incomer* and *A Sparrow's Flight* are set in a recognisable world where, after a catastrophic (possibly nuclear) event referred to as the 'change', communities have reverted to a pre-modern way of life. Within these post-apocalyptic communities, fundamental elements of Western thought, time, space and language, become the object of Elphinstone's deconstructive interrogation, with crucial repercussions on gender definitions, which significantly return in the pre-historic setting and plot of *The Gathering Night*.

At the beginning of *The Incomer*, virtually nothing is known of the past and characters do not seem to have a clear notion of the nature of the 'change'. The act of decoding past history seems, nevertheless, crucial to the community haunted by the ignorance of its own roots. Questions about the past are signalled also by the 'absolute orality' of the community. In the society described in *The Incomer*, texts are perceived with a mixture of interest and fear. When Bridget, the most literate person in the community of Clachanpluck, attempts to decode the damaged script of books salvaged from the past, she is puzzled by missing words in a book of poetry, which, in her words, is 'about what everybody knows, but the words are put together very differently, like music'.[37] The texts are in fact excerpts from T. S. Eliot's 'Burnt Norton' (1935), and these transtextual allusions to the *Four Quartets* support Clachanpluck's problematic relationship with the enigma of its time: 'All time is unredeemable' (Elphinstone, *The Incomer*, p. 59).[38] Decontextualised – 'There is no context now' (p. 55), says George, another member of the community – and literally fragmented, Eliot's lines are left enigmatically suspended, open to interpretation, as is the epigraph to the novel, also borrowed from Eliot's *Quartets*:

> We shall not cease from exploration
> And the end of all our exploring
> Will be to arrive where we started
> And know the place for the first time.

Launching the quest is, significantly, the evocative journey metaphor conjured in Eliot's lines, a journey whose epistemological function is that of rediscovering the known world. Such interrogation is, in Elphinstone's novel as in Eliot's poem, linked to the problematic knowledge of the past. The cryptic space of the past is projected on the geography of *The Incomer*, and, in particular, the forest, which, more than anywhere, evokes the 'change': the forest, which frequently carries otherworldly qualities in ballads such as 'Tam Lin' and 'Thomas the Rhymer',[39] is the other space within the other space of Clachanpluck. The epic tones of the openings in Chapters 2 and 19 echo the first two verses of the Gospel of St John, exposing the forest's metaphysical quality:

> *In the beginning there was the forest. The forest covered all the land, and the land became alive with the creatures of the forest. Everything that lived was part of the forest, and each being knew that the forest was not complete without every one of them.* (p. 8)[40]

> *In the beginning was the land. The land was sufficient to itself, and flourished through timeless years in the strength of its own dream. The land nourished itself, drawing water down from the sky and offering back the same water to the sea.* (p. 148)

The transtextual allusions add a metaphysical tone to the Edenic descriptions of the forest and the land, and, simultaneously, sinisterly anticipate its inevitable loss. The clearing of the forest sets the conflict between 'the creatures of the forest' and 'the people in the clearing' (p. 8). The italicised font used in the passages quoted suggests their independence from the main narrative: whether legends or secondary-world narratives such as dreams or visions, the paratextual and transtextual strategies used in these passages amplify the notion of the forest's otherness: 'like *Frankenstein*', Armitt suggests, '*The Incomer* reveals and reveils its monstrous secret through the embedding of a number of storytelling voices, whose clashing fragments remythologise past tales of creation and creativity'.[41] The second passage also articulates the important link between the forest as archetypal locus of knowledge and man's ability to control the environment through language: 'The power of words was theirs, and by a word they could change everything' (p. 148); but language-driven knowledge, seemingly different from the forest's pre-symbolic wisdom, is threatened by man's limitations and *hubris*: ultimately, the parable seems to suggest, the symbolic order generates 'Time' and 'Space', devising 'lines, and limitations', 'where there had been only infinity' (p. 149).

The drastic changes that occurred in the forest indicate the environmental preoccupations that have underpinned Elphinstone's early novels, her collection of short stories, *An Apple from a Tree*, and, more recently, *The Gathering Night*. As Emily claims, the cause of the change is 'only people' (p. 114), who have built houses and cleared the forest's natural greenery. The ecological agenda, however, retains the metaphysical significance of the forest, which embodies the unknown other, an enigma for the community of Clachanpluck, but also 'A place of knowledge, for the place where consciousness is brought to birth is in the dark' (p. 118). The integrity of such knowledge is cracked by the climactic episode of *The Incomer*: Patrick's rape of Anna. The event brings together all the strands of Elphinstone's investigation, as the violation takes a universal meaning: the rape of a woman is also the re-enactment of the past generations' figurative rape of the land. The partition between the natural world of the forest and the 'human' world of Clachanpluck causes the separation of genders: the women go to the forest, while the men stay in the village. The curse is cleared only after two highly ritualised episodes, which significantly take place in the forest. First, Patrick's death (which may have been suicide or sacrificial execution by Emily or all women) takes place in the forest:

> The shadow was very near to him now. The movement was not so much a thing heard as a vibration that ran through the earth beneath him. It was too dark to see. But he was conscious of eyes holding him, drawing in. [. . .] They were very near. (p. 170)

The episode remains ambiguous, as Elphinstone, perhaps to intensify the sense of mystery in the narrative, plays with the possibilities of Patrick's suicide as a result of his guilt, or an execution performed by unknown justice-makers. Either way, the rape and its punishment become 'symbolic of old, bad ways', Gifford comments, 'somehow bound up with the reasons for the fall of the old world':[42] the ritualised quality of the execution is underpinned by the reference to 'the shadow' at the beginning of the passage, and the enigmatic shift to the collective pronoun 'they' by the climactic end of it.

The second episode reveals that the forest retains, in the end, some positive energy, and its status as a place where wisdom and regeneration originate from. It is in the forest that Emily's daughter, Fiona, experiences an epiphanic moment of self-empowerment, as she realises, towards the end of the novel, that she is in control of her existence, as the newly designated leader of the matriarchal community: 'This is my land, and I will create a world where this thing shall not be' (p. 221). The significance of this episode must be seen in relation to the complex discourse on gender that runs as a subtext throughout the story. There is, as Gifford notes, a 'strong feminism' embedded within the post-apocalyptic vision presented in *The Incomer*. But the eco-feminist ideology which may underpin Elphinstone's other world is not without its problems. While Armitt argues that a 'palimpsestic undercurrent of lesbianism' exists within the novel, homoerotic desire is not always positively fulfilled, as is the case with the awkward relationship between Emily and Naomi.[43] While lesbianism is apparently dismissed on one level, possibly because 'too much the same' (p. 116) undermines notions of feminine identity based on difference, it is the exercise of enforced heterosexual desire, in the act of rape, that ultimately threatens female power within the community. Significantly, when Patrick rapes Anna, the violent act assumes the apocalyptic dimension – 'A whole world disintegrating' (p. 155) – of linguistic chaos – 'Words that meant nothing. Meaningless because not human' (p. 155)'. The curse, cast upon the community, is significantly visualised as a sinister 'thing [that] hovered and spread' (p. 219) over the forest. The rape erodes the possibility of communication between genders; after the women are driven away from Clachanpluck, George explains to Naomi: 'My words aren't the same as your words' (p. 166). In this context, then, the earlier lesbian encounter between Anna and Fiona, which significantly, as Armitt reminds us, takes place 'in a cave within the forest',[44] resonates of a new form of feminine subjectivity, one not necessarily based on same/other opposition:

> The darkness of the cave was quite opaque, giving away not the vestige of a shape or presence, or of anything substantial within at all. But it was not alien. It was like looking into a mirror, except that mirrors only reflect the light. Perhaps the opposite of a mirror, thought Fiona, whatever that may be. Mirrors make everything back to front, so perhaps the opposite is just the way I have been all the time. (p. 41)

The ambiguous episode, resonating echoes of Lacan's 'mirror stage', is a further example of how the forest becomes a place of wonder in two ways: it is the palimpsestual location that resonates with the community's uncanny past, but also a forward-looking place of self-discovery, the heterotopia that allows the subversion of established norms to support a different kind of future. Although a sense of mystery still lingers over the community of Clachanpluck, the possibility seems implied that characters will be able to deal with their ignorance of the past and positively embrace the unknown future.

Elphinstone's second novel, *A Sparrow's Flight*, takes the transtextual dimension of *The Incomer* further. Drawing the notion of a contaminated land from Eliot's *The Waste Land* (1922), the novel introduces imagery from popular traditions and creates thematic and transtextual links with several quest romances, including *Parsifal* and *The Holy Grail*, and related texts such as James Frazer's *The Golden Bough* (1890–1915; first abridged edn 1922) and Jessie Weston's *From Ritual to Romance* (1920), both also cited in *The Waste Land*. A sequel to *The Incomer*, the story revolves around Thomas, Naomi's travelling companion, and is set against the post-apocalyptic landscape of Thomas's empty lands. Scant references to the past hint that the change has particularly affected Thomas's community, who have lived as outcasts ever since. As Thomas explains:

> Before the world changed [. . .] these lands were among the most beautiful on earth, and many people prospered here. But in the days of the old

world, it was as you say. There were men in this country who pursued power, with no regard for life, or for what was fitting for this world.[45] (Elphinstone, *A Sparrow's Flight*, p. 84)

As in *The Incomer*, Elphinstone's left-wing politics and environmental pre-occupations support the narrative subtext, as human selfishness and the greed generated by capitalist ideology are responsible for the change and its cata-strophic consequences. Humans have introduced a new mysterious element into the world, which is fatal to the survival of their own species. Although it is not stated in the narrative, some kind of nuclear radiation has contaminated the empty lands with serious genetic consequences to its inhabitants (p. 86).

While the history of the empty lands reflects the author's environmental concerns, its otherworldly location is evocative of the supernatural locations of the ballad tradition; in *A Sparrow's Flight* Thomas's journey towards the mys-terious empty lands after seven years of absence acquires a supernatural aura through the association with 'Thomas the Rhymer' and the seven-year journey to 'fair Elfland'.[46] Magic makes the ballad's ending ambivalent: after receiving 'the tongue that never lies' (Lyle, *Scottish Ballads*, p. 134), as a gift from the Fairy Queen, Thomas's destiny is, nevertheless, left unknown. In Elphinstone's novel, Thomas is a professional magician, but in the empty lands, as in the ballad, the borderlines between magic and the real are far from clear: 'All we produce is dreams' (Elphinstone, *A Sparrow's Flight*, p. 36), Thomas admits, the implication being that the truth and the real are both unknowable: 'if you don't know the truth you invent dragons' (p. 83).

Throughout the journey, which significantly, as with many journeys to other worlds in the ballad tradition,[47] starts with the passage over a body of water, a strange sense of supernatural otherworldliness pervades the mysteri-ous empty lands. Just before reaching Thomas's community, Naomi imagines the empty lands to be populated with fantastic chimeras and sees 'primroses sprouting the flowers of fantasy, and outlandish plants bearing no relation to anything in the world outside' (p. 95). The climax of the journey, a ritual dance celebrating the time elapsed from the change, is conveyed through a spe-cific set of magical imagery.[48] Though framed within a specific time and place setting, the dance acquires a universal significance, where individual identities seem lost within the grander scope of the event: as Naomi notes, 'They were all outside themselves that night' (p. 179). The archetypal character of the ritual seems further underpinned by the dancers' costumes inspired by the traditional Tarot; at the centre of the performance is the hybrid 'Fool', though the natural elements of the costume, 'leaves, young and green as springtime' (p. 180), could also be a reference to some kind of green man; other figures evocative of the Tarot's major arcana, follow the Fool's act, including 'The Magician', 'Death', 'The Stars', 'The Moon', 'The Sun', and finally, 'The

World', at whose feet, Thomas, dressed as 'The Hanged Man', collapses, putting an end to the dance:

> A scream of anguish tore the music apart. The circle broke, disintegrated. The Hanged One pitched forward, falling on the trampled grass. He screamed again. The music shattered into fragments. His third scream filled the whole air with pain. Then he lay silent, unconscious at the feet of the World. (p. 182)

While the ritual bears clear references to the quest motif – progressing from the Fool being 'the innocent at the beginning of the journey' (p. 178) to 'The Hanged One', wearing a mask looking 'two ways at once, as one who stands upon a threshold' and bearing 'the innocence [. . .] of one who has completed the journey and has returned unscathed' (p. 181) – Elphinstone's choice of specific images from the Tarot opens her text also to other archetypal myths of death and resurrection. At the beginning of A Sparrow's Flight, Thomas is 'The Magician': associated with creative power, the magician, though human, is a man who resembles the Maker's ability to give life and transform. 'The Magician' represents fertility, the origin of life, bears the number one in the Tarot pack and, according to some theorists, 'if the Fool is the Nothing which, so to speak, precedes the Beginning, the Juggler is the Beginning itself'.[49] Though not explicitly revealed, 'The Fool' of the ritual dance may also be performed by Thomas, who, at the beginning of the story, admits to being 'a professional fool' (p. 14). The embodiment of folly and insanity, 'The Fool' signifies a state beyond human nature, the ecstasy that connects man with god.[50] 'The Fool' is also associated with Parsifal,[51] 'the child whose father is dead and who is brought up by his mother in seclusion, ignorant of the ways of the world,'[52] establishing, in turn, an indirect link between Parsifal and Thomas. Like Parsifal, Thomas is on a quest, and is virtually fatherless, as nothing is known about his father;[53] both characters appear to have platonic relationships with women, something that, again, relates them both to the bisexual/neutral Fool in the Tarot.[54] Parsifal is a nephew to the Fisher King, whose illness is linked to that of his land, while his recovery is linked to the Grail:[55] the ancient beliefs concerning the death of the king/god, the legend of Parsifal and the Quest for the Holy Grail and the restoration of the land return crucially in Eliot's The Waste Land (1922), which also bears references to the Tarot. Indeed it is, admittedly, from her reading of Eliot's poem that Elphinstone borrows the theme of a deserted land and the use of Tarot imagery.[56] Before the end of the performance Thomas is The Hanged Man, one of the Tarot arcana adopted by Eliot in The Waste Land, and another reference to:

> the theme of the dying and rising god as expounded in Frazer's Golden Bough, the god whose death and resurrection each year was the

guarantee of the annual rebirth of the crops, and by analogy the life after death for men.[57] (Cavendish, *The Tarot*, p. 106)

The transcendent quality of the seven-year dance in the empty lands is further emphasised by his collapse in front of the dancer who is performing 'The World', another reference to traditional Tarot packs, where 'The World' is usually depicted as a female dancer. In the other world of *A Sparrow's Flight*, the images of the Tarot, whose origin is unknown, represent, much like the fragments from Eliot's *Quartets* in *The Incomer*, the vestigial memory of that remote past, which Elphinstone's characters are concerned with and haunted by. The ritual dance, then, unveils itself as quintessential heterotopia, blending two kinds of Foucault's theory – the theatre and the archive – in the otherworldly palimpsest of the empty lands: the dance not only has a celebratory/exorcising function, but becomes an alternative form of expression that exceeds the limits of the symbolic. Concern with language, already encountered in *The Incomer*, is followed up with Naomi's intellectual search for the music of the past in *A Sparrow's Flight*: the main drive for Naomi's own quest is the opportunity to discover more about the classical music from the past. The decodification of the sheet music becomes invested with wider significance, contributing to a much more universal understanding of the human predicament: 'It didn't matter how difficult it was, or how long it took her. She was beginning to work out the patterns in the unknown music, and they were unprecedented' (p. 174). The act of decoding marks the fulfilment of Naomi's quest, the end of her journey through the past and its mystery: as Gifford remarks, it 'shows Naomi that something can be salvaged from there [the past], which can lead her in the future to a richer music' than she has known.[58] As in *The Incomer*, *A Sparrow's Flight* ends as it begins, with a journey, suggesting that to the nomadic subjects of her quest romances, meaning cannot be pinned down to stable roots, but is perpetually travelling along unfamiliar routes, as the quest continues onwards.

Inspired by the reading of Icelandic sagas, *The Sea Road* is mainly based upon the original *Eirik's Saga*, which tells the story of Eirik the Red's first settlement in Greenland in AD 982. Gudrid, the novel's protagonist, features as a minor character in the saga: the main plot, the journeys to the Green Land [sic], the episode of the plague and Gudrid's two marriages are all present in the original saga, which, however, has Gudrid 'unversed in magic'. A devout Christian,[59] in the saga Gudrid refuses, despite her natural disposition and teaching by the sorceress Halldis, to deal with the pagan practices still widespread in the Green Land. In *The Sea Road*, in contrast, Gudrid practises magic even after her conversion to Christianity, and the tension generated between the supernatural world of the pagan Green Land and the Christian world of Southern Europe constitutes the most significant drive of Elphinstone's rewriting. This is reflected, as explained in more detail later, also on the structure of Elphinstone's narrative palimpsest: following a device frequently used in Scottish Gothic texts such as Hogg's *Justified Sinner* and Stevenson's *Jekyll and Hyde*, Gudrid's first-person narrative is edited and transcribed by an editor, the Icelandic priest Agnar Asleifarsson, whose correspondence with other representatives of the Church, is set against Gudrid's stories from the pagan world of Northern Europe.

As the title suggests, the plot of *The Sea Road* revolves around journeys by sea, at the time of the eleventh-century Viking raids. The *Praefatio*, written by Agnar in the third person, introduces Gudrid's story by way of an excerpt from a letter received by Cardinal Hildebrand:

> This woman, apparently, is one of those who have gone *beyond* the confines of the mortal world, in the body. She has dwelt for over a year in the lands *outside* the material world. She has talked with *demons* and the *ghosts* of the dead.[60] (Elphinstone, *The Sea Road*, p. 3; my emphases)

In the pseudo-theological context of the narrative frame, the tone of the preface, suggestive of the Cardinal's scepticism and his intention to use Gudrid's story to defend his thesis against heresy, undermines, nevertheless, any claims to dogmatic knowledge. The implicit critical discourse on the reliability of dogmas raises, instead, a sense of hesitation suspiciously akin to Todorov's definition of the fantastic and supported by Gudrid's childhood memories of her native Iceland:

> I grew up in the lee of Stapafel, and the spirits of Snaefel behind it always lurked in the background of my childhood. [. . .] The gods walked up there, and on tempestuous nights, we could hear Thor battle with the demons who live in the heart of the mountain. Snaefel is full of lesser spirits too: goblins, elves, trolls, all kinds of unknown things. I've seen them often, but always from the corner of my eye. (p. 19)

The geography of Iceland, much like that of Scottish ballads and traditional tales of the supernatural, hosts a plethora of immanent divinities, whose world seamlessly adjoins the world of humans and is indissolubly bound to the distinctive character of the land: 'The tales in such northern traditions are created out of a sense of the inhospitability and the omnipresence of the land', Manlove remarks, and populated by 'gnomes, dwarves, orcs, or trolls, part of the geology, of the rocks'.[61] Significantly, however, the apparent continuity between the material world and supernatural beings is not without questions, as Gudrid is quick to warn that 'If you look straight at any of those folk they change shape at once into twisted lava columns, so you're never quite sure of what you've seen' (p. 19). The subjectivity of the supernatural features of Gudrid's Iceland foreshadows the more fundamental interrogation of monolithic definitions of truth and the real, which underpins the entire narrative: that the boundaries between the imagination and the world of spirits are not clear is further supported by Gudrid's admission that her soul is 'shaped like Stapafel', the haunted volcano of her childhood, and that 'No change of place or religion can change that' (p. 19).

While the paratext of *The Sea Road* includes a seemingly modern map before Agnar's *Praefatio*, the narrative refers to the Green Land as uncharted territory. As *terra incognita*, the Green Land is, in the eyes of Agnar and other members of the Christian community, a haunted territory at the margins of the 'material world' (p. 3). Borrowed from the original saga,[62] the events that occur in the Green Land after the outbreak of a fatal disease, which claims the life of Gudrid's first husband, are described in a lengthy third-person passage (pp. 128–33). Whereas in Iceland the other world of fairies appears to be integrated within the world of ordinary things, in the Green Land death introduces a much more disturbing other world:

> *The ghosts are watching over the lands of Thorstein the Black, because every night new souls are added to their number. The sickness sweeps through the settlement, and each time a person dies its soul is torn from its body and drawn into the throng.* (p. 128)

As the farm turns into a ghost-possessed liminal space, the hybrid coalescence of different belief systems is such that '*Some are helped on their way with tears and blessings, a few have the mark of a cross made over them, and all are sent with the protection of charms and offerings*' (p. 128). The differences in the rituals applied to death, however, appear void in significance, once '*in the dark space under the rafters*' where '*all these things fade into the same mist*' (p. 128). The erosion of boundaries between different sets of faith occurs simultaneously as the interrogation of what, if anything, separates the world of the living from the other world of spirits, as the case of Grimhild's apparent death suggests: while 'The corpse of Grimhild is rising up, supporting itself against the carved pillar that heads the bed', it is Gudrid who 'stops breathing' and whose 'limbs are like clay, and cannot move' (p. 130). As in Stoker's *Dracula*, where the body of the undead frequently appears more vital than those of its living witnesses, the ghost-ridden world of *The Sea Road* subverts the ontological premises of life and death, ultimately exposing the epistemological limits of both scientific and theological discourse.

The passage referring to the pestilence outbreak in the Green Land is rendered, like other shorter interventions in the main text, in a separate, third-person italicised section of the text: this suggests that the events are not a direct transcript of Gudrid's memories, but a mediated version, probably edited by Agnar. The tension between the supernatural other world of Gudrid's story and the real world of the narrative frame operates a subversive function on the primary narrative level, the story of Agnar and Gudrid; after her departure from Bracciano for Iceland, the strength of Agnar's orthodoxy, as he reveals in the 'Postscriptum', appears shaken: 'Suddenly my world is full of questions, in a way that it hasn't been since I read the forbidden works of the Infidel, out of the locked cabinet in the library at Reims' (pp. 241–2). Much like the editor of the sinner's Memoirs in Hogg's *Justified Sinner*, Agnar's dogmatic discipline seems weakened and his status destabilised at the end, with a decision to move back to the periphery of the known world, his native Iceland.

As in the narrative palimpsests of Hayton's trilogy examined in the next section of this chapter, the layered textuality of *The Sea Road* raises questions of authenticity and originality. The transtextual dimension of *The Sea Road* self-consciously exposes the problematic notion of mediation of translated worlds. In the virtually 'textless' society from *The Incomer* and *A Sparrow's Flight*, or in the medieval communities from *Islanders* and *The Sea Road*, orality is still the principal form of tradition and the only vehicle of information. Elphinstone's discourse about orality and text becomes particularly relevant in *The Sea Road*, where the narrative is being simultaneously transcribed into a written text from the oral source, and translated from Icelandic into Latin. Moreover, Elphinstone's writing is in English: despite the reader's awareness that the fiction of the novel should be read in Latin, readers of *The Sea Road* read the story in modern English. The other world depicted in Gudrid's narrative is therefore, by definition, to remain enclosed in its foreignness, as Agnar admits: 'Meaning [. . .] lies in the words themselves. Change the words and the sense is no longer the same. To change a text from one language into another is a kind of lie' (p. 6). More so than in Elphinstone's early novels, the self-reflective narrative of *The Sea Road* questions the representative powers of language, exposed as an incoherent set of signs whose decodification is perpetually deferred. Yet, even after her conversion to Christianity, Gudrid's magic relies mainly on language: 'the best charms are just words. They are easy to carry about, and on the whole you don't lose them' (p. 58). Language, it would appear, retains a magical ambivalence, embodying the human desire to know and contain what is foreign and boundless.

QUESTIONING ORIGIN AND GENEALOGY: SIAN HAYTON'S TRILOGY

Prior to the publication of *The Sea Road*, the coexistence of adjoining worlds and clashing belief systems in medieval Europe had already been explored in the three volumes of Hayton's trilogy, *Cells of Knowledge*, *Hidden Daughters*, and *The Last Flight*. This complex set of part mythological, part historical narratives articulates the tensions between the supernatural world of the giant Usbathaden and the 'real' world of tenth-century Christian monks and warriors. As the narratives unravel, boundaries between worlds become progressively more blurred, thus subverting all normative hierarchies (Christian/pagan; male/female; natural/supernatural) set by the Christian monks' primary narrative level. The engendered conflict poses further questions of origin and authenticity: 'The Celtic pagan world is full of supernatural events', Elphinstone comments, 'in which reality signifies something completely different from that of either tenth-century Christian narrator or the twentieth-century reader of a historical novel'.[63] While blurring the boundaries of real and other worlds, the trilogy also interrogates stable parameters of origin, as the complex genealogies outlined in the novels suggest a critical reading of lineage-based identity.

The challenges thus posed to the normative hierarchical order reflect the author's own critical understanding of fixed notions of national identity and belonging.[64] Hayton's biography reveals a hybrid, though distinctly Celtic, cultural background. Born in Liverpool of a Scottish/Gaelic/Welsh mother and an English Jewish father, Hayton's upbringing and literary development was significantly influenced by the Scottish and Welsh oral traditions.[65] While *The Governors*, examined in Chapter 4, reveals echoes of Scottish selkie lore, the Arthurian romances collected in *The Mabinogion* provide the nucleus of the trilogy's stories, along with other traditional Scottish tales, such as 'The Battle of the Birds' and 'The Green Man of Knowledge'.[66] The otherworldly dimension depicted in the three volumes revolves around the patriarchal figure of the giant Usbathaden and his archetypal Gothic fortress, though the volumes set out to interrogate, rather than fix, the reliability of tradition.[67]

The daughters of the Giant Usbathaden all bear names evocative of the Celtic tradition: the giant himself, one of his daughters, Olwen, and her husband Culhuch (or Culhwch in the Welsh tradition) derive from the Welsh tradition: the giant Yspaddaden (or Ysbaddaden) is Olwen's father in 'Culhwch and Olwen', the oldest tale in the Arthurian cycle,[68] and the Welsh version of an international traditional folk tale known as 'The Giant's Daughter'.[69] The tale belongs to *The Mabinogion*, several references to which are found in the trilogy: Kigva and Rhiannon are characters from 'Manawydan Son of Llyr'; two ladies named Essyllt are listed among the 'gentle gold-torqued women' invoked by Culhwch to persuade Arthur to fight for him against Yspaddaden in 'Culhwch and Olwen'; Branwen appears in 'Branwen Daughter of Llyr'. Hayton's overt borrowing from 'Culhwch and Olwen' emerges clearly in relation to Olwen, whose description in the traditional tale quoted below recalls the fair creature of Hayton's narratives:

> Yellower was her head than the flower of the broom, whiter was her flesh than the foam of the wave; whiter were her palms and her fingers than the shoots of the marsh trefoil from amidst the fine gravel of a welling spring. Neither the eye of the mewed hawk, nor the eye of the

thrice-mewed falcon, not an eye was there fairer than hers. Whiter were her breasts than the breast of the white swan, redder were her cheeks than the reddest of foxgloves. Whoso beheld her would be filled with love of her. Four white trefoils sprang up behind her wherever she went; and for that reason she was called Olwen.[70]

Olwen's fair beauty evokes the purity of feelings she embodies in the trilogy. Her description in *Hidden Daughters* bears remarkable resemblance to the traditional tale: 'She has skin as white as the drifting snow and her hair is white-gold like the sun at noon. Her eyes are as grey as the ice on the river and she carries herself as proudly as a swan' (*HD*, p. 141).[71]

The Mabinogion also introduces the problematic notions of birthright and lineage that pervasively appear in the trilogy. In 'Culhwch and Olwen', as in the trilogy, Culhuch's father is Kilidh, though in the Arthurian tale his mother has died and has been substituted by an evil stepmother who seeks revenge against the giant. Culhuch's name relates to his birth in a pigsty in the traditional tale, as in *Cells of Knowledge*:

> When she found she was with child and that her dishonour would be shown to all the world by my birth she ran frantic into the forest. There she stayed, insane, till I was born, and she brought me into the world in a pigsty.[72] (*CK*, p. 148)

A second version of Culhuch's story is given in *Hidden Daughters* by his mother, the queen, Kigva, where the figurative reference to pigs reflects the humiliation she suffered during her pregnancy as a captive of Kilidh's tribe: 'Like the pigs she was tethered to the house by her ankle and like the pigs also she was contented to stay that way till her delivery' (*HD*, p. 28).

The problematic notion of lineage and origin is, from the beginning, delineated as the main question explored throughout the trilogy's complex narratives. Challenges to the 'Law of the Father', embodied by the patriarchal authority of various father figures in the trilogy, are eminently represented by the tasks set by the Usbathaden to annihilate Kynan, who aspires to Marighal's hand in marriage. As well as in 'Culhwch and Olwen' this universal motif frequently appears in traditional quest romances,[73] including the popular Scottish tales 'The Battle of the Birds' and 'The Green Man of Knowledge'; these tales are central to Marighal and Kynan's story in *Cells of Knowledge*: the three tasks the giant imposes on Kynan, the cleaning of the byre, the thatching of the roof and the collection of magpies' eggs, are identical to the tasks set by the giant for the king's son in 'The Battle of the Birds'; the giant's daughter's magical intervention to help her husband-to-be also recurs in all versions of the story and her consequent mutilation appears in both 'The Battle of the Birds' and 'The Green Man of Knowledge', as it does in *Cells of Knowledge*: upon rescuing her from the sea, one of the first things we learn about Marighal is that 'there were only three fingers in her left hand' (*CK*, p. 18).

While the plurality of transtextual references to previous texts, motifs and characters foreshadows questions of originality and authorship, the complex textual origin of the trilogy is also reflected in its narrative form. In *Cells of Knowledge,* the letters sent by Selyf, monk at Rintsnoc (Portpatrick), to the Bishop of Alban (Scotland) and the Abbot Gwydion constitute the primary narrative level. In his letters, Selyf introduces other first-person narrators: two of the giant's daughters, Marighal and Evabyth, and the giant's foster son, Kynan. His own son Hw, who has studied the correspondence to defend his father and the monks' order from the accusation of heresy, has also glossed Selyf's letters. In *Hidden Daughters*, Hw takes over the narrative through his own letters describing his adventures with Barve, another of the giant's daughters. Like his father's, Hw's letters to Dubdaliethe and Ælfrid are also accompanied by a commentary put together by an anonymous editor, referred to as 'Ælfrid's student', though not 'consacrated' because he is a medicine student (*HD*, p. 31). Again, as in *Cells of Knowledge*, Hw's first person narrative is frequently interrupted to incorporate other voices: Barve and Olwen both share their stories with Hw. Finally, in *The Last Flight*, the narrative takes the form of an investigation. Acting as an editor, the monk Josiah collects five first-person narratives, different versions of the same story, as they are told by Guaire, Branwen, Drust, March, Essullt, and the mysterious seven sleepers Josiah meets at the end of the investigation: in his letters to Eugenius Calvus, the reference to Ælfrid and medical knowledge suggest that Josiah is in fact the editor of Hw's letters collected in *Hidden Daughters*.

The coexistence of multiple narratives and points of view enhances the trilogy's palimpsestual structure, which leads to an interrogation of textual authenticity and authorship: while the monks' points of view attribute a realistic and historical value to the stories narrated, their narrative reliability is in turn undermined by the other monks' annotations, which effectively erode any claims to truth and orthodoxy; Hw's annotation that '*We are known to be a contentious order, and cannot agree even among ourselves*' (*CK*, p. 95), placed next to the bishop's questioning of Selyf's unorthodox beliefs of baptism, highlights this point particularly well. The daughters' narrative intrusions into the monks' texts fracture the notional textual unity and coherence further, simultaneously subverting the normative hierarchical order of gender: 'the marginalia suggests that in Hayton's re-vision of the past it is the male voice and text which is marginalised, with the female action for once holding centre, stage and page'.[74] Thus Hw's concerns and his comments about Selyf's vicissitudes with Marighal emerge alongside the main narrative in *Cells of Knowledge*. Similarly, in *Hidden Daughters*, Josiah's critical reading of Hw's narrative exposes more fractures in the monks' dogmatism; when, for instance, the giant's daughters discuss mortality and poverty rates, Josiah notices Hw's irritability:

> *Hw was very angry at all this numbering. He said it was presumptuous, like trying to see into the mind of God. I could not understand his point of view, for I think that numbers are the very way in which God has chosen to speak to us of his mind. I am not alone in this, but Hw has no patience with any idea of mine.* (HD, p. 59)

Most importantly, what the monks' narratives unveil is the threat that their knowledge of Usbathaden's other world poses to Christian orthodoxy. Like other Gothic mansions, from Dracula's castle in Stoker's novel to Manderley in Daphne du Maurier's *Rebecca*, temptation and deception coexist in the topography of the giant's fortress. Retaining both uncanny and marvellous elements, Usbathaden's castle is a source of psychological as well as supernatural wonders: to Kynan, who admits 'he could not tell you [Selyf] half of the mysteries there', the giant's castle is a place of visions – 'I would often see my mother in dreams at night' – and marvellous technology: the giant's slaves 'were globes that flew, singing' and could teach him how 'to use sword and shield' (CK, p. 97). The castle, where 'fires would burn [. . .] winter and summer' (CK, p. 88), conceals a system of sophisticated surveillance and *trompe l'œil*, in the form of metal spy-globes, distorting mirrored walls and concealed secret passages: within the fortress walls, Usbathaden's power is, as Foucault describes it with reference to Bentham's *Panopticon*, 'visible and unverifiable'.[75]

As the complex architectural and technological features of Usbathaden's castle are also an expression of otherworldliness, they simultaneously question definitions of the real. The marvellous subject matter of the daughters' textile works, for instance, self-consciously exposes the erasure of real/fantastic boundaries: 'Some of the looms were hung with weavings of beauty and strangeness that showed beasts and plants and countries which no man could know' (CK, p. 104). The underlying question here refers to the origin of such fantastic creatures, as the possibility that they are real in Usbathaden's world is as acceptable as the possibility that they might just be projections of the daughters' imaginations: ultimately, however, images is all they are, simulacral representations with no clear referent. Toward the end of the first volume, Selyf comments on the luxurious rooms decorated with the daughters' woven works:

> All around us were couches covered with cushions, and the walls were hung with thick, *soft* hangings which were pictures of *strange* animals and flowers, and laughing people in brightly coloured clothes. [. . .] All these pictures had been made by the sisters over the years, and I was filled with wonder to think that these women who had never left their halls could

find so much to weave into their pictures. I do not doubt that it was the *softness* lapping around them that would make them see such *wonderful* sights and dreams. *Truly* it was a place to fill and drown your *senses*, and to tempt the *flesh* with sensations of *delight*. (*CK*, p. 163; my emphases)

The sensual dimension of the giant's world, as Hw's marginal commentary points out – '*It is good that you were able to resist this luxury, Selyf*' (*CK*, p. 163) –, threatens to subvert Selyf's discipline, whose 'simple soul is stricken by such riches' as those found in the giant's library, a receptacle of treasures comparable to 'the great Abbey in Rome' (*CK*, p. 163). What Selyf's language implies, particularly in the last line of the quotation above, is the subversion of truth: the Christian understanding of truth as God's promise of a purely spiritual world is here translated in the apparently material world of the giant's castle. The possibility that what Selyf sees in the castle is the effect of mere magical illusion leads such questioning further.

Against both direct and mediated experience of Usbathaden's magical other world, the Christian brothers' letters reveal the unstable foundations of Christian orthodoxy: 'Christianity is not unified or monolithic', Christopher Whyte remarks of the treatment of belief in the trilogy, 'but an ideology in a state of flux, a multiplicity of belief systems alternating or coexisting under a single name'.[76] Allusions to Islam throughout the trilogy, including the reference to the cave at the beginning of Kigva's narrative in *Hidden Daughters*, support the idea of other centrifugal forces within a notion of (Christian) monotheism. In the Quran as in *Hidden Daughters*, the concept of rebirth underlies the initiation ritual performed by Kigva and the seven sleepers in the cave. Other references to the seven sleepers appear in Josiah's allusion to the cave and seven tiny men at the end of *The Last Flight* (*TLF*, p. 257).[77] References to Islam are endorsed by another mysterious figure, the 'wood man', who appears and disappears throughout the trilogy. In *The Last Flight*, his encounter with Selyf, who attempts to exorcise him, reveals the wood-man's association with Islam:

> Prophet, if believing women come to you and pledge themselves to serve no other god beside Allah, to commit neither theft, nor adultery, nor child-murder, to utter no monstrous falsehoods of their own invention, and to disobey you in nothing just or reasonable, accept their allegiance and implore Allah to forgive them. Allah is forgiving and merciful. (*TLF*, p. 124)

While to Selyf he is an apparently possessed human being, the wood-man also presents demonic qualities. Upon seeing him in the forest, Drust first 'could see *nothing*', then 'a face' appears 'among the *greenery*' (*TLF*, p. 120; my emphases). These details, together with Drust's comment that the face 'was very brown from the sun and hung about with tangled grey hair' (*TLF*, p. 120)', support a view of the wood-man as a green man or tree-spirit figure. In his psychoanalytical reading of the green man in relation to Kingsley Amis's novel of that title, Robin Sims suggests that, akin to Lacan's 'thing', 'the green man signifies both a life-force in nature and its opposite'.[78] In *The Last Flight* anthropomorphic trees are responsible for the individual sexual initiations of Drust and Essullt. In Drust's account, the 'tree-woman' presents female sexual characteristics in the shape of 'twin mounds' and 'a ridge running down the length of it like a spine' (*TLF*, p. 132). The event is significantly haunted by the wood-man's prophetic words: 'Women are your fields. Go, then into your fields and do as you would like' (*TLF*, p. 132). In Essullt's account, the first encounter with the wood-man reinforces his hybrid affiliation to Islam –'Allah's earth is vast', he claims – and pagan tree spirits:

> There was a face, but it seems to be part of a tree. Studying the creature carefully I realised that it was, in fact a man but his cloak and jerkin were made of bark, and his hat was woven out of green branches. [. . .] In the gloom of the forest it was scarcely possible to distinguish him from the undergrowth he stood in. (*TLF*, p. 230)

The description echoes the kind of imagery recurrent in church carvings, which, as Sims rightly notes, blurs the boundaries between humanity and nature:

> The green man represents something at once utterly removed from humanity, located in the darkness of the forest, which is at the same time inside humanity, so that the human face can be (metaphorically perhaps) disfigured by branch or vine-like growths that extend from the lips, or come from within.[79]

Later, the wood-man reappears as he takes a more active role in Essullt's sexual initiation with a tree 'hung with bones and bits of cloth', as she recalls:

> The wood-man came round to my back and loosened my girdle, unfas-tened my shift, and stripped me to the skin. I could offer no resistance. He guided me round the fire to the bedecked tree and I saw with horror that one of its lower branches was carved into the shape of a phallus and was pointing toward my loins. [. . .] All I knew was the firm hand of the wood-man as he drew me toward the tree. (*TLF*, p. 237)

As a demon, his appearance to Kigva in *Hidden Daughters*, foreseeing the curse on her people and her land if she stays with Kilidh's people (*HD*, p. 16), prefigures the wood-man's subversive role in the genealogies of the trilogy. *Cells of Knowledge* and *Hidden Daughters* begin with Kilidh's and Kigva's narratives retelling the story of their (unfair) union. Placed at the beginning of the first two volumes of the trilogy, the 'Scenes' prefigure the problematic dual 'origin', acquiring greater resonance in relation to the interrogation of patriarchal authority and genealogy. In the two 'Scenes', these complex issues are emphasised through the use of juxtaposed points of view: in Kilidh's story, the queen (Kigva) is only the warrior's occasional lover; in Kigva's story, the loss of her royal status is linked, according to the wood-demon's prophetic words, to the uprooting of her tribe's settlement 'high in the moorland' to Kilidh's 'lower lands', where her 'voice will mean nothing' (*HD*, p. 16). Kilidh and Kigva's union is, in a sense, the original sin, registering the transition from the seemingly matriarchal system of Kigva's nomadic clan to the patriarchal order of Kilidh's reign. Significantly, Culhuch, the offspring of Kigva and Kilidh, is responsible for Usbathaden's death: the spear used to kill the giant, according to Culhuch, 'has been a sacred relic in my mother's family since time began' (*CK*, p. 155), though upon extracting it from his stomach, Usbathaden claims 'maternal' rights over the weapon: 'I made this spear myself [. . .] and it has returned to its maker like a child to its *mother*' (*CK*, p. 155; my emphases). Creating a direct link between Usbathaden and Kigva, the remark tightens the bond between the two principal sets of lineage in the trilogy; the battle for power between Culhuch and the giant becomes therefore the battle between the matriarch (Kigva) and the patriarch (Usbathaden).

That the giant's demise is linked to his own genealogy is, of course, reinforced by the challenges posed earlier in the story by Marighal's marriage to Kynan, Kilidh's son, and Usbathaden's own foster son. As Marighal explains to Kynan, Usbathaden's 'desire in bringing you to his stronghold was to find a son for himself' (*CK*, p. 105), because 'The children of his line were all female', Kynan learns from the giant himself, 'and this was a source of much grief to him' (*CK*, p. 98). The problematic absence of mothers and male offspring poses further questions about Usbathaden's genealogy: Hw is suspicious about Marighal's lineage, especially when she does not mention her father's name (*CK*, p. 18), nor her mother's (*CK*, pp. 19, 39). Marighal later explains that their mothers died in childbirth and 'did not live to see us grow' (*CK*, p. 107), while Usbathaden mentions his 'immortal bride', whom he left 'to seek dominion over mankind' 'many generations ago' (*CK*, p. 130); the possibility remains open of an incestuous relationship between the giant and his daughters, as noted in one of Hw's glosses: '*We know who the father of this group is, but who are their "mothers"? I fear we do not need to look far*' (*CK*, p. 144). The giant's incestuous relationship with his daughters is also suggested in the context of the magic Marighal performs to help Kynan in his third task: explaining to Kynan that the tree was one of the giant's metamorphic incarnations, she adds that 'My part in it was to make you a road, for *only his own kin could combine with him* to make more branches, so *I merged my substance with his*' (*CK*, p. 158; my emphases). The ambiguous relationship is further questioned, however, by the belief that the loss of virginity of any one of his daughters would inevitably cause the giant's death (*CK*, p. 105).

The interrogation of origin and lineage is also interlinked, at the primary level of the narrative, with the early Christian resistance to celibacy, as seen in the disputed legitimacy of marriage among the monks at Rintsnoc (*CK*, p. 95). Significantly, while in the preface to the first letter Hw declares himself to be 'nearest kin to Selyf' (*CK*, p. 15), later, Selyf himself laments to the blacksmith Grig the danger of losing his 'line', should the son he has 'vowed to disown' (*CK*, p. 167) perish in his battle against the pagans in Orkney. Grig, who has served the giant his weapons and who has acted as Marighal's own foster father, also discloses an ambivalent origin:

> It is said that we were not born of woman, but that the earth herself bore us as seeds in her body. Our gestation took many years, nor is there a mention of a father in our begetting. When the time came for us to see the light of day my mother tore herself open in the same way she does in the south. In those places she sometimes twists and writhes and gaping holes appear in her body, and trees fall like blades of wheat. One time we were flung out of her womb, not as infants, but as stones which turned soft over a period of years, and turned into ourselves. (*CK*, p. 166)

Set against Usbathaden's motherless genealogy, Grig's fatherless ancestry subverts the patriarchal order that the giant, Christian monks and male warriors all articulate in different ways, underpinning the gender preoccupations associated with the complex patterns of genealogy presented in the trilogy: 'There is [. . .] no simplistic male/female schema to the trilogy', Gifford notes, as Hayton 'deliberately blurs the boundaries between the two, for her overall aim is to create an equality of space for her Celtic female alongside the male, a space which conventional histories would not allow'.[80] The erosion of binary oppositions becomes particularly manifest in the last section of *The Last Flight*, where Usbathaden's and the human world merge in the incestuous union of Essullt and her nephew, Drust. As Marighal explains, there will never be a child from their unnatural union and yet, it is necessary that they stay together 'or the world will be destroyed within the year' (*TLF*, p. 261).[81] The union thus performs a ritualistic function:

> It was not the coupling of a man and a woman. Naked, they lay side by side and pressed themselves together. By and by there appeared from the side of each something like a hand that reached across the space between them. The hands met, clasped each other and grew wider till the whole side of the man meshed and tangled with that of the woman. (*TLF*, pp. 260–1)

Evocative of a utopian genderless body, the androgyny conjured in the last image suggests a holistic annihilation of sexual difference and proposes an idealised reconciliation of the trilogy's pervasive gender conflicts and apparent misogyny: at the end of *Cells of Knowledge,* Hw is afraid of meeting the giant's daughters because 'they change shape so easily' (*CK*, p. 137), and at the beginning of *Hidden Daughters*, he admits his concerns about Usbathaden's family: '*There can be no doubt that their existence itself is unlawful, and that it is our duty to contain their power*' (*CK*, p. 87). The link between Hw's mistrust of women and Christian prejudice is clear: '*a comb drawn through your hair will summon spirits. I have seen them and heard them when my mother combed her hair, but she was a good Christian and at once prayed for their departure*' (*CK*, p. 94). Christian orthodoxy and patriarchy converge in the prejudice against the pagan women presented in *Hidden Daughters*. Behind the mysterious disappearance of Olwen's children is, as Barve explains, Kigva's revenge against Usbathaden's betrayal that led to her ruin (*HD*, p. 227), though it is Olwen, significantly, who suffers Culhuch's insinuation of her involvement in witchcraft: 'I do not know what infamous rites she practises but I have heard of rituals where they drink the blood of children as joyfully as if it were fine wine' (*HD*, p. 169). The second volume of the trilogy, however, also signals the collapse of Hw's apparent misogyny, and his gradual embracement of a more positive – if limited – appreciation of womankind: 'Is not this wonderful evidence of the goodness of the Creator, that after Eve he gave us Mary?' (*HD*, p. 200), he asks, as he contemplates on the feast of the Annunciation. Overall the trilogy explores the progressive crumbling of patriarchal authority at the same time as it interrogates the ideological foundations of religion; as Whyte puts it:

> Gender roles interact with belief systems as narrative patterns do. An ideology specifies the behaviour appropriate to each sex, puts configurations of the masculine and the feminine and substantiates them through narratives of how they came to be, through what may be called an ontology of gender.[82]

While the tension generated by the daughters' problematic relationships with the Christian monks interrogates, along with the pervasive questioning of origins, essentialist parameters of gender, the conclusion to Hayton's trilogy settles for the idealised ending of utopia. Hayton could be suggesting that, as Gifford proposes, 'These women *have* to fall into the world of man, so that [. . .] a new world can evolve from the female-male and Celtic-Christian confrontation'.[83] The circular structure nevertheless adds poignancy to the (perhaps) incongruous resolution of the conflict: Kigva's quest for revenge, launched at the outset, thus ends with the reconciliation of the feminine/masculine, demonic/human principles in a genderless, hybrid whole: though conclusive in its cyclic repetition, the symbiotic union retains echoes of the archetypal challenge to authority where the story began.

The Romantic Quest: Alison Fell's *The Mistress of Lilliput*

The quest is a central motif of *The Mistress of Lilliput,* a highly self-conscious pastiche based on Jonathan Swift's *Gulliver's Travels* (1726). Not strictly fantasy fiction, the settings of Swift's satire deploy nevertheless the notion of other worlds to address political questions about Gulliver's (and Swift's) homeland; arguably drawing its plot from the quest romance, *Gulliver's Travels* engages also with a critique of romance on many levels: when the queen's palace burns in Lilliput, and a very masculine Gulliver is able to extinguish the fire through urination, the blame is significantly placed on 'the carelessness of the Maid of Honour, who fell asleep while she was reading a Romance'.[84] The episode establishes direct links between the romance genre, feminine reading and the dangers of *fire*, metaphorical or otherwise: 'the association with the feminine indicates that prose fiction is considered 'suspiciously feminine', Mary-Anne Doody argues, 'Novels of all kinds were going to be treated more and more negatively at the mid-eighteenth century'.[85] As a sequel pastiche, *The Mistress of Lilliput* explicitly draws both on the romance quest elements embedded in Swift's narrative and on the implicit critique of romance, which Swift's satire articulates, to produce a self-consciously feminist transposition of the most traditional form of feminine romance: the love quest. In doing so, *The Mistress of Lilliput* sets the quest for love against the story of Gulliver's return to England and his wife's journey following his mysterious disappearance. The apparently formulaic approach to the love quest hides a subversive discourse of authority and empowerment, which, as Michael DePorte reminds us, is an important subtext of Swift's text:

> Concerns with power are obviously central to the *Travels*: Gulliver's enormous power in Lilliput; the power of everything and everybody except Gulliver in Brobdingnag, [. . .]; the power of technology on the flying island, of necromancy in Glubbdubdrib, and of reason in Houyhnhnmland; not to mention the power Gulliver hopes to exert as author [. . .].[86]

In relation to gender, power is overtly problematic throughout the *Travels*: if in Lilliput Gulliver's heroic masculinity finds the appropriate – albeit temporary – winning context, the hyperbolic world of Brobdingnag challenges the conventional attributes of the male hero, while, in the land of Houyhnhnms, he becomes, at last, a much weaker and humbler, 'domestic' man: 'the hero of every adventure has taken on the feminine role'.[87] Gulliver's progressive feminisation poses questions about the relationship of gender and power in Swift's narrative, and particularly in the last section of the *Travels*, which, Jeanette Winterson notes, signals the insurgence of emotional turmoil in the previously passionless Gulliver. Significantly, in the land of horses, Gulliver's surrender to the feelings he nurtures for his Master is suggestive of a gender shift, as Captain Gulliver appears suddenly 'weakened' by the awakening of love: the male quest leaves Gulliver's self ambiguously disempowered, emasculated in relation to androcentric and patriarchal parameters of masculine identity.[88]

In more than one sense, *The Mistress of Lilliput* articulates the hierarchical subversions of the *Travels* further, as it positions the journey into the other world in the context of its heroine's quest for self-determination. In doing so, Fell's romance subverts the expectations of the conventional quest, which, as Frye notes, excludes women from any active role, reducing the female role to that of passive supporters of male success: '[woman] achieves no quest herself, but she is clearly the kind of being who makes a quest possible'.[89] While the traditional quest maps out a journey of masculine identity through masculine cosmogony, the feminization of the quest romance, as Dana A. Heller remarks, involves the revision of gender hierarchy, a process that starts with the metaphorical and literal journeys into the *terra incognitas* of world(s) woman knows only through their masculine representations: 'Questing, a woman dares to reinvent herself. Unfamiliar, indiscreet, she "lights out" into strange continents, collecting out of the darkness stories never heard before'.[90] To the female heroine, who has only experienced a passive role, the notion of a journey in itself becomes an exploration of limits and a voyage of self-discovery, if not self-empowerment, even though the journey, as Heller remarks, is often 'thwarted or impossible'.[91]

Parallel to the journey into the masculine other world is the journey into the 'dark continent', as Freud would have it, of feminine subjectivity and sexuality.[92] The female body becomes the principal embodiment of heterotopia, the place where normative knowledge and power institutions can be subverted. Exploiting the conventions of erotic historical romances,[93] *The Mistress of Lilliput* links the sexual quest to the journey motif from the beginning of the *Bildungsroman*: immediately after Mary's sixteenth birthday, her mother 'prepared to launch her ship upon the sea of marital prospects' (Fell, *Mistress of Lilliput*, p. 21).[94] Rather than encouraging further explorations into her awakened sexuality, Mary's puritanical marriage to Gulliver castrates her desire: after confessing to her spouse her enjoyment of his company in the alcove, Mary's timid attempt to prolong such pleasures receives a 'stern frown' (p. 31). Willing, as Mary appears to be, to embrace the passive role of ideal femininity, her curiosity nevertheless challenges her placid acceptance of patriarchal rule in marriage. Such inner conflict is expressed through the schizoid perspective of Mary's favourite doll, significantly named Lady Mary, who tells the story.[95] The doll's ironic commentary becomes the expression of Mary's latent resistance to 'an oppressive feminine standard that obstructs their journeys toward self-knowledge', which, in Heller's words, 'occurs frequently in the form of internalized combat against an enemy that lives within the female psyche'.[96] Thus what Mary Gulliver represses, Lady Mary reveals as the concomitant insurgence of Mary's intellectual and sexual appetite for new worlds:

> Attentive as she was, like many of her sex my mistress was more interested in the mysterious continents of her own nature than in regions farther flung; in this matter, thinking to find a fellow-mariner with whom to pore over her charts and align her sextant to the angle of the stars, she had, for better or worse, appointed Mr Gulliver the Captain of her Heart. (p. 35)

Interwoven with the *Bildungsroman* of *The Mistress of Lilliput*, Mary's quest for intellectual and sexual development starts with the journey she undertakes to retrace the steps of Gulliver, who, she believes, has returned to Houyhnhnmland. That the southbound ship Mary and her doll board is named after Aphrodite, the Greek goddess of love, is in itself suggestive of the dual purpose of her quest. The notion of two juxtaposed Aphrodites – the Heavenly and the earthly – (p. 69) reverberates the binary oppositions – virgin/whore, mind/body, reason/madness – of the basic masculine/feminine dichotomy and the schizoid conflict that Mary addresses during her quest. It is worth remembering that the ship, which, along with the colony and the brothel, Foucault defines as an example of 'heterotopia',

> is a floating piece of space, a place without a place, that exists by itself, that is closed in on itself and at the same time is given over to the infinity of the sea and that, from port to port, from tack to tack, from brothel to brothel, it goes as far as the colonies in search of the most precious treasures they conceal in their gardens.[97]

The heterotopic space of the Aphrodite, and the journey it signifies, launches the interrogation of patriarchal gender categories by subverting, from the start, the home/away dichotomy; in resisting the devoted wife's supporting, though passive, role – including the tracing of '*his progress* across the globe' 'on *his* charts' and the 'caretaking' of 'the objects in *his* Cabinet' (p. 38; my emphases) – that Gulliver had designed for her during his previous absence, Mary's departure alters the 'balance' of the relationship, even before the inevitable break-up.

The dissolution of Mary's patriarchal marriage begins on board the Aphrodite, where the co-habitation with the sailors inverts the gaze dynamics by drawing attention to scopophilic and voyeuristic drives for the construction of feminine subjectivity. At home, the notion that, even *in absentia*, Gulliver's gaze is 'Like the head of the Argos with his hundred eyes' (p. 40) suggests the manipulative deployment of self-surveillance as a mechanism of patriarchal oppression. The journey, however, exposes the power dynamics of the gaze, positioning Mary both as a spectator – albeit through the mediated perspective of Lady Mary – and as the object of fetishistic adoration in Lilliput. The doll's voyeuristic observations point to the inverted scopophilic address, which allows the female gaze to enjoy the sight of male bodies: 'I was quite overcome with excitement', Lady Mary comments, 'my lips bone dry, my cheeks flushed up like autumn apples, and [. . .] *my eye* ransacked the feast spread *before me*' (p. 81; my emphases).

Lilliput, conversely, seemingly reinstates the patriarchal reduction of the female body to object of male scopophilic desire; the result is a notion of femininity split into the holy Madonna – Lady Mary is the object of a sacred worship – and the whore: while the surface of Mary's body is first turned into a 'Popular Pleasure Palace', subsequently her inner anatomy becomes the object of detailed investigation. To the Sadeian members of the Queen Bee Society the giant body landed ashore represents not only the ultimate frontier of visual pleasures, but also, through voyeurism, the opportunity to assert their masculinity. Performed by the curiously named Edesad, the exploration of the giantess's genitalia is expressed in the parodic tone of a mock epic: 'when he saw the infernal colours of the place, its pinks and purples, crimsons and carmines, he thought he had been swallowed up by the mouth of Hell itself' (p. 139). Filtered through the lens of Edesad's scrutiny, female anatomy is enshrouded in the mist of the 'dark continent', exposing, simultaneously, the doomed fallacy of his quest: 'Conquering her', Cixous writes, 'they've made haste to depart from her borders, to get out of sight, out of body'.[98] Based on the active/passive Freudian dichotomy, the necessity to 'colonise' the female body can only lead to a precarious notion of masculine empowerment. Significantly, the reference to the Medusa is a powerful reminder of the castration fear, which underpins the voyeuristic functions of conventional cinematic representations of the female body:[99] 'Weak-limbed and divided against himself, the *champion* sank down against the slippery sides, certain that he had glimpsed in the abyss the horrible head of a *Gorgon*, and he with no shining shield to counter its accusing *gaze*' (pp. 140–1; my emphases). The episode also resonates the search of Gulliver's pockets in Part 1 of Swift's *Travels*, an intrusion that Gulliver seemingly accepts with good will: 'I was ready to strip myself, and turn up my pockets before him' (p. 16). Yet, in Swift's text, the search is literally manipulated by Gulliver, who is not willing to reveal all:

> I took up the two Officers in my Hands, put them first in my Coat-Pockets, and then into every other Pocket about me, except my two Fobs, and another *secret Pocket* which I had no Mind should be searched, wherein I had some little Necessaries of no Consequence to any but my self. (pp. 16–17; my emphases)

While the body-search and the Lilliputian Gentlemen's incomplete inventory reinforce, as it has been noted, Swift's self-conscious critique of authentic generic conventions,[100] the episode exposes the authority of 'The Mountain-Man' and,

simultaneously, reverberates subconscious fears and Oedipal tensions in relation to his body and sexuality,[101] made more explicit by the resonance of the
male gaze metaphor: among other 'Conveniences', Gulliver's secret pocket
holds his spectacles. Exposing the misogynist/patriarchal subtext of Freudian
psychoanalytical theories of male and female sexuality in relation to the male
gaze, the erotic narrative of *The Mistress of Lilliput* retains the psychological
ambiguity of Swift's text, while it subversively fulfils the conditions for Mary's
sexual emancipation; ironically set against Gulliver's prudish sexuality, the
violation of Mary's body unlocks the other world within her own body:

> If the incursions of the Queen Bee Club had made a negligible impact,
> here she encountered a first-rate fit, slick and sizeable, and no sooner
> had the device advanced than it retreated, and then, relinquished, was
> restored again, and famously received, till Manatee and matron rocked
> not recklessly but with the rhyme and reason of a piston driven by an
> engine, back and forth, with such a clack and clatter that she might
> have thought herself a child again, encompassed by the hectic rhythm of
> machines. (Fell, *Mistress of Lilliput*, pp. 160–1)

The erotic subtext of the narrative is reinforced by the coexistence of other
romances within the narrative of *The Mistress of Lilliput*, including the
unhappy love of Lady Mary and Bluebottle and Mary's union with French
botanist Antoine Duchesne, whose correspondence with Mr Moll (the historical cartographer and a fictional friend to Mr and Mrs Gulliver) is included in
the narrative palimpsest of the romance. Far from reinstating the conventions
of traditional romance, the narrative presents Antoine as the embodiment of
an anti-masculine hero: emotional and passionate, he is juxtaposed to Gulliver,
who is rational and controlled. When Antoine discovers that his experiments
on Chilean strawberries cannot lead to reproduction because the plants are not
hermaphrodite, his distress exposes his (feminine) sensitivity: 'I sulked like a
jilted lover; I took no food for days. But finally, impelled by Cupid's dart you
might say, I saw that the mountain must go to Mahomet, and directly took the
ship from St. Malo' (p. 68). Antoine's botanical quest for the perfect match
reveals an important gender subtext: 'I aim to create hybrids, or half-breeds
if you prefer, from the conjunction of two different species of the same genus'
(p. 276); while Duchesne's quest implicates the overcoming of binary notions
of gender, Gulliver is said to 'suffer an oppression of spirits which stems from
the inequities of his native country, where the marital system is abhorrent to
him' (p. 256); 'regular as clockwork' (p. 313), 'starkly pale, with narrowed
lips and closely shaven pate' (p. 314), his self-enclosed (pseudo-) scientific
research reveals his lack of interest in romance: 'On not a single graph was
Wife inscribed', Mary noted upon visiting his workshop, 'or *love* or *loneliness*,
so single-minded was this sovereign of the void' (p. 320).

It is significant that Gulliver lives in the hospital island of Ogé (the reverse of Ego), whose topography is suggestive of the emotional desert it stands for: 'If Sumina was airy and azure, and its sister island damp and occluded, their cousin was fiercer by far, for what spread before them was a landscape of blistering barrenness' (p. 303). The subversive romance of *The Mistress of Lilliput* is underpinned by the unstable geography of its settings; while Mary's first encounter with Antoine takes place on Sumina, it is on the nearby Amina that the romance unravels: the two anagrams conceal references to the masculine *animus* and feminine *anima*, as they articulate a dialectic polarity of the two opposing principles. The volatile territory of Amina resists a stable topography and does not appear on Mr Moll's official charts. It is seemingly Mary's desire that allows for the island to exist from the beginning of the story: '*her* own island, however evanescent, was in all ways more substantial than Mr Moll's' (p. 59; my emphases). Later Lady Mary reveals that Amina 'bashfully resists discovery' (p. 335), while Mary learns that the inhabitants of Amina 'believe that in Chaos lies *her* consistency, in Formlessness *her* form' (p. 336); significantly, a definition of chaos taken from Ovid's *Metamorphoses* is what Mary assertively identifies herself with, when she breaks up with Gulliver:

> I would say I am '*a formless lump, unfashion'd and unfram'd*', and you may name me Chaos if you will, but I would rather be a foolish fleshly woman than a perfect paragon, for such a one you seem to seek. (p. 334)

The notion of chaos supports Mary's refusal to be styled and conform to prescribed notions of femininity, ultimately reclaiming the female body's autonomy from the male gaze's scrutinising control.

Gender subversion, which paves the road for the romance's happy ending, is intrinsically linked to the quest and a critical reading of static 'roots': 'true union [. . .] begins at home', Lady Mary comments, 'though some may travel countless leagues in search of it, and anchor, all expectant, at the most exotic islands' (p. 348). While Lady Mary 'do[es] not often dwell upon [my] motherland, which was no mother [to me]' (p. 229), the repressive culture of Presbyterian Scotland emerges as the subtext behind Mary's uprooting. The goal of the quest, ultimately, promotes the supremacy of chaos over charts, emotion over reason, and the utmost resistance to Mr Knox's 'litany of forbidding' (p. 230), as the conclusion sees Mary and her doll settled in the other space of Duchesne's homeland:

> Reader, if the Queen of Scots began her life as a *Marie* and ended it more drearily as *Mary*, my fate was to be the converse, for having disembarked at Le Havre, and subsequently journeyed south to the Duchesne estates at Solutré, I was surrendered to the care of Monsieur Antoine's little ward Céleste, the daughter of his widowed sister Marguerite. Her

eyes were blue and limpid as her name, and her heart unclouded by the bitter legacy of black-browed Mr Knox, whose trumpetings unthroned an earthly queen and sought to tear the very name of woman from the heavens. (p. 350)

As previously seen in Elphinstone's and Hayton's novels, through the subversion of existing hierarchies, the romance of *The Mistress of Lilliput* articulates an inward quest for (self-) knowledge and empowerment; simultaneously, epistemological strongholds are undermined as the waste lands of Naomi's quests and the marvellous dimension of Usbathaden's world point to the interrogation of categorical boundaries of seen/familiar and unseen/foreign worlds and, particularly in Usbathaden's other world, carry out the wider ontological preoccupations of postmodernism. As it interrogates the boundaries of the real, the otherworldly draws attention to the problematic nature of all binary oppositions, including, of course, gender.

NOTES

1. J. R. R. Tolkien, *Tree and Leaf* [1964] (London: Harper Collins, 2001), p. 10.
2. Fred Botting, 'In Gothic Darkly: Heterotopia, History and Culture', in David Punter (ed.), *A Companion to the Gothic* (Oxford: Blackwell, 2001), pp. 3–14 (p. 12).
3. Manlove, *Scottish Fantasy Literature*, p. 12.
4. Nicole Goisbeault, 'African Myths', in Pierre Brunel (ed.), *A Companion to Literary Myths, Heroes and Archetypes* (London: Routledge, 1988), pp. 24–9; see also the section 'Morality and Aesthetics in the Ritual Archetype' in Wole Soyinka, *Myth, Literature and the African World* (Cambridge: Cambridge University Press, 1976), pp. 1–36.
5. See Françoise Graziani, 'Discoveries', in Brunel (ed.), *Companion to Literary Myths*, pp. 317–24.
6. See Ronald Hutton, *The Pagan Religions of the Ancient British Isles* (Oxford: Blackwell, 1991), p. 184.
7. Margaret Elphinstone, 'Contemporary Feminist Fantasy in the Scottish Literary Tradition', in Caroline Gonda (ed.), *Tea and Leg-Irons: New Feminist Readings From Scotland* (London: Open Letters, 1992), pp. 45–59 (p. 46).
8. Lowry Charles Wimberly discusses both the motif of the journey to and the locations of Other worlds in the ballad tradition of Scotland and England. See Lowry Charles Wimberly, *Folklore in English and Scottish Ballads* (Chicago: University of Illinois Press, 1928), pp. 108–38.
9. Walter Scott, *Minstrelsy of the Scottish Border*, ed. Thomas Finlayson Henderson, 4 vols (Edinburgh and London: William Blackwood and Sons, 1902), vol. II, p. 352.
10. J. M. Barrie, *Peter Pan in Kensington Gardens* [1906], reprinted in *Peter Pan in Kensington Gardens and Peter Pan and Wendy*, ed. Peter Hollindale (Oxford: Oxford University Press, 2008), p. 30. Further references to this edition are given after quotations in the text.
11. Manlove, *Scottish Fantasy Literature*, p. 89.
12. George MacDonald, *Phantastes* [1858] (Grand Rapids: Eerdmans Publishing, 2000), p. 33.
13. Manlove, *Scottish Fantasy Literature*, p. 86.

14. Marina Warner, *Fantastic Metamorphoses, Other Worlds: Ways of Telling the Self* (Oxford: Oxford University Press, 2002), pp. 171–96.
15. Lewis Carroll, *The Complete Sylvie and Bruno*, in *The Complete Illustrated Lewis Carroll* (Ware: Wordsworth Classics, 1997), p. 464.
16. For a more extensive discussion of Mitchison's text, see my essay 'Crossing Dream Boundaries: Decoding Nonsense and Fantastic Ambiguities in Naomi Mitchison's *Beyond this Limit*', in Pauline McPherson, Christopher Murray, Gordon Spark and Kevin Corstorphine (eds), *Sub-versions: Cultural Status, Genre and Critique* (Newcastle: Cambridge Scholars, 2008), pp. 135–48.
17. Elphinstone, 'Contemporary Feminist Fantasy', p. 50.
18. Scott Brewster proposes 'the borderline condition as a pronounced feature of Scottish Gothic'; see Scott Brewster, 'Madness, Mimicry and Scottish Gothic', *Gothic Studies* 7: 1 (2005), pp. 79–86 (p. 84).
19. Manlove, *Scottish Fantasy Literature*, pp. 11–14.
20. Lucie Armitt, *Theorising the Fantastic* (London: Arnold, 1996), p. 8.
21. Brian McHale, *Postmodernist Fiction* (London: Routledge, 1987), p. 75.
22. McHale, *Postmodernist Fiction*, p. 45.
23. Michel Foucault, 'Of Other Spaces', trans. Jay Miskowiec, *Diacritics*, 16: 1 (Spring 1986), pp. 22–7 (p. 23).
24. Foucault, 'Of Other Spaces', p. 25.
25. Lucie Armitt, *Where No Man Has Gone Before: Women and Science Fiction* (London and New York: Routledge, 1991), p. 7.
26. Gérard Genette, *Paratexts: Thresholds of Interpretations*, trans. Jane E. Lewin (Cambridge: Cambridge University Press, 1997), p. 2.
27. Genette, *Paratexts*, p. 2.
28. Genette defines 'transtextuality' as 'all that sets the text in a relationship, whether obvious or concealed, with another text'. See Gérard Genette, *Palimpsests* [1982], trans. Channa Newman and Claude Doubinsky (Lincoln: University of Nebraska Press, 1997), pp. 1–5.
29. McHale, *Postmodernist Fiction*, pp. 56–7.
30. Adam Thorpe, 'Love in the Mesolithic Era', *The Guardian*, Review Section, 25 July 2009, p. 8.
31. See Alan McGillivray, 'Interview with Margaret Elphinstone', *Laverock*, 1 (1995), 29–38 (p. 29).
32. Margaret Elphinstone, 'Waylaid by Islands', *The Bottle Imp* 2 (November 2007). Available at: http://www.arts.gla.ac.uk/ScotLit/ASLS/SWE/TBI/TBIIssue2/Waylaid.html (accessed 3 September 2009).
33. Drawing on the concept of nomadic cultures, in a figurative sense Rosi Braidotti refers to the 'nomadic subject' to indicate a different approach to the 'post-modern/industrial/colonial' subject 'blurring boundaries without blurring bridges'. See Rosi Braidotti, *Nomadic Subjects: Embodiment and Sexual Difference in Contemporary Feminist Theory* (New York: Columbia University Press, 1994), p. 4.
34. Gilles Deleuze and Féliz Guattari, *A Thousand Plateaus* [1980] (London: Continuum, 2004), p. 7.
35. See McGillivray, 'Interview with Margaret Elphinstone', p. 29
36. McHale, *Postmodernist Fiction*, p. 66.
37. Margaret Elphinstone, *The Incomer* (London: Women's Press, 1987), p. 58. Further references to this edition are given after quotations in the text.
38. The passages are quoting T. S. Eliot's First Quartet, 'Burnt Norton'. See T. S. Eliot, *Four Quartets*, in *The Complete Poems and Plays of T. S. Eliot* (London: Faber and Faber, 1969).

39. Wimberley points out that notions of the forest as Other world and magical trees in ballads such as 'Tam Lin', 'Thomas the Rhymer', 'Kemp Owyne' and 'Alison Gross' may represent the vestigial 'evidence of an old tree cult'. See Wimberly, *Folklore in English and Scottish Ballads*, p. 124.

40. Compare with King James Bible, St John 1: 1–2: 'In the beginning was the Word, and the Word was with God, and the Word was God. The same was in the beginning with God'.

41. Lucie Armitt, 'Space, Time and Female Genealogies: A Kristevan Reading of Feminist Science Fiction', in Sarah Sceats and Gail Cunningham (eds), *Image and Power: Women in Fiction in the Twentieth Century* (London: Longman, 1996), pp. 51–61 (p. 59).

42. Douglas Gifford, 'A New Diversity', *Books in Scotland* 26 (Winter 1987), p. 11.

43. Armitt, 'Space, Time and Female Genealogies', p. 57.

44. Armitt, 'Space, Time and Female Genealogies', p. 57.

45. Margaret Elphinstone, *A Sparrow's Flight: A Novel of a Future* (Edinburgh: Polygon, 1989), p. 84. Further references to this edition are given after quotations in the text.

46. 'Thomas the Rhymer', in Emily Lyle (ed.), *Scottish Ballads* (Edinburgh: Canongate, 1994), pp. 132–4 (p. 134). Further references to this edition are given after quotations in the text. For different versions of the ballad see F. J. Child (ed.), *English and Scottish Popular Ballads*, 5 vols (Boston and New York: Houghton, Mifflin, 1882–98), vol. 1, pp. 317–29.

47. See Wimberly, *Folklore in English and Scottish Ballads*, p. 108.

48. See Douglas Gifford, 'Contemporary Fiction II: Seven Writers in Scotland', in Douglas Gifford and Dorothy McMillan (eds), *A History of Scottish Women's Writing* (Edinburgh: Edinburgh University Press, 1997), pp. 604–29.

49. Richard Cavendish, *The Tarot* (London: Michael Joseph, 1975), p. 67.

50. Folly, as suggested by the reading of St Paul and others, signifies a higher state of humanity, closer to divinity. For this and other interpretations of 'The Fool' and a general discussion about the Tarot, see Cavendish, *The Tarot*, pp. 67–70. See also Robert Wang, *An Introduction to the Golden Dawn Tarot* [1996] (Hammersmith: Thorsons, 2001).

51. See Jessie L. Weston, *The Legend of Sir Perceval: Studies upon its Origin, Development and Position in the Arthurian Cycle*, 2 vols (London: David Nutt, 1906–9), *The Quest for the Holy Grail* (London: G. Bell and Sons, 1913) and *From Ritual To Romance* [1920] (Garden City: Doubleday and Company, 1957).

52. Cavendish, *The Tarot*, p. 66.

53. See Weston, *The Legend of Sir Perceval*, vol. 1, p. 65.

54. See Cavendish, *The Tarot*, p. 70.

55. See Weston, *The Legend of Sir Perceval*, vol. 1, pp. 57–75.

56. See Germanà, interview with Margaret Elphinstone, in 'Re-working the Magic', pp. 333–4.

57. Cavendish, *The Tarot*, p. 106.

58. Gifford, 'Contemporary Fiction II', p. 605.

59. 'Eirik the Red', in Gwyn Jones (ed.), *Eirik the Red and Other Icelandic Sagas* (Oxford: Oxford University Press, 1980), pp. 126–57 (p. 135).

60. Margaret Elphinstone, *The Sea Road* (Edinburgh: Canongate, 2000), p. 3. Further references to this edition are given after quotations in the text.

61. Manlove, *Scottish Fantasy Literature*, p. 2.

62. Compare with Jones (ed.), *Eirik the Red*, pp. 142–3.

63. Margaret Elphinstone, 'The Quest: Two Contemporary Adventures', in Christopher Whyte (ed.), *Gendering The Nation: Studies in Modern Scottish Literature* (Edinburgh: Edinburgh University Press, 1995), pp. 107–36 (p. 110).

64. Germanà, interview with Sian Hayton, 2003, in 'Re-working the Magic' (2004), pp. 353–66 (p. 355).

65. See Germanà, 'Re-working the Magic', p. 357. Scottish and Welsh oral traditions are an important source in Hayton's fiction, as in her unpublished work as a playwright: 'Mirthful Mournings on the Death of Elspeth McEwan', written in 1996–7 and performed in Kirkcudbright in 1998, tells the story of the last woman burned as a witch in Dumfries; 'The Last Dream of St Cuthbert' was written in 2000.

66. 'The Battle of the Birds' was recorded from the oral Gaelic tale recited by John MacKenzie in Argyll (1859); see J. F. Campbell (ed.), *Popular Tales of the West Highlands* (London: Alexander Gardner, 1890), vol. 1, pp. 25–63; 'The Green Man of Knowledge' was recorded from Geordie Stewart, a traveller from Aberdeenshire, by Hamish Henderson; see A J. Bruford and D. A. MacDonald (eds), *Scottish Traditional Tales* [1994] (Edinburgh: Birlinn, 2007), pp. 80–97.

67. See Douglas Gifford, 'Contemporary Fiction II', pp. 613–15; see also Elphinstone, 'The Quest', p. 108.

68. See Peter Berresford Ellis, *Dictionary of Celtic Mythology* (London: Constable, 1992), pp. 223–4. See also Miranda Jane Green, *Celtic Myths* (London: British Museum Press, 1993), pp. 35–6.

69. See Rachel Bromwich and D. Simon Evans (eds), *Culhwuch and Olwen: An Edition and Study of the Oldest Arthurian Tale* (Cardiff: University of Wales Press, 1992), p. xxvi. Stith Thompson and Antti Aarne classify this tale as 'Six Go Through the Whole World' (no. 513A) under folktales of supernatural helpers. See Stith Thompson, *The Folktale* (New York: Holt, Rinehart and Winston, 1946), pp. 54, 280. See also Antti Aarne, *The Types of the Folktale: A Classification and Bibliography*, trans. Stith Thompson (Helsinki: Academia Scientiarum Fennica, 1964), p. 181.

70. Bromwich and Evans, *Culhwuch and Olwen*, p. 93.

71. Sian Hayton, *Hidden Daughters* (Edinburgh: Polygon, 1992), p. 141. Further references to this edition are given after quotations in the text (abbreviated to *HD*).

72. Sian Hayton, *Cells of Knowledge* (Edinburgh: Polygon, 1989), p. 148. Further references to this edition are given after quotations in the text (abbreviated to *CK*). Compare with: 'The boy was baptized, and the name Culhwch given to him because he was found in a pig-run', 'Culhwuch and Olwen', in *The Mabinogion*, ed. and trans. Gwyn Jones and Thomas Jones (London: Everyman, 1994), p. 95. Welsh 'hwch' was interpreted as pig in the manuscript of 'Culhwuch and Olwen'. See Bromwich and Evans, *Culhwuch and Olwen*, p. xxx.

73. 'In stories of this kind the hero succeeds in accomplishing a number of apparently impossible tasks, placed as calculated impediments in his way by a giant who knows that he himself is fated to die when the daughter marries, and therefore he will be prepared to do all he can to prevent her marriage taking place'. See Bromwich and Evans, *Culhwuch and Olwen*, p. xxvi.

74. Gifford, 'Contemporary Fiction II', p. 613.

75. Michel Foucault, *Discipline and Punish: The Birth of the Prison*, trans. Alan Sheridan (Harmondsworth: Penguin, 1977), p. 201.

76. Christopher Whyte, 'Postmodernism, Gender and Belief in Recent Scottish Fiction', *Scottish Literary Journal* 23: 1 (May 1996), pp. 50–64 (p. 58).

77. The legend of the Seven Sleepers of Ephesus refers to seven young men who wake up after a long time spent sleeping in a cave. The story is recorded in *The Quran*

(Surah 18, verse 9–26), Paul the Deacon's *History of the Lombards* (late 790s) and Jacobus de Voragine's *Golden Legend* (1260–75).

78. Robin Sims, 'Facing the Thing: The Green Man, Psychoanalysis and Kingsley Amis', *Critical Survey* 19: 2 (2007), pp. 82–100 (p. 93).

79. Sims, 'Facing the Thing', p. 94.

80. Gifford, 'Contemporary Fiction II', p. 613.

81. Sian Hayton, *The Last Flight* (Edinburgh: Polygon, 1993), p. 261. Further references to this edition are given after quotations in the text (abbreviated to *TLF*).

82. Whyte, 'Postmodernism, Gender and Belief', p. 58.

83. Gifford 'Contemporary Fiction II', p. 614.

84. Jonathan Swift, *Gulliver's Travels* [1726], ed. Robert A. Greenberg, 2nd edn, (New York: Norton and Company, 1970), p. 37. Further references to this edition are given after quotations in the text.

85. Margaret Anne Doody, 'Swift and Romance', in Christopher Fox and Brenda Tooley (eds), *Walking Naboth's Vineyard: New Studies on Swift* (Notre Dame, IN: University of Notre Dame Press, 1995), pp. 98–126 (pp. 99–100).

86. Michael DePorte, 'Swift, God and Power', in Fox and Tooley, *Walking Naboth's Vineyard*, pp. 73–97 (p. 78).

87. Jeanette Winterson, 'Introduction', in Jonathan Swift, *Gulliver's Travels* (Oxford: Oxford University Press, 1999), pp. v–xii (p. ix).

88. See Felicity A. Nussbaum, 'Gulliver's Malice: Gender and the Satiric Stance', in Jonathan Swift, *Gulliver's Travels* [1726] (Boston: Bedford Books at St Martin's Press, 1995), pp. 318–34. See also Susan Bruce, 'The Flying Island and Female Anatomy: Gynaecology and Power in *Gulliver's Travels*', *Genders* 2 (1988), 60–76. See also Sandra M. Gilbert and Susan Gubar, *The Madwoman in the Attic: The Woman Writer and the Nineteenth-Century Literary Imagination* (New Haven and New York: Yale University Press, 1979), pp. 31–3.

89. Frye, *Anatomy of Criticism*, pp. 322–3.

90. Dana A. Heller, *The Feminization of Quest-Romance: Radical Departures* (Austin: University of Texas Press, 1990), p. 1.

91. Heller, *The Feminization of Quest-Romance*, p. 14.

92. Freud, *The Question of Lay Analysis* [1926], *SE*, vol. 20, pp. 177–258 (p. 212).

93. See Kay Mussell, *Fantasy and Reconciliation: Contemporary Formulas of Women's Romance Fiction* (Westport, CT: Greenwood Press, 1984), pp. 41–2.

94. Alison Fell, *The Mistress of Lilliput or The Pursuit* (London: Doubleday, 1999), p. 21. Further references to this edition are given after quotations in the text.

95. As I have argued elsewhere, the doll's name is a reference to Lady Mary Montague, whose irreverent poetry embodied a proto-feminist response to the misogynist subtext of Swift's work. See my chapter 'Re-writing Female Monstrosity: Schizoid Misogyny in Alison Fell's *The Mistress of Lilliput* and Emma Tennant's *Two Women of London*', in Adalgisa Giorgio and Julia Waters (eds), *Women's Writing in Western Europe: Gender, Generation and Legacy* (Newcastle: Cambridge Scholars, 2007), pp. 102–17.

96. Heller, *The Feminization of Quest-Romance*, p. 13.

97. Foucault, 'Of Other Spaces', p. 27.

98. Hélène Cixous, 'The Laugh of the Medusa', trans. Keith Cohen and Paula Cohen, *Signs* 1: 4 (Summer 1976), pp. 875–93 (p. 877).

99. See Mulvey, 'Visual Pleasure and Narrative Cinema', p. 14.

100. 'Thus the Lilliputian inventory of Gulliver's possessions is incomplete because the authors miss his secret pocket'; see 'Preface', in Frederick N. Smith (ed.), *The Genres of Gulliver's Travels* (Cranbury, NJ, and London: Associated University Presses, 1990), p. 20.

101. As Frank Stringfellow reminds us:

> In Freudian theory [. . .] the blindness stands for castration, the mutilation of another valued organ; and this connection is at least hinted at in 'A Voyage to Lilliput' by the fact that in his secret pocket Gulliver keeps a pair of spectacles as well as the 'other little Conveniences.' We recall, too, that almost from the beginning of part 1 Gulliver has been obsessed with protecting his eyes from injury, and at his most aggressive moment, when he steals the fleet of Blefuscudians, his only fear is the threat to his eyes.

See Frank Stringfellow, *The Meaning of Irony: A Psychoanalytic Investigation* (Albany: State University of New York Press, 1994), p. 59.

Chapter 3

WITCHES, DEMON LOVERS AND FEMALE MONSTERS

And it should be noted that there was a defect in the formation of the first
woman, since she was formed from a bent rib, that is a rib of the breast,
which is bent as it were in a contrary direction to a man.[1]
Heinrich Kramer and James Sprenger, Malleus Maleficarum

You only have to look at the Medusa straight on to see her. And she's not
deadly. She's beautiful and she's laughing.[2]
Hélène Cixous

A significant part of the Scottish heritage for women writers now is the
figure of the dangerous woman. In twentieth-century writing she may
sometimes seem to align herself with a feminist perspective, but she
refuses to become quite ideologically sound. She is too sinister for that.[3]
Margaret Elphinstone

In April 1944 a spiritual medium was arrested in Portsmouth, tried under the
1735 Witchcraft Act and consequently incarcerated in Holloway prison for
nine months. The medium became known as the last person to be tried for
witchcraft in Britain. Her name was Helen Duncan and she was Scottish.

The strange case of Helen Duncan is the most recent layer of an important
historical palimpsest in Scottish culture: the most recent survey to date confirms that figures relevant to witch trials in Scotland accounted for almost 4000

accusations resulting in at least 1500 executions.[4] Scottish literature abounds in references to witches and unsettling *femmes fatales*, of which the 'rigwoodie hags' in Robert Burns's *Tam O' Shanter* and the bewitching spinster of Muriel Spark's *The Prime of Miss Jean Brodie* (1961) are only the most celebrated examples. Not exclusively Scottish, 'mad, bad and dangerous' female creatures, however, occupy a prominent position in Western myth, art, medical discourse and, of course, literature. This chapter will explore the range of subversive female characters presented in Galford's *The Fires of Bride* (1986) and *Queendom Come* (1990), Spark's *Symposium* (1990), Thompson's *Pandora's Box* (1998), and Smith's *The Accidental* (2005). As with the other chapters in this study, the analysis of the selected novels will unveil their ambivalent approach to this cultural motif; highlighting the pervasive influence of some traditional qualities of the dangerous woman on the contemporary Scottish cultural and literary canon, the analysis simultaneously challenges those conventional paradigms, opening the narratives to a post-structuralist critique of gender binarisms and a postmodern interrogation of the real and the 'truth'. In this respect, Galford's and Spark's novels disclose a parody of the traditional Scottish/Celtic witch closer to the models found in the Scottish cultural tradition, whereas Smith's and Thompson's texts move away from the traditional trope to engage with deconstructive critiques of gender categories (Thompson) and a complex reflection on the postmodern loss of the real (Smith).

From Greek mythology to science fiction dangerous women play significant (though simultaneously peripheral) roles. Archetypal temptresses such as Hesiod's Pandora and the Biblical Eve, emerging prominently as originators of evil, have been subject to consistent efforts of narrative dissemination. In her multifarious embodiments, the pervasive popularity of the dangerous woman reveals the ambiguous politics sustaining such representations. Though extraordinary power is somehow bestowed upon this female archetype, her supernatural faculties stand on shaky moral grounds, laying bare the ambivalent duality inherent in female empowerment. This is apparent in the recurrent dichotomies that juxtapose virtuous female characters to their malicious counterparts: in Greek myth, the Sirens' treacherous song and the Gorgon's petrifying beauty are opposed to the Sibyls' divine wisdom; in the traditional fairy tale, the fairy godmother's benign generosity counteracts the tricks played by the evil stepmother (who can be a witch, too); in the androcentric world of mainstream science fiction, 'masculinised' female characters are typically opposed to their 'alien' counterparts, whose 'otherness' represents all that is outside the white, middle-class, male, heteronormative community.[5] Such ambivalent treatment of female/feminine power persists throughout centuries of visual and literary representation, simultaneously unveiling, it will be seen later, patriarchal conservatism in relation to binary gender categories and their feminist critique.[6]

Homer's malevolent Sirens are mentioned in *Malleus Maleficarum* (1484), the fifteenth-century textbook on witchcraft written to support witch-hunts and persecutions that occurred parallel to the rise of cultural and scientific awakenings across Europe: 'The notion that witchcraft was a real and heinous crime is not a medieval or Dark Age idea', Walter Stephens rightly remarks, 'Witchcraft theory and the persecution of witches are Renaissance phenomena, and they lasted into the Age of Reason'.[7] The *Malleus* considered the question of female propensity to 'Evil Superstitions' and, therefore, witchcraft, aiming to prove the devil's appeal to women on the essentialist grounds of sexual/gender difference. The authors list a number of 'facts', supported by Biblical/classical references, to demonstrate that 'in these times this perfidy is more often found in women than in men' (Kramer and Sprenger, *Malleus Maleficarum*, p. 44). The catalogue includes female lack of 'moderation in goodness or vice',[8] and their impressionability, making women particularly prone 'to receive the influence of a disembodied spirit' (p. 44); their 'slippery tongues', too, make them 'unable to conceal from their fellow-women those things which by evil arts they know' (p. 44); finally, despite the claim that 'All kingdoms in the world have been overthrown by women' (p. 46), the authors conclude that women are 'feebler both in mind and body' and that 'it is not surprising that they should come more under the spell of witchcraft' (p. 44).

Implicit in the misogynist ideology that underpins the *Malleus* is a barely suppressed fear of female sexuality, and its subversive effects on masculine subjectivity: with regard to the high incidence of witchcraft among women, 'the *natural* reason', the authors explain, 'is that she is more carnal than a man, as is clear from her many carnal abominations' (p. 44), adding that, as Cicero would argue, 'a woman is beautiful to look upon, contaminating to the touch, and deadly to keep' (p. 46). Female beauty is acceptable as long as she is the object of the controlling male gaze; when she strays from the literal and metaphorical enclosures designed for her body by patriarchal authority, she becomes a threat to the very foundations of masculine power. 'Excessive' beauty, then, could be a good enough reason to be a candidate for the stake, as could be the 'wrong' colour of hair, coupled with the unmarried status of many of the victims.[9] It is hardly surprising that, of the three main categories of vice related to women, infidelity, ambition and lust, the first and the third relate to women's uncontrolled sexuality, while the second merely reinforces the authors' awareness of women's unsettling potential to subvert the Law of the Father. Though exceptions occurred, available evidence suggests that the 'average' witch in early-modern Europe was older than fifty years of age, female and often unmarried.[10] Although the early-modern witch-hunt that took place in Europe and America between mid-fifteenth and mid-eighteenth centuries was an extremely complex cultural phenomenon, it is not erroneous to argue that misogyny and patriarchal anxieties about female subversion were important factors in the social context of witch-hunts.

Along with 'fornicatresses' and 'adultresses', the *Malleus* lists midwives among the categories of women most at 'risk' of being seduced by the devil. The links between the reproductive function of the female body and the cultural history of witchcraft in modern Europe supports an understanding of the cultural resonance that the witch holds, particularly in pre-Christian Scotland and Ireland. Fertility plays a significant function in the worship of female Celtic divinities. Some evidence suggests that in the ancient Celtic belief system goddesses occupied a more prominent position than their male counterparts: 'One of the remarkable features of Scottish mythology is the predominance of goddesses', Donald MacKenzie claims, 'They are greater and stronger than the gods'.[11] The Celtic goddess's commanding status, possibly bearing positive associations with female fertility, stems from the distinctive link between the female divine principle and earth. In ancient Celtic societies land and national identity are both associated with the body of the goddess and her earthly proxy, the queen: 'all political power', Claire French argues, 'was originally invested in the tribal goddess and her agent, the queen'.[12] The important link between female goddesses and land is also reinforced by other considerations about its ambivalent manifestations. MacKenzie draws a distinction between the Goddess, or hag, the Gaelic *Cailleach*, and the Giantess, a malevolent divinity. Another writer, Robert Lawrance, differentiates between the Gaelic *glas-stig* ('grey hag') and *Bean-shith* ('Fairy woman').[13] The 'hag' is an ambivalent character of Scottish lore: she is a healer and would be of assistance especially in childbirth, a trait which she shares with the early-modern witch; at the same time she can mould mountains, fight against and kill human heroes. Anne Ross's important study of 'Divine Hags' emphasises the ambivalent morals of the Celtic hag, who 'is at once creator and destroyer, gentle and fierce, mother and nurturer':[14] the ambivalent nature of the Celtic hag embodies the dualism of the Celtic divinity system.[15] As Ross pointed out, the Divine Hag 'has a long ancestry and an incredible longevity' (p. 162), which, as oral sources suggest, survived until the late twentieth century. Many of the surviving tales reinforce the notion that the *Cailleach* is a powerful woman, a murderer, but also a healer (a healing stone is also called *cailleach*) and associated to land through her connection with harvesting rituals.[16] The *Cailleach*'s ambivalent affiliation to the land is also underpinned by its association with negative influences to natural cycles of land productivity.[17]

Significantly, such ambivalent ties to land fertility and productivity emerge in many Scottish stories about witchcraft.[18] The shape-shifting body of the witch – typically linked with animals such as the raven, the hare or the cow – is also coupled with infertility, milk turned sour and, ultimately, death, as summarised in this reference to early-modern witchcraft in 'The Witch of Cnoc-Na-Moine':

> In those days there existed women called witches possessed of a super-natural power, which to-day puts the archfiend in the background. [. . .] These witches generally lived without any visible means of support, yet their houses were plentifully supplied with the choicest of viands. Milk, butter, and cheese seemed to have been their chief diets, and curiously they possessed no cows. Their vengeance and malice knew no bounds; they hesitated not at destroying man and beast. Young men and maidens frequently fell victims to their foul play, for the least offence. They could transform themselves into the shape of any animal, but their favourites were a goat, cat, pig, hare and raven.[19]

The witch's ability to change shape in order to perpetrate evil does not, as seemingly implied in this and many stories of the kind, pertain exclusively to older witches. Young women, done wrong by suitors or former lovers, are also responsible for spectacular acts of revenge. In 'A Long Island Witch', for instance, a young woman turns herself into a 'fierce animal' and attacks a man who has 'broken off the courtship'.[20] Similarly, in the story of 'Mor Bhan-Fair Sarah' two witches are said to have been 'two of the handsomest girls in the whole country-side': their experiments with black magic are seemingly linked to their competition over the love of one man.[21]

The persistence and variety of women gifted with supernatural powers – be they repellent hags or charming maidens – should not lead to easy assumptions of female emancipation in Celtic societies. Although 'the prominence given to goddesses in Scotland is suggestive of matriarchal customs and conditions' in pre-Christian Scotland,[22] the notion of a Celtic matriarchy is in fact problematic: 'Goddess worship', French rightly argues, does not necessarily entail a privileged position for women'.[23] The ambivalence of such complex gender politics in Celtic cultural and religious systems has been manifestly exposed in Hayton's trilogy analysed in the previous chapter: the problematic notion of origin/lineage originates from the female ambivalent resistance to/collusion with the Law of the Father epitomised by Kigva's archetypal story and embedded in the parallel stories of the giant's daughters.

Beside her important historical and cultural incidence, particularly reso-nant in Scotland, the witch assumes a symbolic significance exceeding the boundaries of national cultures. As stipulated at the beginning of this chapter, despite the continuum running through Celtic mythology and the persist-ence of a strong presence of female divinities in the Irish and Scottish cultural traditions, the witch represents a universal metaphor and a 'popular' feature across Western cultures: 'Witchcraft and sorcery in various forms appear to have existed from the dawn of human history', John Widdowson argues, 'and throughout the ages the witch has been regarded as a figure of fear'.[24] As with bogeymen, evil fairies and ogres, spoken references to witches have always acted as tools for control and censorship of unacceptable human behaviour. Although Widdowson does not make this claim explicitly in his case study, his analysis of the linguistic and cultural references to the 'witch figure' used to enforce control and discipline may also be read in line with the pervasively misogynist ideology that the witch embodies in a patriarchal context: with her shrivelled, sterile and deformed body, the witch's otherness voices a threat to normative social structure – including the nuclear family – thus defying social convention and established authority.[25] The physical description of many of the witches accounted for in Widdowson's (Newfoundland) case studies reflect such bias:

> These women are usually old and often reclusive; they live alone, or speak, dress or act oddly in some way. These are traits shared by many other threatening figures and they emphasise various types of abnormality or deviation from accepted cultural norms of behaviour and appearance.[26]

The witch's abnormality is arguably linked to her anti-maternal function. Disconnected from its reproductive function, unlike the ancient Celtic goddess of pre-Christian times, in a patriarchal context the witch's rapacious sexuality and/or sterility come to epitomise the anti-feminine principle. In resisting the boundaries of normative femininity, the witch consequently defies the foundations of masculinity and patriarchal authority. By default, the witch is a nocturnal, underground force, operating beyond the boundaries of social acceptability. Her cavernous abode is antithetical to any accepted notions of feminine domesticity and home-making, while her cauldron becomes a sinister transposition of her sterile womb.[27] Take, for instance, Hugh Miller's evocative description of Stine Bheag's house:

> The place was darkened, as I have said, with smoke, but at intervals the flames glanced on the naked walls of turf and stone, and on a few rude implements of housewifery which were ranged along the sides, together with the utensils of a more questionable form and appearance. A huge wooden trough, filled with water, from whence there proceeded a splashing bubbling noise, as if it were filled with live fish, occupied one of the corners; and was sentinelled by a black cat, that sat purring on a stool beside it, and that on every louder splash rose from her seat, and stretched her neck over the water.[28]

In this familiar set-up, the creepy workshop illustrates the witch's anti-feminine attributes. She is, as it has been argued, a 'phallic mother', with many of her (physical) attributes suggesting her inherent 'masculinity': her sharp nose and nails, her broomstick and pointy hood are all equally revelatory of the phallic symbolism associated with the witch's sexualised body.[29]

Rather than impersonating a form of hybrid sexuality, the subversive role performed by the witch, along with other pervasive representations of female monstrosity, is, according to Barbara Creed, in fact linked to male castration anxiety. To the male gaze, the (monstrous) female body is no longer the passive object of the controlling lens of patriarchal power. The female body is frightening not, as Freud would have it, because it is castrated, but because it can in fact castrate: 'These images of woman as monstrous-feminine are alive and well in the contemporary horror film and represented in a variety of ways: witch, archaic mother, monstrous womb, vampire, *femme castratrice*, castrating mother'.[30] It is hardly surprising that second-wave feminist critics, including Cixous and Sandra Gilbert, have identified in the sorceress a representation of subversive female 'otherness'. Much like the 'madwoman', the 'witch' signifies therefore at least two things: the destabilising power of woman's self-determination, and, as a result of such dissidence, her enforced relegation to the peripheries of the social spectrum. In Cixous and Clément's *The Newly Born Woman* the sorceress occupies this ambivalent position: the unofficial performer of abortions and facilitator of extra-marital love affairs against Christian orthodoxy, the anti-establishment witch 'ends up being destroyed, and nothing is registered of her but mythical traces'.[31] In her introduction to Cixous's and Clément's work Gilbert emphasises the pervasive presence of 'the ancient/innocent/fluent/powerful/impossible woman' within a cultural continuum that includes 'Flaubert and Baudelaire, Rimbaud and Apollinaire, [. . .] the *Malleus Maleficarum*, Freud, Genet, Kleist, Hoffman, Shakespeare, and Aeschylus' (p. x). Much like Cixous's other embodiment of feminine subjectivity, the irreverent gorgon of 'The Laugh of the Medusa', the most significant fact about the 'newly born woman' is that she is, as Gilbert puts it in a rhetorical question, 'the one who erupts at, and disrupts, the edge of female consciousness, the liminal zone between sleeping and waking' (p. x). Personified by the uncanny sorceress and the hysteric, the 'feminine role' is simultaneously associated with marginality and a critical subversion of established rules, laws and conventions.

The witch, the hysteric, the dangerous woman, then, become cognate metaphors for the destabilising function of female expression free of patriarchal constraints; opposed to the 'angel-woman', the witch, Gilbert and Susan Gubar argued in their seminal work *The Madwoman in the Attic* (1979), becomes the embodiment of 'Male dread of women, and specifically the infantile dread of maternal autonomy'.[32] As one of the multiple forms of female deviancy – madness, hysteria, rebellion – she represents, the witch takes a critical stance against gender categorisation. Her 'unjustified' femaleness challenges fixed gender roles, erasing the identification of woman as mother or wife, and questioning the phallogocentric foundations of patriarchal gender discourse. In doing so, the madwoman may also, just like the sorceress, become the victimised instrument of conservative agenda, exposed, as Shoshana Felman suggests, by the pervasive cultural affiliation of madness and women: 'Madness and women [. . .] turn out to be the two outcasts of the establishment of readability'.[33]

At the end of the twentieth century, the dangerous (mad) woman personifies the post-structuralist challenge to essentialist readings of sexual difference based on binary oppositions. With their shape-shifting bodies and deviant sexual behaviours, the witch and the madwoman reflect Butler's theoretical resistance to any 'stable notion of gender',[34] eroding the barrier between gender and the established hierarchical order derived from it, and pointing towards a critical reading of gender identity and sexual difference. Such preoccupations with gender categories and the problematic representation of feminine subjectivity are central to all the novels explored in this chapter. In particular, male/female, masculine/feminine oppositions are overtly deconstructed by the queer characters of Galford's *The Fires of Bride* and *Queendom Come* and the demonic women of Muriel Spark's *Symposium*, which explicitly play with the *Cailleach*/witch motif.

Beyond the challenges posed to conventional gender hierarchies, the dangerous woman arguably invites further ontological and metaphysical questioning. That witch-hunts aimed to annihilate the potentially subversive power of women has been demonstrated by historical evidence: 'statistics compiled by historical research reveal that about eighty percent of the victims of witch-hunts were women', Walter Stephens rightly observes, 'The conclusion that witch-hunting was an exercise in "woman hunting" requires a short step'.[35] The belief in witchcraft, Stephens argues engagingly, reveals, however, another speculative layer and a significant metaphysical subtext. During witchcraft trials the insistent search for evidence of the witch's copulation with the devil revealed a preoccupation with the existence of a world beyond the seen. Paradoxically, it is the witch's sexuality and, in particular, her intercourse with non-corporeal creatures that provide the crucial proof of the existence of a spiritual dimension, and therefore of God.[36] Early modern witchcraft theorists tackled the issues that had haunted key Christian theologists including St Augustine and St Thomas Aquinas, that is the problematic substance of angels' and demons' bodies, which, as put by Stephens, could determine the existence of a world beyond that of pure matter: 'Without demonic corporeality, there was no proof that demons were real, and thus the implication was that nature – pure matter rather than spirit – could adequately explain everything that humans experienced'.[37]

If the witch's body personifies the phantom link between the divine and the human, it follows that the dangerous woman, like the ghost trope explored in Chapter 5, becomes the embodiment of liminal otherness. Her in-between status is, once more, useful in deconstructive terms, echoing Cixous's notion that 'Woman un-thinks the unifying'. Such 'unthinking', then, propels the dangerous woman's subversive function beyond its important position in gender theory to embrace postmodernism's wider concerns with the real. In this respect Thompson's *femme fatale* performs a dual purpose in *Pandora's Box* ; on one hand, it demystifies the essentialist binary system of gender/sex differentiation; on the other, through its self-conscious parody of the detective novel, it interrogates the foundations of empirical knowledge and secure notions of the real. The last novel analysed in this chapter, Smith's *The Accidental*, is similarly entrenched in postmodern anxieties about the possibility of knowing the 'truth' and representing the real. Disrupting the dysfunctional routines of four family members, Smith's charismatic seductress, Amber, simultaneously exposes the 'unreal' core of the characters' hyperreal worlds. Marking the end of their existence as simulacra, Amber brings the exciting epiphany of a potentially new world.

QUEERING (HER)STORIES: ELLEN GALFORD'S *THE FIRES OF BRIDE* AND *QUEENDOM COME*

New Jersey-born Ellen Galford's satirical fiction addresses the crucial intersections of marginal identity and female empowerment. The complex interaction of nationality, religion, ethnicity, gender, sexual orientation and migrancy underpins the insider/outsider, native/incomer, central/marginal dialectic oppositions central to her novels. Identity preoccupations in Galford's fiction stem from the author's own concern with self-definition and the negotiation of an identity that does not sit easily in any pre-defined category.[38]

Published in the last two decades of the twentieth century, Galford's novels – *Moll Cutpurse* (1984), *The Fires of Bride* (1986), *Queendom Come* (1990) and *The Dyke and The Dybbuck* (1993) – reflect on the condition of the female subject against patriarchal structures of oppression. At the same time, her self-conscious transpositions of oral and historical traditions challenge 'pre-packaged' versions of national identity and female subjectivity, reflecting on the conflict between authenticity and the performative acts brought on by normative assumptions about gender, nationality, family, class and professionalism: 'Instead of conflating the different identities', Paulina Palmer observes, 'she adopts into a general form of minority otherness and alterity, she foregrounds each one individually'.[39] In doing so Galford's use of satire and comedy playfully inverts and subverts the patriarchal/heterosexual established order, forcing the reader to view contemporary society from the 'other' feminist/lesbian point of view.

The fictional island of Cailleach is the scene for *The Fires of Bride*, a self-conscious travesty of a Gothic novel set against the sinister backdrop of a derelict castle haunted by the ghost of a nun and inhabited by an alleged witch in the person of clan chieftain Catriona McEochan; like the witch of Celtic lore, Catriona is also a 'healer' or, more mundanely, the island's GP. The layered structure of the novel – which is framed by the story of Caledonian TV journalist Lizzie – is also reminiscent of the narrative palimpsests of many Gothic texts, deploying multiple points of view and narrators to increase a sense of textual disorientation through a system of 'box within box of interlocking narratives' and internal repetitions.[40] The island is, by name, the female space of the Celtic hag, or *Cailleach*, but its history – or, as the case may be, herstory – is also linked to the worship of 'Bride, Brigantia, Bridget', 'the triple goddess who brings them poetry, smithcraft and the skills of midwifery' (Galford, *The Fires of Bride*, p. 10).[41] The two powerful female divinities coalesce in the history and the topography of the island; as Catriona puts it: 'Bride belongs to Cailleach. And Cailleach to her' (p. 48). But, as the story develops, it becomes apparent that neither the history nor the topography of the island can be represented or known in any definitive fashion.

The novel displays its preoccupations with the problematic representation of Scotland from the outset – 'Dead boring visuals up there'. Caledonian TV producers are not convinced by the island's marketable potential for a valuable broadcasting product: 'A slow pan along Glen Stereotype, then cut to the shores of Loch Cliché. You've seen one sheep, you've seen them all. And it's always bloody raining' (p. 4). Other familiar Scottish (stereo)types emerge in Lizzie's romantic expectations of Cailleach: 'Lonely castles guarding rocky coasts', 'Ghost stories by the bucketful', 'Inscrutably shawled and barefoot maidens crooning' (p. 9). The 'romantic'/Gothic version of Cailleach's history, however, adjoins other 'political', 'spiritual', 'sexual' histories (and, indeed, herstories) which converge in the multiple strands of the island's historical past, local lore, oral traditions and archaeology: whether based on 'facts' or 'imagination', all sources, it seems implied, are equally unreliable, exposing the reductive edge of one official story. The island's ancient topography – though haunted by ruthless archaeologists anxious to 'crack' the code hidden within its ancient standing stones – appears to resist monolithic interpretations: 'Celtic Twilight', 'X-rated', 'We are Not Alone', 'Herstory', 'Matriarchal Genealogy', 'Paranoid' are the suggestive headings of various possible interpretations Lizzie collects about the Cailleach stone ring: ranging from pseudo-Celtic spirituality to global conspiracy theory, the versions reflect the interpretative layers offered by the cryptic monument, ultimately exposing, once again, its undecipherable status.

The locals' contempt for the scientific theories archaeologists, who include the ironically nicknamed 'Stoney', and historians have come up with – 'all that rubbish they talk about the stones' (p. 12), says bed-and-breakfast owner Ina Isbister – reinforces the pervasive notion of the stones' cryptic essence. Significantly, Ina is also ready to dismiss her own version of the story: the notion of human sacrifices that people used to perform in the Stone Circle, is in fact an old wives' tale: 'that's what my grannie always said, and hers before her, but it's just a load of old superstition and nobody really knows' (p. 13). Superstition plays an ambivalent function: while it seemingly assists in unravelling the island's secret story, it also self-consciously undermines its own bogus foundations. On an island where the local GP is 'on first name terms with all the island's ghosts' (p. 11), all women seem to be in fact entangled with the fabrication of 'traditional' stories and beliefs. Allegedly gifted with second sight, Isa, the blind weaver, also manufactures items of local lore, such as the superstition that the tweed woven with one's hair will bring good luck to the wearer and the owner of the hair on the same day, a belief 'minted by me, right here in this house this morning' (p. 65), or the bogus 'weaving songs', her 'own Gaelic translations of Bessie Smith and Billie Holiday' (p. 179), she performs for Finnish researcher Gretel. Even the apparently authoritative voice of Catriona admits to its own unreliability when it traces the island's history: 'Half of what I say is rubbish, the rest is true. Up to you to sort out what's what' (p. 44).

The most intriguing of Cailleach's secret herstories is disclosed by the ancient Book of Bride, an apocryphal version of the Gospel, revealing the existence of a female goddess, Bride, twin sister to Jesus Christ. The discovery of this text, or the Cailleach codex, as it becomes known, represents the focal point of the novel's narratives, and one dangerous women participate in and benefit from. The central part of the novel travels back in time to focus on Mhairi, the eleventh-century nun who ensures the incognito transmission of the illuminated text and ultimately dies to protect her secret. She is the archetypal ancestor of the subsequent generations of subversive women to populate Cailleach: her entry to the convent follows her refusal to serve her father's will and marry an old earl to consolidate family allegiances. Mhairi's stance against medieval patriarchal conventions underpins the gender conflict that runs through all the narrative layers of *The Fires of Bride*. The nuns of St Bride are held in suspicion of being 'subversive' and 'she-devils' by the male exponents of the Christian Church: their determination not to conform to the strict rules of the Church – including subservience to patriarchal hierarchy – is overtly symbolised by their desire to keep the flame of Bride's fire alight, and, unofficially, by their meticulous transcription of the text of the Book of Bride for the benefit of future destinations. Fixing Bride's story is, however, problematic, as different versions of the story proliferate, even despite the efforts of Mhairi and Bloduedd, another sister, to preserve the original text: 'Sometimes the words are at war with the pictures, sometimes new marginalia appear, and others vanish' (p. 116); the archetypal herstory, the story of Bride, resists closure, manifesting itself in the plurality of persistent – and clashing – superstitious beliefs that survive in Cailleach:

But underneath the surface of the Authorised Version lie tales older than the language they are told in. Grandmothers continue to warn and to gossip, people still puzzle over dreams. Things are done without a reason, like the pinch of salt tossed over the shoulder. Random relics, perhaps or a conspiracy? (p. 110)

If Mhairi is, as Palmer suggests, 'the hub of these interlocking narratives',[42] Maria embodies her late-twentieth-century double. While a mysterious force draws her to the beach every night, like the main character in Hayton's *The Governors*, Maria imagines herself translated into a selkie: 'trapped by a spell in human form, now is the moment when I will turn back into a seal again, and slip into the waves and slide out to sea to find my own kind' (p. 106). Mhairi's ghost appears to her as a solitary seaweed gatherer, but when the spectre visits Maria's house, she is Maria's double (p. 136); their sexual union is described in magical realist tones – 'Her lips, fingers, and everything they touch glow in the darkness': the evocative lesbian love scene explicitly reinforces their bond as each other's double, 'Mirror-images, copper-speckled moonstones, flow together' (p. 139). Like Mhairi, Maria's artwork displays the subversive ideology which reclaims the space once occupied by the nuns ('Stone Circle I') and Bride herself ('Rival Firm'): made of recycled scrapyard materials and placed by the island's landmarks, her sculptures re-mould the island's layered topography and, in a sense, rewrite its past. Repopulating the ghostly remains of the ancient convent and restoring the goddess to her position on the 'other' side of the Kirk, Maria's metallic creation – itself a tribute to Bride's smithcraft – allows the island's missing story to resurface from centuries of censorship and oppression.

Her aesthetic response to the island's history makes a particular impression because it throws light on the incomer/native conflict pervasively present in Galford's fiction: 'The islanders will never accept you. You'll be an incomer 'til you are one hundred and three' (p. 153), is Stoney's warning when Maria reveals her attachment to Cailleach, where the 'incomer' tag lasts a minimum of three generations; to the islanders Maria will always be 'Yon incomer with the red hair' (p. 144). Her sculptures beg the question of legitimacy, claiming, as they do, to rewrite the island's traditional values: 'I realise that an incomer can hardly be blamed for not knowing our ways' preaches minister Murdo MacLeish, 'But she has shown no respect for them. She has blighted our landscape and, what is worse, perverted the morals and time-tested values of this community, with her obscene, vulgar, ugly images' (p. 218). The later revelation that Maria, being his niece, is not, strictly speaking, an incomer, literally kills his determination to repress Maria's voice.

The novel challenges the authenticity of accepted views of Scottish identity and manifestations of Scottish culture. On the occasion of the MacEochan clan gathering, when thousands of self-named North American and Australian Scots invade Cailleach, Ina Isbister observes the ambivalence behind such colourful displays of Caledonian nostalgia when 'Half their people mooched off on the first boat as would take them, the other half were flung forcibly into the sea by the clan chief of the day' (p. 73). To one kind of them, the answer seems to be, Scottish culture is a newly branded product to be marketed and sold over to the other kind of Scottish émigrés, those still hungry for pseudo-Scottish memorabilia. Though Scotty McCrumb's 'Granny's Hielan Hame Industries' are set up to produce Scottish souvenirs – 'Little dolls in kilts. Scenic ashtrays. Teddy bears with sporrans. Shell-craft tie-pins. Elkhorn cigarette-lighters. *Typical stuff*' (p. 169; my emphases) – all items are in fact to be manufactured in the Philippines, only to be customised, 'packaged' and 'branded' in the Outer Hebrides. Such globalised exploitative attempts to (mis)represent Scottish history and culture meet their demise with the dangerous women of Cailleach. While Maria's subversive designs, including 'a mug commemorating the names and death dates of Highland women burned as witches' and a map of Scotland detailing 'NATO bases and American nuclear missile sites' (p. 184), destroy the commercial future of McCrumb's enterprise, the later transformation of the capitalist business into a local cooperative takes a proactive stance against the lucrative commodification of Scottish culture.

The latter is the work of the most dangerous woman in Cailleach: Catriona. Like Maria and Mhairi, Catriona is also linked to Bride; having inherited the healing powers of the goddess, Catriona specialises in obstetrics and gynaecology. Catriona's body, however, is also associated with the *Cailleach*, or Celtic hag: 'With a face like Glencoe on a winter's morning', transvestite Davie/Dinah warns Maria that 'Dreaded Catriona' is 'always up to something funny' (p. 30). Uncanny Catriona represents the discursive convergence of the island's history – as a clan chieftain, her story is inscribed in that of Scotland – and herstory, as she simultaneously personifies the island's underground culture, through the ambiguous *Cailleach*, 'the old Celtic hag, the island's namesake (the sister, rival and one true love of the goddess Bride)' (p. 211). A self-conscious parody of the Scottish witch – adorning her chambers are stuffed seagulls and a black cat – Catriona holds séances with a Victorian planchette (pp. 59–61), but also, more mundanely, drives 'like a demon' (p. 43) and vanquishes red wine stains with a 'magical' potion of white wine (p. 38). Like the witch of many Scottish folk tales, shape-shifting is accounted among her alleged supernatural powers and admittedly she is 'the family changeling', though her self-mocking tone – 'Dropped into the aristocratic cradle by a pack of malevolent pixies, in exchange for the rightful infant heiress' (p. 89) – throws doubts over such a claim. Significantly, Maria's multiple attempts at her portrait fail to fix Catriona's identity, which seemingly resists representation. With the arrival of Mhairi the Seaweed-woman, however, the multiple strands of herstories that have unravelled along the disjunctive routes of Scottish women's history delineated by *The Fires of Bride* finally seem to converge to produce a range of images suggestive of Catriona's subversive power: 'a muscular Flora MacDonald', 'an old witch', 'an angular, monocled Paris salon dyke', 'a Roman empress', 'Mary Queen of Scots' and 'a black-caped vampire queen' (p. 141). The humorous catalogue of powerful impersonations further estranges Catriona's identity; her indecipherability, nevertheless, epitomises the 'essence' of the 'newly born woman', exposing a kind of femininity that resists conventional typologies and, as Clément and Cixous theorised, cannot be easily contained. What links Catriona to the other dangerous women in the novel is her ability to subvert established codes of understanding, behaviour and language. As a twentieth-century reincarnation of the Scottish witch, Catriona defies the power and authority of those who represent the institutionalised norm: the Kirk. Against Reverend Murdo's attempts to hush her voice and censor her scandalous behaviour, the Scottish witch strikes her ultimate victory: when *The Sunday Sentinel* is taken over by the new publications, the '*Scottish Sunday Deviant and Weekly Dissenter*' (p. 221), Catriona delivers the *Cailleach*'s cultural revolution.

Similar preoccupations with censorship of deviancy in patriarchal/heterosexist Britain and a complex understanding of 'identity' constitute the subtexts of Galford's third novel. Set during the 'Blue Reich' – a satirical travesty of Thatcherite Britain – *Queendom Come* revolves around the magical return of Albanna, a 'Proto-Pictish Queen', warrior and 'she-wolf of the North', to 1980s Scotland/Britain. Albanna's awakening to fulfil her promise that she 'would return in a time of trial and trouble'[43] is facilitated by Gwhyldis, the high priestess and representative of the archetypal Celtic witch/healer. Albanna's magical awakening from the past exposes the drastic consequences of Tory politics, before catalysing an imaginary coup to free her people from the PM's dictatorship. Ironically, despite Gwhyldis's 'dream of a script' designed to awake the Queen 'to lead her people in their hour of need' (p. 7), Albanna has failed to rise during the previous hard times – Norse raids, witch-hunts, battles for independence – of Scottish history; the historical references to the Scottish defeats and loss of independence on one hand, and witch-hunting on the other (p. 7), point to the two aims pursued by Galford's satire in *Queendom Come*: whilst Gwhyldis's narrative highlights the tragicomic consequences of privatisation policies in Scotland, it also reflects on the effects and intrinsic bigotry of Conservative policy on gender roles and sexual habits in Scotland/Britain exposed in Section 82, a parodical transposition of Section 28.

Albanna's former kingdom is now part of a larger empire led by a PM and 'her minions'. Beside the Colonial Governor for Scotland, it is the Secretary of State for Style who occupies a chief position as the PM's advisor: the narrative repetitively points to the emphasis placed on 'image' and 'branding' as key components of 1980s political strategy. A crucial part of the government's agenda, the restoration of traditional British values, is revealed to be, in an overt allusion to Margaret Thatcher's 'return to Victorian Values', as archaic as Albanna's anachronistic return:

> Peaky-faced Oliver Twists in old scuffed trainers are rounded up for Compulsory Youth Training Schemes, to patch up crumbling sewer mains or help build the new Tartanland plc All-Weather Leisure Complex in the middle of Glencoe. Tall silk hats are back in fashion for newspaper magnates and major shareholders. Live-in servants once more abound, upstairs and down (their share of the household poll tax is automatically stopped from their wages) and no up-to-date Executive Luxury Flatlet is complete without its foldaway maid's bed in the airing cupboard. And cholera is coming back. (p. 55)

Adjoining the return of nineteenth-century revenants is the erosion of significant slices of the historical landscape of Scotland; the government's privatisation schemes extend to the auctioning of monuments such as 'the Callanish Stones' and even 'Stirling Castle', 'centrally located hilltop site with first-rate motorway connections . . . ideal for shopping complex, time-share development or theme-park' (p. 11). Whilst profiting from the marketable commodification of ancient history, the Scottish cultural industry has re-branded long-established institutions – the Big Mac International Festival is now 'sponsored by a famous American hamburger chain' (p. 43) – and forged 'new' historical sites for the benefit of tourism at the expense of authentic sites, as is the case with the disused Waverley Station (p. 94). The geography of modern Scotland is retraced by a new visitor industry, one that has long lost the appeal of historical and cultural authenticity.

In the satirical context of *Queendom Come*, Albanna's arrival, though intended to subvert the *status quo*, creates the opportunity to underpin conservative campaigns, by providing the ultimate iconic embodiment of a glorious British past. The programme of events, which Albanna is to participate in, including the opening of Ye Olde Texan Oil Town Nostalgia Park 'on the site of a redundant shipyard' in Aberdeen, and a visit to the 'Crofter's Cottage Genealogy Centre' (p. 101), is suggestive of its ruthlessly exploitative ideology. Rather than playing the Blue Reich's game, the queen's return deconstructs in fact notions of authenticity of certain 'historical' foundations to/beliefs about Celtic Britain. For a start, the marketing of Albanna as ancient British queen proves problematic: 'If the name Boadicea bothers you, perhaps we could compromise. Introduce you as Britannia. You see, Alba – such as it was – is now part of Britain, after all' (p. 42). Most significant, in this context, is Albanna's inability to distinguish her own people from their enemies: 'If you're so clever', she eventually asks Gwhyldis, 'just tell me exactly where in this motley population my people are. Exactly which ones am I supposed to be saving? And from what?' (p. 108). To the Pictish queen the binary opposition Scottish/English is utterly meaningless. Morever, even though the Scottish nationalists' enthusiastic response to Albanna's second coming makes the PM uncomfortable, ultimately the novel emphasises their empty threat because, as the Secretary for Style claims, 'Those people are addicted to lost causes' (p. 92). The Scotland that Albanna comes back to is the complex post-colonial nation where other cultures have, despite Conservative attempts to preserve Britishness – 'We cannot allow ourselves to be swamped any further by alien cultures' (p. 87)– changed the nation's cultural substrate. When Dill and Sheila wonder at Albanna's ability to speak modern English, Albanna's response 'And why shouldn't I? I have eaten your food' points to the diversity which the existence of an official language conceals: 'The logic of this escapes them. Strictly speaking, if that's how it works, the lady should now be using a mixture of Italian, Chinese and Gujarati' (p. 25). Much like the parallel herstories of *The Fires of Bride*, what Albanna's journey through time interrogates is the reductive insider/outsider dichotomy: her non-linear history claims, if nothing else, that, far from being stable, notions of identity and belonging are in fact subject to continuous change. Talking to the PM about the ambivalent strategies of her foreign policy, Albanna thus outlines her concerns:

> You send up invisible sentinels to patrol the skies, aim flying metal penises at the homeland of your enemies, and apply all the wonders of your wizardry to sustain eternal vigilance and keep your borders tight. And then you go and dig a great long tunnel under the Channel, so the invaders don't even need to get their coracles wet. Yours is a mysterious tribe indeed. (p. 63)

Though alliances and loyalties may shift in time, Albanna's wisdom is capable of identifying the imperial ideology underlying American foreign policy: 'They don't speak Latin any more, they come from the west instead of east, but otherwise they haven't changed much. Still obsessed with interfering in other people's private business, and fond of eagles' (p. 119).

While the 'launch' of Albanna becomes an important component of the government's political agenda, it also exposes the Reich's Anglocentric marginalisation of the 'Scottish colony'. Albanna's appearance requires 'maps' and 'timelines' to contextualise her origins, because 'According to the latest surveys [. . .] twenty-six per cent [of the English population] still believes that Scotland wakes from its enchanted sleep only to supply the telly programmes for New Year's Eve' (p. 89). But if the carefully presented image of the Celtic queen may well suit the government's agenda, her *voice* is significantly more problematic. Albanna's contribution to the 'Tribute to the British Family' event does in fact reveal uncomfortable truths about the origins of such institutions as the nuclear family. Upon apprehending the meaning of 'marriage', Albanna's matriarchal views appear less than positive: 'Cohabiting with each other throughout the lunar cycle? That's abnormal! Perverted! [. . .] I must say, I am shocked to discover how far your people have deviated from the norm. You should be ashamed of yourselves!' (p. 91).

In response to Albanna's public stance against the patriarchal institution of marriage, the PM orders that the 'facts' be checked by a historian, but, as she is informed that 'Most of them work in Australia and America now', she requests that 'someone *rewrite history*' (p. 92; my emphases). More astutely the Secretary of State opts for an exclusively visual exploitation of Albanna's image: 'Trot her out in full battledress, helmet and spear and all, on appropriate occasions – but keep the chat to a bare minimum' (p. 92). Debarred of her authentic voice, the Celtic queen can still produce the desired effect: that of embodying the empty simulacrum of a forged glorious past.

Albanna's challenges to the traditional nuclear family are made more prominent by the government's attempt to enforce the celebrated 'Victorian values' and eradicate all who stray from the 'norm'. Juxtaposed to the central/ powerful position occupied by Albanna and Gwhyldis in the land formerly known as Alba, a late twentieth-century Edinburgh doctor, Marion Dillon (Dill), is ostracised and (unfairly) dismissed from her position because her homosexuality goes against the 'Sexual Normality Bill', significantly approved on the night of Albanna's awakening on Midsummer's Eve, 'by a House full of adulterers, voyeurs, fetishists and secret spankers' (p. 11). After the crumbling walls of the Royal Infirmary have been taken over by Scothealth plc (p. 30), upon her dismissal Dill is informed that 'A deviant is a deviant. We owe it to our customers to protect them' (p. 31). Ironically, the unpopular 'Sexual Normality Bill' creates more business opportunities such as 'Designer Closets', an agency which provides homosexuals with their perfect heterosexual alter egos: 'a customized heterosexual curriculum vitae, complete with photographs of loving spouse and bouncing babies, plus a complimentary gold wedding band' (p. 54):[44] when the PM's 'cast-iron coiffure' falls victim of a pigeon attack at the Edinburgh Tattoo, 'a team of security-vetted, certified-heterosexual hairdressers extract the bird droppings and repair the Official Hairstyle' (p. 77).

Whilst Albanna's popularity temporarily freezes the sectarianism of Scottish nationalists – 'The armchair rebels, tartan lefties and other wild-eyed fanatics have stopped quarrelling with each other just long enough to notice that the Celtic Queen is once more in their midst' (p. 120) – her sex still proves to be problematic. The male/female opposition is epitomised by the separate factions of worshippers – the female 'witches' and the male 'druids'– competing for their positions on Arthur's Seat. One of the latter, Mr Melville, struck by Albanna's spear at the beginning of the story, 'launches a campaign against the revival of witchcraft in our own time, as exemplified by feminist Goddess-worshippers and other dubious dabblers of hypothetical old religions' (p. 56). The question 'Should the Brotherhood break with sacred tradition and invite to dinner the closest living link with the ancient Bards – in spite of her inconvenient extra chromosome?'(p. 101), however, leads to an interesting argument on sexual difference and gender: 'Surely, they argue, her probable age – not to mention her royal blood and tattooed skin – *unsexes* her' (p. 101; my emphases): Albanna's age, status and appearance may compensate for her biological sex. The government agents, however, attempt to modify Albanna's image in order to make her appearance conform to social norms. On her official visit to the North-British centre 'Albanna [. . .] has topped up her tattoos with some flamboyant touches of face-paint. She also wears a surprisingly conventional Royal hat, and seems to have been taking lessons from Someone in the queenly art of handbag-carrying' (p. 104).

The ensuing *coup d'état* is designed to eradicate widely spread heterosexist and patriarchal ideology of the Blue Reich. Albanna's second appearance on Arthur's Seat, six months after her awakening, delivers the most uncomfortable piece of news: 'This ceremony, gentlemen, is a travesty', she proclaims, 'There is no place for the male sex in religion' (p. 134). That her words speak for generations of Scottish women oppressed by patriarchal conventions is made clear by the subsequent eruption of Arthur's Seat, vomiting a lava made of 'leeks, carrots, lentils, barley and a lot-of stored-up grievances. It is the soup immemorial of all Scottish grandmothers, and there seems to be an inexhaustible supply' (p. 137). Having staged a fake natural disaster to lure the Prime Minister and send her back to Pictish times, the ghosts of victimised 'deviants' – an ironic delegation from the Scottish history of intolerance – are summoned up by Gwhyldis: witches, homosexuals, Covenanters and 'consumptive Romantic poets' lie in the beds of a hospital the PM forgot to have closed down; as Dill puts it: 'History has come to get you' (p. 143).

PLAYING WITH SCOTTISH WITCHCRAFT: MURIEL SPARK'S *SYMPOSIUM*

Spark's treatment of the Scottish witch introduces larger questions of self-agency and subversion, which may be better understood in the wider context which accommodates them. As with Galford's, Spark's biography prompts questions of categorisation and cultural boundaries. Born in Scotland in 1918 from a Scottish Jewish father and an English mother, in 2006 she died in Italy, where she had moved in 1965 after spending time in Africa, America and England. Distancing herself from her Jewish roots and Presbyterian education, Spark formally converted to Catholicism in 1954, having spent the first four decades of her life in a state of spiritual 'indifference', as she revealed in 'My Conversion', an essay she published in 1961.[45] Spark's postmodernist fictions deconstruct stable notions of belonging and national identity, reflecting also Spark's own experience of life away from her native country: Scotland emerges as a state of mind, a fantastic world beyond the contingent boundaries of the real. The revenants of Scotland, and Edinburgh in particular, return in her stories in cycles of nostalgic parting and (fictional) returns, a state which Spark identifies as a vocation: 'It was Edinburgh that bred within me the conditions of exiledom; and what have I been doing since then but moving from exile into exile? It has ceased to be a fate, it has become a calling'.[46] When Spark returns to Scotland in her novels, it is with the intention of questioning the slippage between Scottish culture and the perceptions of Scottishness from the outsider's point of view: ultimately, Spark seems to suggest, Scotland is unknowable. Her memorable Scottish characters, which include Dougal Douglas (*The Ballad of Peckham Rye,* 1960) and Jean Brodie (*The Prime of Miss Jean Brodie,* 1961), share uncanny demonic features, blending their apparent elusiveness with a suggested potential to destabilise the norm. Resisting easy categorisations, these characters also interrogate the 'essence' of Scotland and Scottish culture, fragments of which are interwoven in the narratives through transtextual references to Scottish ballads and lore. In *The Prime of Miss Jean Brodie,* a novel which manifestly exposes the uncanny dark spots of the Scottish capital, Sandy notes that 'there were other people's Edinburghs quite different from hers, and with which she held only the names of districts and streets and monuments in common';[47] similarly, in *The Ballad of Peckham Rye* the evanescent quality of the main character, Scots Dougal Douglas, is conveyed through the pervasive ambivalence upon which his 'fey' Scottishness and sexuality appear to be construed.

The demonic ambivalence of Dougal Douglas and Jean Brodie returns in conjunction with Spark's preoccupation with (female) power in *Symposium,* 'a story', Lorna Sage suggests, 'about original sin and the evil eye'.[48] As with *The Prime of Miss Jean Brodie,* the novel, which is partly set in Fife, displays the author's joint fascination with the *femme fatale* and the origin of evil. In *Symposium* the sinisterly charismatic Edinburgh spinster is replaced by Scottish, red-haired Margaret Murchie, recently married to William Damien: 'Margaret certainly presents as a Scot of gothic splendour, attractive, striking, odd and discomfiting', Alan Freeman comments, 'a Scot of the Scott kind' (p. 134).[49] A series of apparently unrelated mysterious deaths reveal a disturbing pattern: the victims are all female and knew Margaret. Ironically, the only person Margaret overtly wishes to 'liquidate', her mother-in-law Hilda Damien, is 'accidentally' killed by a gang of burglars managed by Charterhouse, Chris Donovan's butler. The other deaths, which may be the responsibility of Margaret's mad Uncle Magnus, remain unsolved, though Magnus reveals that Margaret has the 'evil eye' and that she is 'capable of anything' (p. 60); adding that 'Perhaps she inherited something wild from me' (p. 61), Magnus also relates Margaret's subversiveness to Scottish history: 'Margaret is a Murchie, Covenanting stock who refused to accept the rules of bishops' (p. 82), hinting enigmatically that her manipulative powers may derive from the supernatural vein of her Scottish roots: 'Do you know anything about hypnotism? It's at the bottom of witchcraft' (p. 82). Later, while Magnus suggests selecting a name from 'a list of eligible bachelors' with a pin (p. 111), Margaret remembers that 'At school I was good as Lady Macbeth' (p. 117) and admits to being at least tempted to kill her brothers-in-law: 'If they were my husbands I'd tip prussic acid into their tea' (p. 118).

With the exception of her husband, William, who is (literally?) 'enchanted right-away', all other characters become progressively involved in a parodic witch-hunt, aiming to unveil the dark secrets underneath Margaret's virtuous facade epitomised by her repetitive references to the spurious altruistic philosophy of 'Les Autres': 'That goody-goody type of girl, how could she be real?'(p. 39), questions Hilda; 'There's something quite funny', Hurley admits, 'Her get-up wasn't natural for a young girl at six-thirty on a normal evening. She had green velvet, a wonderful green, and a massive background of red and gold leaves all arranged in pots' (p. 25); her potential beauty – 'Margaret would have been a Titian-haired beauty' (p. 20) – something about the strangeness of her clothes, her red hair and, most oddly, her vampire-like 'protruding' and 'aggressive' teeth amplify a sense of Gothic distortion. The fact that Margaret comes from St Andrews adds further uncanny layers about her persona. When Chris mentions that Hilda felt 'it was very spooky there in Fife [. . .]. Nothing you could put your finger on' (p. 65), Hurley replies: 'Oh, that's Scotland. All the families are odd, very odd' (p. 65). Overtly associated with the archetypal Scottish maniac – 'A female Jekyll and Hyde' (p. 144) – the nature of Margaret's hypothetical crimes remains, as with Jekyll's doppelgänger – 'What were precisely the crimes of Mr Hyde?' (p. 144) – undefined. Yet such elusiveness exaggerates the emphatic impact of her Scottish origin: 'Her witchy propensities are attributed to a mixture of possibly inherited family madness', Sage notes, 'and in a splendidly throwaway fashion – simple Scottishness'.[50] Margaret's foreignness attracts questions about 'otherness', which she may also self-consciously draw towards herself through her obsession with 'Les Autres'. Along with Corby, the Mauritian chef employed by Chris and Hurley for their dinner party – 'Of course Mauritius still has a very primitive element, you know. Their witchcraft. They sense things' (p. 137) – Margaret comes to represent the unknowable other: 'Scottishness becomes the source and explanation of her other-worldliness', Alan Freeman argues, 'and her apparent potential mendacity'.[51]

Though apparently representing one of two two-dimensional clichés – the aggressively ambitious she-devil versus the passively oppressed/repressed feminine angel – each of the female characters in Symposium helps in fact to deconstruct such binary categorisations. Chris Donovan, a rich Australian widow in a relationship with artist Hurley Reed, is 'ageless', 'because she has the money to preserve her looks'(Spark, *Symposium*, p. 22);[52] her friend Hilda Damien, also a widow, is a 'magnate', 'having made her own money through her own cleverness' (p. 23). She is 'above and beyond feminism' (p. 35), but longs to be married again; she is the most powerful woman in the novel and the final victim of the mysterious force that may have also killed Margaret's grandmother and Sister Rose. Lady Helen Suzy, who has 'succeeded' in marrying the rich Lord Suzy, is also revealed to have her own subversive fantasies: upon hearing about St Uncumber, the saint 'to whom people, especially women, used to pray to relieve them of their spouses' (p. 6), she pronounces that she 'might try the Uncumber method' (p. 6); even – or perhaps most importantly – the eccentric nuns at the Anglican Convent of Mary of Good Hope smoke, swear, hold Marxist beliefs, are expert plumbers and (allegedly) karate fighters; they all share a 'subversive' attitude to established views on (gender) politics, religious institutionalism and even celibacy: 'The nuns' historical materialism flies in the face of traditional Christian spirituality', Freeman rightly remarks, 'as well as its moral injunctions against violence, adultery and theft'.[53]

As usual in Spark's fiction, cross-references and a tight system of internal repetitions point to the hidden bonds among unlikely characters. Grace, Margaret's mother, is the seemingly passive recipient of coded gender roles: when Hilda visits Margaret's family in St Andrews, Grace complains that 'It's the third wedding I've coped with' (p. 38). Yet, the fact that she is dressed in 'black and white', like the empowered (masculine) Hilda, seems to imply that, as Hilda's alter ego, she holds covert strength. Within the incestuous textuality of the story, as in all of Spark's plots, unlikely connections slowly emerge, hinting at the novel's allegorical title; 'symposium' refers to the intricate connections that link apparently distant people, who unknowingly share more than they appear to on a surface level: the repetition of the phrase 'I want to look nice' (p. 100), simultaneously enunciated by Ella and Margaret as they prepare for the focal event in the novel, the dinner party, endorses such underground connections. As Craig rightly observes, the narrative is suggestive of the ambiguous boundaries that separate self and other:

> The arbitrariness of the relation of self and other which Margaret suffers from is itself a function of the breakdown of the relations of self and other of which she is part: it is a world where people and things are so confused that the book starts with a male character declaring 'This is rape!' in reference to a burglary of his home.[54]

Yet the opening sentence of *Symposium* also emphatically draws attention to the subtext of violation of the female body. As with Craig, Lady Suzy is also surprised by Lord Suzy's metaphor of choice. In a letter to Pearl, Lord Suzy's daughter and Helen Suzy's former school-friend, she attempts a psychoanalytical explanation: 'He says he's been raped, how would he know about rape? In

fact in a funny psychological way he wants to be raped, they say we all do!!!'
(p. 73). Sexual fantasies – often with a sadomasochistic nuance – are pivotal
to the ways in which the characters in *Symposium* interact with each other.
Though sex is never openly performed, the narrative revolves around various
unconsummated desires. In this respect female sexuality is surrounded by an
aura of suspicion. During his honeymoon with Margaret, William humorously
compares Italian cities to loose women – 'Venice is a whore' (p. 19); 'Florence
is a harlot' (p. 20) – suggesting the misogynist slant of an anti-female discourse.
William's comments are indicative of the identification of moral corruption
and crime with female sexuality. Could he perhaps be subconsciously thinking
of Margaret as one such professional temptress? Their first casual encounter,
strategically concocted – as Hilda rightly suspects – by Margaret, by the fruit
section in Marks and Spencer, is an overt parody of Adam's temptation in the
Garden of Eden. Identified with the archetypal 'bad' woman of the Christian
world, Margaret personifies the female 'other', unjustifiably held in suspicion
because, being Scottish/female/outsider, she deviates from multiple normative
assumptions.

Identity is subject to manipulation, construed as it is upon the mediation of
stories, gossip, rumours and clichés, which point to the self-reflective core of
Symposium, as a hub of fantasy-fuelled stories. The fact that the truth about
Margaret emerges by a process of relentless mediation means that no character has 'full' control over or understanding of her agenda. Ultimately what
Symposium claims is that the truth can never be fully disclosed, but only represented through endless distorted and fragmented variations around a common
theme. Ernst Hunziger complains about TV's lack of authenticity: 'Can't the
television make it more convincing?' (p. 16). But all main characters disclose
deep connections to the strategies of representation: Hurley Reed is an artist;
Roland Sykes is an investigator; Annabel is an assistant TV producer; before
marrying William, Margaret works in TV research; William is an expert in
artificial intelligence; Hilda is a media tycoon. Margaret's identity is therefore
built upon layers of mediation provided by documentaries, TV footage and
articles. As Flora, one of Margaret's sisters, concludes, the prejudice surrounding Margaret lacks substantial authenticity, as it relies on the fabrication of
(unfounded) stories by the media:

> My sister is naturally very down to earth. As you know the earth is mag-
> netic, Margaret attracts people like the press and the television. Her hair
> is naturally red. There is nothing at all to prove anything against her. I
> hate it when people come here to interrogate us. (p. 127)

Flora's statement also suggests that, ultimately, only inexplicable forces
determine one's destiny. In Margaret's case – as in many Scottish witchcraft
stories – the detail of her red hair exposes her otherness. Significantly Spark

disseminates traces of traditional witch-lore in the form of transtextual quotations from the Scottish witchcraft ballads 'Kemp Owyne' (used by Magnus to address Margaret):

> O was it a wer-wolf in the wood,
> Or was it a mermaid into the sea,
> Or was it a man or a vile woman,
> My true love that mis-shapit thee? (p. 108)

and 'Allison Gross':

> Awa', awa', ye ugly witch,
> Haud far awa' an' lat me be!
> For I wouldna ance kiss your ugly mouth
> For a' the gifts that ye could gie. (p. 143)

thus highlighting the textual links between the Scottish witch and narrative representation. Such references support the construction of Margaret's identity as that of a transtextual palimpsest of Scottish witchcraft. Whilst apparently empowering the Scottish witch throughout the story, as previously done in *The Prime of Miss Jean Brodie*, *Symposium* simultaneously exposes Margaret's helplessness under the weight of other mysterious forces – God/Spark – even though the witch (temporarily) 'challenges the author, and starts to play providence on her own account'.[55] Though allowing her dangerous woman enough scope to fulfil the first part of her plan – her marriage to William – ultimately Spark wrecks the Scottish witch's subversive agenda, at last revealing her own sinister tricks.

BETWEEN GENDERS: ALICE THOMPSON'S *PANDORA'S BOX*

Thompson's second full-length novel, *Pandora's Box,* also deploys a plethora of transtextual references to articulate a radical interrogation of sex/gender categories. A blend of classical myth, Biblical and literary references creates a supernatural story of death and rebirth, mediated through a pastiche of Greek mythology and Christian iconography. Thematically, the story of Pandora's artificial birth through the skill and the scalpel of plastic surgeon Noah also establishes parallels with other classical and Gothic parodies of divine creation from Ovid's 'Pygmalion' to Mary Shelley's *Frankenstein* (1818), and especially the postmodernist renditions of Carter's *The Passion of New Eve* (1977) and Gray's *Poor Things* (1992). As the title suggests, the transposition of the Greek myth of Pandora loosely informs the content of the story, simultaneously providing the basis for critical revision: the myth of Pandora is turned upon itself to interrogate the links between female beauty/body and gender identity, as the narrative revision displays preoccupations with the impact of male gaze and desire on gender categorisation.

Unlike *Justine* and *Pharos*, where references to the Scottish doubles and the ghost-story tradition, respectively, seep through the transtextual palimpsests of Thompson's narratives, *Pandora's Box* is less overtly touched by a distinctively Scottish cultural tradition while, on the whole, its generic boundaries are hard to define. Though 'playfully cast in the genre of crime fiction',[56] as Susan Sellers writes, it is hard to constrain this complex novel, which simultaneously flirts with the conventions of science and crime fiction, magical realism and fantasy, within the conventional boundaries of a single genre. With *Justine* and *Pharos*, however, both character and novel share a resistance to categorical definition, their complexities amplified through continuous allusions to other texts and self-consciously exposing the subversive discourse of transtextual rewriting. The novel's epigraph is from Hesiod's *Works and Days* and recalls how Pandora, 'an evil thing in which they may all be glad of heart while they embrace their own destruction',[57] was sent to earth by Zeus as punishment. As Pandora, whose name ironically means 'all gifts', personifies divine revenge, she also, like the Biblical Eve, discloses the misogynist discourses underlying both myths: the roots of Thompson's *Pandora's Box* are located in the anti-female discourses embodied by the archetypal dangerous woman.

The narrative opens with the discovery of a 'shadowy figure' surrounded by flames and standing in the shape of a star outside Dr Noah Close's house. The unidentifiable body points to the male gaze/desire subtext of the narrative: to the scientist, the body is a riddle which challenges the limits of empirical knowledge; to the plastic surgeon, the unidentified body constitutes a blank canvas, potentially allowing him unlimited freedom in his reconstruction of Pandora's body. In these terms the assignation of a female sex must be read as a projection of Noah's desire over the creature he will, later, be able to claim as his own:[58]

> Her body became a landscape over which he had to cross, but he saw it in terms of square inches. The limitations of the future lay within the circumference of his immediate world. He took on her body a moment at a time. He was remoulding her not with the touch of human flesh but with the caress of the knife, the prickle of the needle – medical science had become *an act of love*. (Thompson, *Pandora's Box*, p. 10; my emphases)

As surgery – and scientific knowledge – replaces divine creation, the life-giving process establishes an ambivalent bond between creator (Noah) and creature (Pandora) and reverberates echoes of other problematic narratives of (artificial) creation including Shelley's *Frankenstein*: this bond is simultaneously entrenched with psychoanalytical questions of language and desire. The complex creator/creature desire-based bond is explicitly uncovered by Pandora's provocative question, the only one she ever asks, when Noah surprises her in his own house: 'Don't you realise how much you need me?'

(p. 19). His naming of Pandora becomes a parody of the account of creation in Genesis,[59] and evoking Biblical authority, Thompson underlines Noah's statements as unilateral expressions of his own will and love: 'He liked the idea that he had created her, forged her out of fire. [. . .] He called her his wife. He called her Pandora' (p. 21). Noah marries his creation before she has a name: the naming, significant in the references it makes to the account of creation in *Genesis* and the Greek myth of Pandora, is the second act of ownership which Noah, whose own name is reminiscent of the Biblical patriarch and his grand quest, exercises over his creature. As in the Greek myth of Pygmalion, 'he has created female life as he would like it to be – pliable, responsive, purely physical'.[60]

As Marina Warner notes, while the myth is clearly linked with the institution of marriage, 'Pandora is a most subtle and complex and revealing symbol of the feminine, of its contradictory compulsion and peril and lovableness'.[61] Pandora's inability to communicate underpins her subordination to the Law of the Father negatory of female autonomous signification, and her belonging to Noah's patriarchal world as (dangerous) 'other'. Their impossible communication erodes, in fact, the full exercise of Noah's authority, as he admits: 'His love for her had made him fragile, cut him open so his heart showed' (p. 27). As such, Pandora's resistance to Noah's control is the first significant act of rebellion she performs against her maker; her secretive weaving and strange collection of glass animals – a transtextual allusion to Tennessee Williams's treatment of the female other in *The Glass Menagerie* (1944), as well as a metaphorical reference to the witch's affiliation with the animal world – question the authenticity of Noah's creation:

> He became convinced that she too was made of glass, like the glass case, that he could see straight through her. Inside there was a part of herself she retained, she kept safe and to herself, which she would never let out, like one of the glass animals, that stood in the glass case and refracted the light. (p. 24)

Throughout the second section of the novel, other narrative parodies of creation reiterate the intimate bond between male desire and female beauty, exposing the ambiguous foundations of fixed gender categories. After Pandora's disappearance, psychic detective Venus Dodge's vision of the missing Pandora is conveyed through the classical myth of Venus's birth from the sea, pointing to the ambivalent convergence of the two myths. The fact that the seawater of the original myth, however, is transformed into a bloody river foreshadows the destructive force that Pandora personifies:

> Once there was a river of blood which flowed through the desert thick and still moving. No natural life inhabited the river or lived in its

vicinity. [. . .] one night, limbs, structures, protuberances, began to grow upwards out of this blood. These forms came together in the shape of the body of a woman. Her body had the kind of beauty that is translucent and as she rose up out of the river it was as if she were made of glass. (pp. 69–70)

The 'river of blood' also reveals the forceful imposition implicit in the creation of Noah's scalpel: Pandora's glass-like body, in opposition to Venus's fluid journey out of water, has been (violently) carved into her flesh by the surgeon's scalpel. Where Venus's beauty is arguably 'natural', Pandora's is forcedly man-made.

Linked to the critical exploration of female beauty is the interrogation of the identification of sex and gender categories. Pandora's existence is enshrouded in sexual ambivalence since Noah's first recovery of 'the body [. . .] so charred he could not tell whether it was man or a woman' (p. 4); Pandora's secretive embroidery work, presented as an uncanny parody of feminine domesticity, interrogates sex/gender categories further:

Curious to see the work, Noah lifted up the sheet, and with his eyes followed the gentle fluid curves of the stitched woman, skin the colour of snow. But to his shock, he saw that Pandora had added on to the *faceless* woman's pubic area a huge *phallus*, surrounded by coarse, dark, pubic hair, each hair beautifully stitched, the tip of the erected penis stitched soft as red velvet. (pp. 28–9; my emphases)

The unidentified body (Pandora's self-portrait?) signals the explicit interrogation of gender categorisation, which in turn erodes the foundations of empirical evidence and scientific discourse. The fallacy of Noah's essentialist views is exposed through his unreliable subjectivity and desire-led gaze, which frames and informs the narrative. In his eyes Pandora is, to use Clément's words, 'absent, hence desirable; a dependent nonentity hence adorable', but also a reminder that men enjoy playing with dolls.[62] Noah's reaction to Pandora's artwork suggests a psychoanalytical reading of the episode: the phallus draws attention to its disembodied position, forcibly pointing to Noah's own fear of female-induced castration: 'the phantasy of the castrating mother undermines Freud's theories that woman terrifies', Creed argues, 'because she is castrated and that it is the father who alone represents the agent of castration within the family'.[63] Like the 'gaze of the Medusa', the trope of the 'castrating woman' represents a crucial challenge to a phallocentric (and Freudian) understanding of sexual difference and passive femininity. Here Pandora's hermaphrodite representation interrogates the solidity of binary readings of sexual and gender identities. Echoing Butler's reading of Beauvoir's argument that 'one is not born, but rather becomes a woman',[64] Thompson's implicit contention supports Butler's view that 'woman itself is a term in process, a constructing that cannot rightfully be said to originate or end'.[65]

Pandora's sexual ambivalence embodies the unstable parameters behind both biological sex and cultural gender; rather, Thompson appears to suggest that sex, like gender, is a cultural construct. This is reinforced in the playful mocking of the detective story conventions; in spite of Noah's assumptions about her sex, Venus contravenes the laws of genre/gender: rather than using rational deduction – typically identified with masculinity – she relies primarily on psychic visions – subverting the principles of rational/masculine knowledge. Significantly, however, the final evidence is physical: 'Her naked body was curled up in a ball as *pale* and *pink* as a naked baby rat. He couldn't understand how he had ever been fooled into thinking such a *puny* body had ever belonged to a man' (p. 62; my emphases). It becomes apparent then that the understanding of biological sex depends on stereotyped binary oppositions of power distribution between genders: her masculine strength and status make Venus a man, in Noah's eyes; conversely, feminine harmlessness and vulnerability are revelatory of her female sex.

Strongly reminiscent of Carter's *The Passion of New Eve*, the carnivalesque backdrop of the club where Noah meets Lazarus pushes the deconstructive gender subtext into the foreground. Lazarus, evocatively named after the man whom Jesus resuscitates from the dead, is akin to Pandora, whose life, along with her sex assignation, Noah has restored into her body. The club, which hosts a crowd of sexually ambivalent punters, is ironically named 'Keep the Faith', while the interior decor showcases blasphemously cross-dressed and transgendered religious icons: 'Black beards had been painted on to the stone faces of the Virgin Marys and the statues of Christ were wearing various doll-size sequinned dresses' (p. 94). The transgendered space of 'Keep the Faith' prompts Noah to ask the crucial question 'What does being a woman mean?' (p. 102). Such overt critical interrogations increase in urgency upon Noah's visit to Lazarus's home, another space that Thompson's extensive symbolism layers with discursive statements. Gender signification/representation is embedded in the architecture of the estate; at the bottom of the swimming pool is a mosaic depicting another Greek goddess, Athena, born out of Zeus's head: like Venus and Pandora, this myth portrays the rise of a female subject as a projection of male fantasy. As Creed notes,[66] however, Athena is also Medusa's daughter, sporting the Gorgon's head on her shield, after Medusa's death by Perseus's hand. The image of Athena, goddess of war, in Lazarus's estate, is another symbolic act of resistance against patriarchal constructs of femininity. The grotesquely surreal space of the house, which is crowded with bone sculptures, also reveals a fountain with a statue of the goddess Pandora, which strikes Noah for 'the resemblance the statue had to his dead wife' (p. 113). The multiplicity of reflections in the pool and fountains underpins the symbolic function of the house, whose external walls are also covered in mirrors 'reflecting the lights of the town' (p. 111); the house, like the club, is hyperreal: no real forms correspond to these simulacral images, anticipating the solution to the riddle of Pandora's disappearance: 'You forged her from fire', Lazarus claims, 'How can you expect loyalty from a phantom of your own imagination?' (p. 139). Pandora, it would appear, is nothing but Noah's simulated fantasy.

As the embodiment of ideal female beauty and feminine passivity, Pandora's existence is framed within the constrictive boundaries of male desire: as outlined in Mulvey's seminal article, 'The determining male gaze projects its phantasy onto the female figure which is styled accordingly'.[67] In Thompson's re-working of the myth of Pandora, the male gaze – and all it stands for – is questioned and subverted by the gaze of the 'other' – be it that of Pandora/ Lazarus or Venus Dodge. Thompson's claim that 'gender is an imposition' may be understood therefore as a response to Butler's definition of gender performativity as the 'relation of being implicated in that which one opposes'.[68] *Pandora's Box* exposes the fragile foundations of sexual difference and gender definition within a phallogocentric system of representation. In this revision of the Greek myth, rather than personifying divine revenge, Pandora embodies the ambivalent resistance against the constraints of archetypal misogynist/ patriarchal readings of womanhood and femininity; as the *tabula rasa* replaces the archetypal dangerous woman, the *femme fatale* trope brings together aspects of post-structuralist gender theory and postmodern ontological uncertainty. While *Justine* is, as discussed in the next chapter, a book of blank pages, Pandora's box is here purposefully emptied: the dangerous woman remains a metamorphic creation, whose definition retains a magical openness.

THE RANDOM ENCHANTRESS: ALI SMITH'S *THE ACCIDENTAL*

The arrival of a mysterious stranger disrupts the lives of a twenty-first-century British family: the inciting incident of Smith's third novel uses the plot-catalyst familiar to twentieth-century film and fiction preoccupied with the contingency and absurdity of (modern) life.[69] As with *Pandora's Box*, Smith's *The Accidental* plays with the trope of the female demon, though rather than gender categories and female subjectivity more emphasis is placed on postmodernist concerns with authenticity, the boundaries of the real and the foundations of 'truth': '*The Accidental* becomes a book about what is real and what isn't'.[70]

The novel revolves around a dysfunctional middle-class family, whose disaffected lives Amber MacDonald, the 'accidental' temptress, disrupts with her seemingly random arrival at their Norfolk holiday home. In this novel, as in Spark's *Symposium*, the dangerous woman's powers are never fully explained: though the consequences of her actions leave a tangible legacy, Amber resists definition, ultimately remaining an unsolved riddle: 'A traditional mystery',

Louise France remarks, 'holds it [the novel] together: who is Amber, where did she come from?'.[71] The last (Amber's?) words of the novel stipulate 'I'm everything you ever dreamed',[72] suggesting that Amber, who is, on many levels, bound to the world of cinematic representation, is, like Thompson's Pandora, nothing but a figment of the imagination.

Her own story – told in the magical realist, postmodernist style of first-person intersections at 'the beginning', 'the middle' and 'the end' of the main story – begins with her own conception on a bar table in a cinema, the Alhambra, 'Palais de luxe, [. . .] place of my conception, for which I was named' (p. 211), 'just short of a century after the birth of the Frenchman whose name translates as Mr Light' (p. 205). This ironically self-conscious account of 'beginning', simultaneously reminiscent of Salman Rushdie's *Midnight's Children* (1981) and Laurence Sterne's *Tristram Shandy* (1767), serves the purpose of introducing Amber/Alhambra as a character who inhabits the interstitial space between history – hence the cultural references, from the student revolution to the Beatles and *The Sound of Music*, to the (late) 1960s – and the imagination. Suggestive of red/light – 'Red means passion, or something on fire' (p. 206) – both her names also playfully point to her metamorphic, elusive form: Amber – 'Amber means lamps lit in the dark' (p. 206) – and Alhambra – Arabic for 'red fortress', 'a palace made of palaces' (p. 305), 'Heaven on earth' (p. 306), 'a top-of-the-range but still affordable five-door seven-seater people-carrier' (p. 306), and 'a derelict old cinema packed with inflammable film stock' (p. 306). In her quintessential otherness, Amber is the unsettling reminder of repressed desires and fears. Indeed in her appearance is a coalescence of familiar and unfamiliar, known and unknown, an uncanny blend of unfathomable, evanescent qualities: 'Her strange looks', Philip Tew comments, 'are also seen differently by various family members, indicating her chameleon status' and with it her multifarious power.[73] Michael Smart, a university lecturer with a propensity for love affairs with female students, notices 'She had an accent that sounded foreign' (p. 65), whilst his wife, Eve, who initially believes Amber to be one of Michael's student lovers, also observes that 'She looked vaguely familiar, like someone you recognize but can't remember where from' (p. 89). To Astrid and Magnus, Eve's children from a previous relationship, Amber is 'kind of a woman but more like a girl' and 'very beautiful, a little rough-looking, like a beautiful used girl off an internet site' (pp. 21, 55). Despite the disruptive influence and the long-lasting legacy of Smith's 'barefoot delinquent angel',[74] by the end of the story 'It is hard to remember', Astrid is forced to admit, 'exactly what Amber looked like' (p. 226).

Yet, to all four characters, Amber is *enlightening* in different ways. To Michael, Amber is 'an epiphany' (p. 76): 'He had seen the light. He was the light. He had been lit, struck like a match. He had been enlightened. He was photosynthetic' (p. 77). A subversive transposition of the Christian Logos,

Amber becomes the signifying principle of Michael's previously obscured world: 'Because she was light itself. Amber, walking through the world, lit the world, took the world, made it, and after her everything in it faded' (p. 165). The encounter triggers Michael's creative vein; the mysterious stranger 'had entered him like he was water', he observes, 'Like he was a dictionary and she was a word he hadn't known was in him' (p. 62). Literally intoxicated by her, Michael's imagination becomes obsessed with the semantic nuances of amber/Amber:

> Amber was an exotic fixative. Amber preserved things that weren't meant to last. Amber gave dead gone things a chance to live forever. Amber gave random things a past. Amber could be worn as an amulet. Gypsies used amber as crystal ball. Fishermen braved oceans with just a net to harvest amber. (p. 163)

Eve, a writer of fictional biographical books, imagines a range of picaresque roles to suit Amber– 'A tramp'; 'A gypsy kind of person'; 'A skilful freeloader who lived by charming her way into people's houses to eat' – though she is forcibly led to admit that 'She was charming' (p. 98). To Eve, too, Amber's dangerous light is significantly reminiscent of the flames used to burn subversively charismatic women at the stake, evoked in the reference to Ingmar Bergman's *The Seventh Seal* (1957):

> history held that to be quite so animally magnetic wasn't always so safe and in a different age she'd have been publicly flayed for it or dragged humiliatingly through the village and stuck in the stocks, or chained to a post outside the local church with all her hair shaved off like that girl in the Bergman film, the film where death was following the medieval knight and the plague was making everyone go mad. (p. 178)

On Eve's children, Amber casts the radiance of emotional and sexual awakening. Twelve-year-old Astrid, who has been called a lesbian by the school bullies, is forced to reflect upon (her own) femininity and sexuality. Obsessed with meticulous accuracy and hygiene, Astrid's claim that 'to be a size fourteen' [. . .] is gross' (p. 24) displays a problematic bond with her mother – and her body – whilst her fascination with Amber's physical appearance is drawn to her lack of conventional traits of femininity: 'she isn't wearing any make-up. It is weird. Her underarms aren't shaved. There is hair there, quite a lot. Her shins and thighs and the backs of them are also not shaved' (p. 21). From their first outing, significantly sealed by Amber's evocative offering of an apple, Amber becomes not only the archetypal temptress, who slips beside her in bed, but the catalyst of Astrid's longed-for emotional awakening: 'Astrid feels her own bones underneath the warm breath, thin and clean there like kindling for a real fire. She thinks her heart might combust right out of her chest id est the happiness' (p. 135). To Magnus, Amber is a clever sexual initiator, in his (mathematical) terms, 'Amber=angel' (p. 142) and 'The line going from Amber's eyes to his at one precise moment had the most unbelievably beautiful gradient in the world' (p. 142). More than anything else, Amber is a first lover who makes the reconciliation between Magnus's emotional and rational selves a cogent possibility.

Amber's symbolic light illumines the path towards an increased awareness of the real, the loss of which all the characters appear to be mourning, before her unexpected arrival. Haunting Magnus's narrative is the suicide of a fellow sixth-former, victim of a practical joke which Magnus participated in: 'He did it. Magnus is God' (p. 40). But playing God casts a nihilistic shadow over Magnus's guilt-ridden world: 'There is actually no God. There is only Magnus' (p. 40). In this simulacral world, where 'People are nothing but shadows' (p. 144), Magnus conjures up his own double as a manageable hologram, a creature purely made of light, in place of the 'real Magnus', 'all bulk, big as a beached whale, big as a floundering clumsy giant'(p. 38). Self-enclosed in her own world, Astrid's film recordings similarly disclose her desire to find the real (and hold) the truth of her origin: obsessed by her desire to pin down the identity of her biological father, Astrid compulsively records dawns, because they signify the 'beginning of beginnings' (p. 124), a reference simultaneously to one of her father's letters to her mother and also her own beginning, suggestively linked, via her parents' names, Adam and Eve, to the archetypal 'dawn of time'. Before Amber's arrival, Michael's philandering behaviour also reveals the symptoms of an ontological crisis: 'Had he had her or had she had him?' (p. 71), he wonders after a quick sexual encounter with Philippa Knott, one of his students, and 'Would Rachel have been more authentic?' (p. 71): the lacklustre string of affairs, which fails to fulfil Michael's lust for new conquests, highlights the ontological black holes of his existence. Critical questions of authenticity equally invest Eve's 'autobiotruefictinterviews' (p. 81), a successful series of fictional/biographical interviews with dead people. Despite her success as a writer, Eve's writer's block discloses deep anxieties about the validity of her work, which, like Michael's affairs, seems to develop in patters of alienating replication; significantly, but for Quantum, her (simulating) running machine, nothing has any meaning left, as Eve begins to interrogate the boundaries of real/imagined worlds: 'Was dream a reality? Was reality a dream?' (p. 187). Haunting Eve, like Astrid, is the question of origin and the identity of her own father, living in America with his other family. Such subconscious preoccupations emerge uncontrollably when Amber's accent, Scottish like Eve's mother's, rekindles nostalgic memories of her Scottish childhood in the fictional interview Eve has with herself:

What was Scotland to Eve? Eve's mother knelt on the rug in front of the electric fire in the front room in the house in Welwyn Garden City playing records on the big box-shaped record player. The voices of men came out of the box. They sounded like they were dead already but that they'd died valiantly for love or for loss, that the breaking of them had been worth it. (p. 94)

As in Eve's nostalgic reminiscence of her Scottish childhood, so is the key to all the characters' alienated selves buried in the memories of the past, both near and far: the unearthing process launched by Amber's arrival serves to bring these into the light of the present.

By playing with the fragile bonds that link the disaffected members of the Smart family, Amber propels their individual tensions forward, forcing each individual to embrace the real. Though, if her identity as Alhambra is to be believed, she may be 'born free' (p. 105), Amber, as Sophie Ratcliffe suggests of its creator, 'seems to be very much of this world';[75] proof of Amber's interplay with authenticity is the comic humour created by Amber's unashamed frankness, epitomised by her open intention to 'ravish him [Magnus] sexually then bring him back safely' (p. 143). Amber, unlike Eve, does not refrain from telling the truth as it is. Not only does Amber accuse Eve of being 'fake', but also, by kissing her, offers Eve's reluctant self an epiphanic moment of self-revelation:

There, everything was different, as if she had been gifted with a new kind of vision, as if disembodied hands had strapped some kind of headset on to her that revealed all the unnamed, invisible colours beyond the basic human spectrum, as if the world beyond her eyes had slowed its pace especially to reveal the spaces between what she usually saw and the way that things were tacked temporarily together with thin thread across these spaces. (p. 202)

The random encounter with the stranger compels Eve to rethink the parameters of her approach to the real and the truth and take 'a gap from her own history': 'Who is to say what authenticity is? Who is to say who owns imagination?' (p. 286), she wonders, unable to find an answer to this compelling question.

After their return to a burgled home, the responsibility of which is attributed, without evidence, to Amber, Smith follows the characters in the slow progress of new beginnings: 'By the end, everything, including the story of the stranger on the doorstep, is ready to begin again'.[76] Eve is at last forced to be true to herself:

She had been refusing real happiness for years and she had been avoiding real endings for just as long, right up to the moment she had opened the front door on her own emptied house, her own cupboards stripped of their doors, her own unpictured walls and unfilled rooms, no trace of her left, nothing to prove that Eve Smart, whoever she was, had ever been there at all. (p. 295)

Her journey takes her back to America, a random stranger knocking unexpectedly on the door of a stranger's home, which could have been her father's. The ending, fashioned as the blank canvas of a new beginning, merges Amber's journey with that of Eve, who, like the stranger who turned up on her doorstep in Norfolk, 'decided she'd sleep in the car' (p. 303).

A similar process, begun since Amber's arrival at the holiday home, invests the rest of the family: 'Something about Amber at the centre of it like an axis is what is holding them all together right now in this room', Magnus had observed in Norfolk, 'keeping everything going around, stopping everything from fragmenting into an exploded nothing that shatters itself out into the furthest reaches of the known universe' (p. 152). Correspondingly, Magnus's darkened vision of a world of 'Broken people' (p. 149) is gradually replaced by the discovery of the human ability to relate to other people, epitomised by his emphatic celebration of the word 'and' (pp. 154–5). He concludes 'Amber=true. Amber=everything he didn't even know he imagined possible for himself' (p. 153). That Amber is the carrier of 'truth' is also implied in her dramatic – and yet anticlimactic – dropping of Astrid's camera from a bridge onto the motorway lane, thus putting an end to Astrid's escapist narrative of deferral and initiating a process of playful self-examination: 'It nearly makes her laugh out loud, how small and white and angry the face in the mirror looks' (p. 119). Back at the empty family home, the 'Amber effect' lingers in the new monochromatic world of red clothes, bedcover, carpet, toothbrush that 'Astred' (p. 223) selects to mark the beginning of a new (emotional) phase in her life:

> The sky is red, a storm is coming and all the cute chipmunks in the world are potential firebombs. But for now Big Ben is still standing, like a tower that tells what time it is, and so are the Houses of Parliament, and so is Tate Modern, and the Eye, and the river is just the same old grey water with the sky dawning red above it, red all over the city of London, red through the window of Astrid's room. (p. 235)

While the reassuring continuity of the familiar sights of Astrid's London is simultaneously infused with new light, Michael, on 'official leave' from his academic position, is hit by the sudden awareness that 'Tottenham Court Road was nothing but a mirage and the streets radiating off it were the product of a bereft and infected imagination', and that 'The real world was elsewhere, like she was' (p. 273). His fall is, however, followed by the possibility of rising again, embracing a new life. Having abandoned his clichéd past for good, he remains, at last, a sensitive father to Astrid and Magnus, working on a sequence of poems called 'The Lady Vanishes'.

As the post-lapsarian family adjusts to the new light that Amber has cast on their world, Smith's novel reveals the glimpse of a possible move away from the simulacral cage of postmodernity; the source of real light may still be unobtainable, but characters may rejoice, at least, in the spectral particles of a new whole they are invited to share. In this sense, though as elusive as the demon lover in Thompson's *Pandora's Box*, like a twenty-first-century parody of Mary Poppins, the temptress of *The Accidental* restores some kind of balance to the broken household, which, significantly, remains motherless at the end of the story.

What Amber shares with the bewitching women of Galford's and Spark's novels examined in this chapter is the destabilising function of the archetypal sorceress: while exposing the fallacy of rigid categorical thinking, the modern witch is invested with the devastating power held by the traditional *Cailleach*; the seeds of a different kind of knowledge can only germinate in the aftermath of her destructive force.

NOTES

1. Heinrich Kramer and James Sprenger, *Malleus Maleficarum*, trans. Montague Summers (New York: Dover Publications, 1971), p. 44. Further references to this edition are given after quotations in the text.
2. Cixous, 'The Laugh of the Medusa', p. 885.
3. Elphinstone, 'Contemporary Feminist Fantasy', p. 45.
4. See Lizanne Henderson, 'The Survival of Witchcraft Prosecutions and Witch Belief in South-West Scotland', *Scottish Historical Review* LXXXV, 1: no. 219 (April 2006), pp. 52–74 (p. 56); see also Christina Larner, C. H. Lee and H. V. MacLachlan, *A Sourcebook of Scottish Witchcraft* (Glasgow: University of Glasgow, 1977); Christina Larner, *Enemies of God: The Witch Hunt in Scotland* [1981] (Edinburgh: John Donald, 2000); Stuart MacDonald, *The Witches of Fife: Witch-Hunting in a Scottish Shire, 1560–1710* (East Linton: Tuckwell Press, 2002), and Julian Goodare, Lauren Martin, Joyce Miller and Louise Yeoman (comps), *The Survey of Scottish Witchcraft* (Edinburgh: University of Edinburgh, 2003). Available at: http://www.shc.ed.ac.uk/Research/witches/index.html (accessed 13 January 2010).
5. Many early SF narratives, including Thomas Gardner's 'The Last Woman' (1932), reflect such essentialist views of gender and a paranoid attitude towards female emancipation. Despite the conventional view of SF as masculine genre, male supremacy is in fact frequently interrogated in many twentieth-century texts, such as C. L. Moore's 'Shambleau' (1933), Francis Stevens's 'Friend Island' (1918) and Leslie F. Stone's 'The Conquest of Gola' (1931); Naomi Mitchison's *Memoirs of a Spacewoman* (1962) was, as often with Mitchison's work, ahead of its time, portraying a society in which women are emancipated from the biological shackles of procreation. For a more comprehensive discussion of gender preoccupations in science fiction, see Helen Merrick's insightful survey, 'Gender in Science Fiction', in Edward James and Farah Mendlesohn (eds), *The Cambridge Companion to Science Fiction* (Cambridge: Cambridge University Press, 2003), pp. 241–52.
6. See the introduction to Gilbert and Gubar, *The Madwoman in the Attic*, and Barbara Creed, *The Monstrous Feminine: Film, Feminism, Psychoanalysis* (London: Routledge, 1993).
7. Walter Stephens, *Demon Lovers: Witchcraft, Sex and the Crisis of Belief* (Chicago: University of Chicago Press, 2002), p. 125.

8. Kramer and Sprenger, *Malleus Maleficarum*, p. 42.
9. Lydia Gaborit, Yveline Gusdon and Myriam Boutrolle-Caporal, 'Witches', in P. Brunel (ed.), *A Companion to Literary Myths, Heroes and Archetypes*, pp. 1163–78 (p. 1165).
10. Brian P. Levack, *The Witch-Hunt in Early-Modern Europe*, 2nd edn (London: Longman, 1995), p. 147.
11. Donald A. Mackenzie, 'A Highland Goddess', *Celtic Review* VII (1911–12), pp. 336–45 (p. 336).
12. Claire French, *The Celtic Goddess: Great Queen or Demon Witch?* (Edinburgh: Floris Books, 2001), p. 20.
13. Robert Lawrance, 'The Legend of Lianachan, or a Story of "the Grey Hag"', *Celtic Monthly* XI (1902–3: July 1903), pp. 196–7 (p. 196).
14. Anne Ross, 'The Divine Hags of the Pagan Celts', in Venetia Newall (ed.), *The Witch Figure* (London: Routledge and Kegan Paul, 1973), pp. 139–64 (p. 140).
15. Ross, 'The Divine Hags of the Pagan Celts', p. 140.
16. Several oral sources confirm the persistence of this ancient belief in the late twentieth century. See, for instance: Dougald Smith, 'Cailleach Cachailith Na Feusag' (Argyll, Islay: 1953); Ewen Currie, 'An Saighdear MacCorcadail's Chailleach Bhuana' (Ardnahoe, Islay: 1953); Ella Walker, 'Taigh Na Caillich' (Breadalbane, Glenlochy: 1964); Margaret Stewart 'Last Sheaf' (Lochtayside: 1964): records of the above are held in the Archive of the School of Scottish Studies at the University of Edinburgh.
17. E. C. Watson, 'Highland Mythology', *Celtic Review* V (July 1908), pp. 48–70 (p. 65).
18. Some early anthropological studies have linked witchcraft to pre-Christian fertility cults. See Margaret Murray, *The Witch-Cult in Western Europe* (Oxford: Clarendon Press, 1921), *The God of the Witches* (London: Sampson Low, Marston, 1933) and *The Divine King of England* (London: Faber and Faber, 1954). See also Levack, *The Witch-Hunt in Early-Modern Europe*, pp. 18–19.
19. George Morrison, 'The Witch of Cnoc-Na-Moine', *Celtic Monthly* VI (May 1898), pp. 159–60.
20. See MacIain, 'A Long Island Witch', *Celtic Magazine* X (July 1885), pp. 433–4.
21. Anon., 'Some Stories about Witches', *Celtic Magazine* XIII (December 1887), pp. 92–4.
22. Mackenzie, 'A Highland Goddess', p. 344.
23. French, *The Celtic Goddess*, p. 41.
24. Widdowson, John, 'The Witch as a Frightening and Threatening Figure', in Venetia Newall (ed.), *The Witch Figure* (London: Routledge and Kegan Paul, 1973), pp. 200–20 (p. 200).
25. Lydia Gaborit, Yveline Gusdon and Myriam Boutrolle-Caporal, 'Witches', in Pierre Brunel (ed.), *A Companion to Literary Myths, Heroes and Archetypes* (London: Routledge, 1988), pp. 1163–78.
26. Widdowson, 'The Witch as a Frightening and Threatening Figure', p. 209.
27. The link between the domestic kitchen and witchcraft is supported by Levack, who argues that women's predominant presence in the kitchen may have contributed to their association with the magical practices of witchcraft in early-modern Europe:

> As cooks they not only had the opportunity to gather herbs for magical purposes, but they also had the skill to turn them into potions and unguents. It is no accident that witches were often portrayed standing over cauldrons, for it was in such vessels that many of the agents of sorcery were in fact concocted.

See Levack, *The Witch-Hunt in Early-Modern Europe*, p. 138.

28. Hugh Miller, *Scenes and Legends of the North of Scotland or the Traditional History of Cromarty* (Edinburgh: Nimmo, Hay and Mitchell, 1889), pp. 282–9 (p. 286).

29.
> There is a motif occurring in certain primitive mythologies, as well as in modern surrealist painting and neurotic dream, which is known to folklore as 'the toothed vagina' – the vagina that castrates. And a counterpart, the other way, is the so-called 'phallic mother', a motif perfectly illustrated in the long fingers and nose of the witch. (Joseph Campbell, *The Masks of God: Primitive Mythology*; Harmondsworth: Penguin, 1976, p. 73)

Scottish witches, in particular, are fond of their 'hattocks' ('little hats'), which they use to be transported, as featured in the humorous 'London Again!'; see A. J. Bruford and D. A. MacDonald (eds), *Scottish Traditional Tales* (Edinburgh: Polygon, 1994), pp. 383–6 and p. 479n.

30. Creed, *The Monstrous Feminine*, p. 166.
31. Hélène Cixous and Catherine Clément, *The Newly Born Woman* [1975] (London: I. B. Tauris, 1996), p. 5.
32. Gilbert and Gubar, *The Madwoman in the Attic*, p. 34.
33. Shoshana Felman, 'Women and Madness: The Critical Fallacy', *Diacritics* 5: 4 (Winter 1975), pp. 2–10 (p. 6).
34. Butler, *Gender Trouble*, p. 9.
35. Stephens, *Demon Lovers*, p. 3.
36. See Stephens, *Demon Lovers*, p. 17.
37. Stephens, *Demon Lovers*, p. 86.
38. See Ellen Galford, contribution to the Scottish panel at the Modern Languages Association conference (1993), quoted in Caroline Gonda, 'Another Country? Mapping Scottish/Lesbian/Writing', in Whyte, *Gendering the Nation*, pp. 1–24 (p. 7).
39. Paulina Palmer, 'Ellen Galford's "Ghost Writings": Dykes, Dybbucks, and Doppelgängers', in Claire M. Tylee (ed.), *'In the Open': Jewish Women Writers and British Culture* (Newark: University of Delaware Press, 2006), pp. 65–78 (p. 67).
40. Paulina Palmer, *Contemporary Lesbian Writing: Dreams, Desire, Difference* (Buckingham: Open University Press, 1993), p. 106.
41. Ellen Galford, *The Fires of Bride* (London: Virago, 1986), p. 10. Further references to this edition will be given after quotations in the text. For background information on the Celtic goddess Bride and her Christian correspondent St Brigid see also French, *The Celtic Goddess*, pp. 37–8.
42. Palmer, *Contemporary Lesbian Writing*, p. 106.
43. Ellen Galford, *Queendom Come* (London: Virago, 1990), p. 27. Further references to this edition will be given after quotations in the text.
44. As well as the prejudice of the authorities in power, Galford is here also obliquely attacking the readiness to accept discriminatory policies displayed by members of the gay and lesbian community, as noted by Paulina Palmer: 'She also criticizes the small minority of lesbians and gay men who, instead of joining their fellows in demonstrating against the Section, choose to collude with their oppressors by exploiting for mercenary motives the fears of the gay community'. See Paulina Palmer, *Contemporary Lesbian Writing*, p. 89.
45. Muriel Spark, 'My Conversion', first published in *Twentieth Century* CLXX (Autumn 1961); republished in Joseph Hynes (ed.), *Critical Essays On Muriel Spark* (New York: J. K. Hall, 1992), pp. 24–8 (p. 24). See also Norman Page, *Muriel Spark* (Basingstoke: Macmillan, 1990), pp. 5–7; Judy Sproxton, *The*

Women of Muriel Spark (London: Constable, 1992), pp. 13–16. For a critical discussion of Spark's work as a Catholic novelist, see Martin McQuillan (ed.), *Theorizing Muriel Spark: Gender, Race and Deconstruction* (Basingstoke: Macmillan, 2002), pp. 1–11.

46. Muriel Spark, 'What Images Return', in Karl Miller (ed.), *Memoirs of a Modern Scotland* edited by (London: Faber and Faber, 1970), p. 151.

47. Muriel Spark, *The Prime of Miss Jean Brodie* [1961] (London: Penguin, 2000), p. 33.

48. Lorna Sage, 'Seeing Things from the End', first published in *The Times Literary Supplement* (21–7 September 1990); reprinted in *Critical Essays on Muriel Spark*, pp. 275–8 (p. 275).

49. Alan Freeman, 'A Bit of the Other: Symposium, Futility and Scotland', in McQuillan, *Theorizing Muriel Spark*, pp. 127–38 (p. 134).

50. Sage, 'Seeing Things from the End', p. 276.

51. Freeman, 'A Bit of the Other', p. 134.

52. Muriel Spark, *Symposium* [1990] (London: Virago, 2006), p. 22. Further references to this edition are given after quotations in the text.

53. Freeman, 'A Bit of the Other', p. 133.

54. Craig, *The Modern Scottish Novel*, p. 108.

55. Sage, 'Seeing Things from the End', p. 276.

56. Susan Sellers, *Myth and Fairy Tale in Contemporary Women's Fiction* (Basingstoke: Palgrave, 2001), p. 103.

57. Alice Thompson, *Pandora's Box* (London: Little Brown, 1998), epigraph. Further references to this edition are given after quotations in the text. The full account is found in Hesiod, *Works and Days*, lines 47–105.

58. See Sellers, *Myth and Fairy Tale*, p. 105.

59. See Genesis 3:20.

60. Susan Gubar, ' "The Blank Page" and the Issues of Female Creativity', in Gilbert and Gubar, *The Madwoman in the Attic*, pp. 73–93 (p. 73).

61. Marina Warner, *Monuments and Maidens: The Allegory of the Female Form* [1985] (London: Vintage, 1996), pp. 214–15.

62. Cixous and Clément, *The Newly Born Woman*, p. 67.

63. Creed, *The Monstrous Feminine*, p. 151.

64. Beauvoir, *The Second Sex*, p. 295.

65. Butler, *Gender Trouble*, p. 33.

66. See Creed, *The Monstrous Feminine*, p. 166.

67. Mulvey, 'Visual Pleasure and Narrative Cinema', p. 11.

68. Germanà, unpublished interview with Alice Thompson in 'Re-working the Magic', pp. 374–87 (p. 380); Butler, *Bodies that Matter*, p. 241.

69. Reviewers of *The Accidental* have noted a number of potentially influential sources for the novel's plot. Lucy Hughes-Hallett notes the similarities between Smith's novel and Pier Paolo Pasolini's *Theorem*, released the year of Alhambra's birth (1968), in which 'a vagrant who may be an angel, or a criminal maniac (or both), makes an inexplicable appearance in the home of an apparently commonplace family'; Sophie Ratcliffe points to Smith's affinities to Iris Murdoch and, in particular, *An Accidental Man* (1971), which contains the episode of a child killed in a road accident used by Amber's confessional narrative. See Lucy Hughes-Hallett, 'Fiction: *The Accidental* by Ali Smith', *The Times* (22 May 2005). Available at: http://entertainment.timesonline.co.uk/tol/arts_and_entertainment/books/article523700.ece (accessed 10 December 2009); and Sophie Ratcliffe, 'Life in Sonnet Form', *Times Literary Supplement* (20 May 2005), p. 19.

70. Louise France, 'Life Stories', *The Observer*, 22 May 2005, Available at: http://www.guardian.co.uk/books/2005/may/22/fiction.bookerprize2005 (Accessed 10 December 2009).
71. France, 'Life Stories'.
72. Ali Smith, *The Accidental* (London: Hamish Hamilton, 2005), p. 306. Further references to this edition are given after quotations in the text.
73. Philip Tew, *The Contemporary British Novel*, second edition (London: Continuum, 2007), p. 212.
74. Hughes-Hallett, 'Fiction: *The Accidental* by Ali Smith', p. 19.
75. Ratcliffe, 'Life in Sonnet Form', *Times Literary Supplement*.
76. Hughes-Hallett, 'Fiction: *The Accidental* by Ali Smith'.

Chapter 4

DOUBLES: BODILY DUPLICATIONS AND SCHIZOID SELVES

Love is the name for the desire and pursuit of the whole.[1]

Plato

Oxymoron was ever the bravest figure, and we must not forget that disorderly order is order after all.[2]

G. Gregory Smith

Scotsmen feel in one language and think in another.[3]

Edwin Muir

Duality is departure and return. [. . .] It is bisexuality, and dual nationality.[4]

Karl Miller

SEEING DOUBLES: FROM PLATO TO DECONSTRUCTION

West coast/east coast. Highlands/Lowlands. English/Scots. Scots/Gaelic. Celtic/Rangers. Even, perhaps, Dolly the sheep: the proliferation of doubles seems endemic to all levels of Scottish culture, past and present, visible in its historical sectarianism, political and geographical divisions and linguistic fragmentation. The double is a manifestation of the hybrid space of the postcolonial nation: in this sense, duality speaks of binary patterns of differentiation and, simultaneously, blurs the discernment between the terms of the proposed opposition; with its destabilising power, the double points in fact to the heterogeneous essence of (national) identity. The double personifies a translated self, a traumatic sense of fracture and dislocation. It embodies the notion of being other than oneself: whilst interrogating the self/other dichotomy, duality forces the self's confrontation with the other. Retracing the pervasive duality of Scottish culture, the six novels examined in this chapter – Fell's *The Bad Box* (1987), Hayton's *The Governors* (1992), Atkinson's *Behind the Scenes at the Museum* (1995), Emma Tennant's *The Bad Sister* (1978) and *Two Women of London* (1989) and Thompson's *Justine* (1996) – also inform the traditional motif with feminist/postcolonial questions of gender/national identity and postmodernist preoccupations about the real.

The cultural ramifications and ideological implications of one of the most prominent motifs in Western thought are manifold. In *Symposium* Plato discussed the origins of love as the longing for one's other half, from which one has been separated ever since the gods parted the original four-limbed bodies into two halves. Greek mythology teems with many other narratives infused with double imagery and motifs:[5] most famously the myth of Narcissus gave its name to a range of psychoanalytical studies of self-eroticism, first theorised by Havelock Ellis and Paul Näcke and later defined by Freud's influential study on narcissism.[6] Man's fascination with his own duality, according to Otto Rank, is linked to belief in the afterlife: primitive man recognised in his shadow or his reflected image the presence of his immortal part, in other words, the soul.[7] Christianity, with its strong emphasis on dual oppositions – body/soul, good/evil, God/man, man/woman – translates the pagan shadow into the Guardian Angel.[8] In folk tradition the double perpetuates uncanny associations with evil or ill luck;[9] as Paul Coates reminds us: 'its appearance marks the imminence of death'.[10] This is definitely the case in Scotland, where the apparition of a 'wraith', or one's double, implies the forthcoming death of the self or somebody close to the witness of the uncanny event.[11]

Pervasively present in myth, religion, philosophy and popular culture for millennia, the literary double, Coates reminds us, flourishes in the nineteenth century; while Romantic preoccupations with the boundaries and positioning of the self brought the double to the forefront of aesthetic representation, post-Romantic and late Victorian concerns about the (colonial) other emerged in the *fin de siècle*. In the early twentieth century such concerns with the inherent divisions of the modern self surfaced in the alienated subjects of Woolf's, Lawrence's and Forster's fictions, while the parallel development of psychoanalysis brought the multiple levels of the self into the centre of scientific investigation. In his 'Dissection of the Psychical Personality' (1933), Freud made some important points about the divided structure of personality:

The ego can take itself as an object, can treat itself like other objects, can observe itself, criticize itself, and do Heaven knows what with itself. In this, one part of the ego is setting itself over against the rest. So the ego can be split; it splits itself during a number of its functions – temporarily at least. Its parts can come together again afterwards.[12]

Freud identified three main components of personality, the ego, the superego and the id, describing the last as 'the dark, inaccessible part of our personality'.[13] While drawing his conclusions from pathological case studies, Freud also stressed that the crucial split belongs in *all* personalities, and that no 'sharp frontiers' separate the different components. Ultimately, he concluded, 'three tyrannical masters' compete for power over the ego: the super-ego (conscience), the id (repressed instincts) and the external world. Lacan elaborated further on the subject of the ego's schizoid split and the conflict with the external world catalysed by the rise of the signifier. Lacan's mirror stage represents the moment when the subject perceives his/her own *imago* as 'other', an instance where the mirror becomes the liminal boundary separating the subject from its own representation as 'other':

Indeed, for the *imagos* – whose veiled faces it is our privilege to see in outline in our daily experience and in the penumbra of symbolic efficacity – the mirror-image would seem to be the threshold of the visible world, if we go by the mirror disposition that the imago of one's own body presents in hallucinations or dreams, whether it concerns its individual features, or even its infirmities, or its object-projections; or if we observe the role of the mirror apparatus in the appearances of the double, in which psychical realities, however heterogeneous, are manifested.[14]

In Lacan's system, the mirror stage is the paradoxical phase whereby the child becomes aware of its own image, and therefore of its own self and existence autonomous from that of the mother. Simultaneously, however, the mirror image speaks of the trauma of this (sudden) epiphany, revealing its alienating function: 'the image', Sean Homer explains, 'comes to take the place of the self',[15] launching the 'imaginary' stage of language, followed, in the Lacanian system, by the rise of the symbolic order. The birth of the ego is, therefore, associated, from the start, with the notion of being 'other': 'the ego emerges at this moment of alienation and fascination with one's own image';[16] the first glimpse of one's identity derives from the actualisation of self as other.

As the double implies the traumatic dissociation of a complex sense of identity, such inner tensions – and their representations – proliferate within the collective unconscious of 'divided' cultures: 'Stories that deal explicitly with the Double', Coates argues, 'seem in the main to be written by authors who are suspended between languages and cultures'.[17] In the Scottish cultural context,

Hogg's *Justified Sinner* and Stevenson's *Dr Jekyll and Mr Hyde* epitomise the pervasive tradition of duality in Scotland. Both narratives engage with unstable binary oppositions: reason and madness, objective knowledge and subjective perception, real and imaginary alter egos; the fragmented structure – and in Hogg's text the sustained interpretive ambiguity – of the two texts reinforces the unsettling function performed by the double in Scottish fantasy.

In 1919 G. Gregory Smith coined the phrase 'Caledonian Antisyzygy' to accommodate 'the very combination of opposites' or 'a reflection of the contrasts which the Scot shows at every turn'.[18] What for Smith was a distinctive trait of Scottish culture and identity, to other thinkers of the Scottish Renaissance was a concern; Hugh MacDiarmid lamented the schizoid divide as the pervasive malaise of Scottish culture: 'Our national culture', he claimed, 'suffers from all the ills of split personality'.[19] MacDiarmid argued that the neglecting of Scots and Gaelic in favour of English had distanced the Scottish poet from the world of experience, depriving Scottish literature of authenticity and closeness to the 'sensuous and material world'.[20] At the other end of the debate about language, against MacDiarmid's 'Plea for Synthetic Scots',[21] Edwin Muir contended that the introduction of standard English in sixteenth-century Scotland had drastic consequences on the development of its own national culture, relegating Scots to the lower levels of popular culture and stripping Scotland of 'the prerequisite of an autonomous literature', that is, in Muir's words, 'a homogenous language'.[22] Exposing the problems in Muir's linguistic essentialism, Christopher Whyte has suggested that 'the most appropriate interpretation of Muir's view may be as a *taking in of the colonial wound*',[23] a recognition of the coloniser/colonised hierarchical discourse through the polarised view of Scotland's bilingualism. Significantly, Muir's contention that 'Scotsmen feel in one language and think in another', and the anxieties that it concealed, has been more recently paraphrased by Emma Tennant, who attributed the recurrent prominence of the double in Scottish literature to the nation's intrinsic split: 'The whole subject of the double', she claimed in an interview, 'came into Britain via Scotland [. . .] Scotland was split – between two languages, split between being Scottish and being English'.[24] An inherent aspect of the Scottish cultural and literary tradition, the notion of being simultaneously English and Scottish, Tennant argued, persists in contemporary manifestations of the Scottish psyche: 'I think it's Scottish to be split, to talk in one way and have to go South to make your living'.[25]

The sense of nostalgic dislocation which Tennant shares with Muir in her experience as a Scottish émigré resists, in a sense, postcolonial notions of fluid heterogeneity and hybridity – as opposed to the Scottish/English binarisms – as integral qualities of late twentieth-century and early twenty-first-century Scottish identity. While a notion of division still lingers in contemporary debates on Scottish identity, rather than duality, it is a plurality of voices and traditions, as Cairns Craig suggests, that make up the polyphonic narratives of post-devolution Scotland: 'Traditions are not the unitary voice of an organic whole but the dialectic engagement between opposing value systems which define each other precisely by their intertwined oppositions'.[26] It is within this post-devolution context that the six novels examined in this chapter address the paradox inherent in the Scottish double, building upon and simultaneously eroding binary approaches to identity, cultural belonging, and the strategies to represent these complex issues.

Whilst expressing complex notions of national and cultural affiliation, in the examined novels – and, particularly, *The Bad Sister*, *Two Women of London* and *Justine* – the double articulates preoccupations with a schizoid feminine subjectivity and binary gender definitions. Deconstructive gender discourse has exposed the dualism that has underpinned gender categories in Western thought. In *The Newly Born Woman* Cixous reflected on such pervasive binary hierarchies, suggesting that 'If we read or speak, the same thread, or double braid is leading us throughout literature, philosophy, criticism, centuries of representation and reflection'.[27] The pervasive duality of Western thought and social norms leads to the crucial question, 'Is the fact that logocentrism subjects thought – all the concepts, the codes, the values – to a two-term system, related to "the" couple man/woman?'[28] Cixous's answer to this important question exposes reductive gender definitions based on simple man/woman binary oppositions:

> One can no more speak of 'woman' than of 'man' without being trapped in an ideological theatre where the proliferation of representations, images, reflections, myths, identifications, transform, deform, constantly change everyone's Imaginary and invalidate in advance any conceptualization.[29]

Like Cixous, Luce Irigaray's *This Sex Which Is Not One* (1977) follows a similar deconstructive trajectory: using female sexuality to make a point about gender definitions, Irigaray refutes Freudian reading of female sexuality as 'lack': 'So woman does not have a sex organ? She has at least two of them, but they are not identifiable as ones. [. . .] Her sexuality, always at least double, goes even further: it is *plural*'.[30] The plurality of female sexuality erodes the patriarchal foundations of gender hierarchies, arguing that the female sex '*is neither one or two*' and that 'she cannot be identified either as one person, or as two. She resists all adequate definition'.[31] Woman is, to Irigaray, 'other in herself', simultaneously embodying, in post-structuralist fashion, duality and the overcoming of duality:

> One would have to listen with another ear, as if hearing *'another meaning' always in the process of weaving itself, of embracing itself with*

words, but also of getting rid of words in order not to become fixed, congealed in them.[32]

Second-wave feminism is particularly concerned with the linguistic strategies deployed to address sexual difference. 'How can one define this sexual difference?', Julia Kristeva wonders, 'It is not solely biological; it is above all, given in the representations that we ourselves make of this difference. We have no other means of constructing this representation than through language, through tools for symbolizing'.[33] Such symbolising function is never, in Kristeva's system, detached from the semiotic order of language, while the boundaries between symbolic and semiotic languages become particularly blurred when the female body splits into two, during pregnancy. It is then that the female subject becomes aware of the ambivalent maternal space, as exemplified in *The Governors*, where self and (m)other coexist in 'the same continuity differentiating itself'.[34]

The overcoming of binary oppositions advocated by deconstructive discourse reveals its ambivalent attitude towards binary differentiation: 'Deconstruction is an entertainment of duality', Miller rightly suggests, 'At the same time, it is clear that it also intent on ending it – on finishing with the double and with the dominion of opposites'.[35] If gender cannot be defined in terms of binary oppositions, then the notion of *écriture féminine* rests also on ideological indeterminacy: in relation to sexual difference and writing, Cixous's deconstructive approach, Elphinstone explains, 'argues [. . .] for a more fluid concept of multiple, heterogeneous *différance*, a *différance* which for her is the measure of genuine women's writing, a writing free from patriarchal hierarchies and oppositional constructions'.[36] The notion of *écriture féminine* is not without its problems, relying as it does on the binary opposition it refutes; moreover, while Cixous's theory attempts to resist definition, it also poses homogenising threats to the 'category' of women's writing. Moving away from biological sex/gender categories and concentrating on complex readings of sexuality, Butler's queer reading calls on a dynamic theory of 'performative' gender, a 'relation of being implicated in that which one opposes, [. . .] that is not a "pure" opposition, a "transcendence" of contemporary relations of power, but a difficult labor of forging a future from resources inevitably impure'.[37] The inherent impurity of gender definitions is linked to language, or the strategies and codes used to express sexual identity, which, in Butler's view, is simultaneously 'determined' and socially 'constructed'. Ultimately, if deconstruction promotes the annihilation of binary difference, underlying texts such as Thompson's *Justine* is the radical question whether it is at all viable to use the elusive 'women's writing' as a homogenous critical category.

As seen in the previous chapters, textuality – both as transtextuality and paratext – plays a significant role in the representative strategies of non-realist texts. The self-conscious references to previous texts (particularly in *The Bad Sister* and *Two Women of London*), the coexistence of two or more typefaces (*The Bad Box*, *The Governors*), the use of 'footnotes' and blank pages (*Behind The Scenes at the Museum* and *Justine*) amplify, at a textual level, the sense of narrative fragmentation and/or duplication that belongs in the content of the stories. It could be argued that duality is in fact encrypted in 'the mere act of writing', which, Margaret Atwood reminds us, 'splits the self into two'.[38] The investigative essence of writing informs literary texts with the self-referentiality which, as Jonathan Culler puts it, makes it 'a mode of writing distinguished by its quest for its own identity'.[39] This becomes particularly crucial in post-modernist fictions, here including Atkinson's *Behind the Scenes at the Museum* and Thompson's *Justine*, which capitalise on self-conscious strategies reflecting upon their fictional status. Simultaneously, these texts contrive to annihilate textual thresholds between inside and outside, reader and author, real and 'imagined' worlds. Royle relates the literary uncanny to a form of 'telepathy' which 'haunts literature in the form of strange coincidences, doubles, uncanny communication or sharing of thoughts or feelings [. . .]'.[40] This could be read in line with Baudrillard's notion of 'simulation', the quintessential mode of post-modernist hyperreal, a dimension where (textual) representation effectively replaces the real: 'It is no longer a question of imitation, nor of reduplication, nor even of parody. It is rather a question of substituting signs of the real for the real itself'.[41] With its emphasis on the simulated and mediated real, particularly visible in *Two Women of London* as well as *Justine*, Scottish postmodernist fiction self-consciously points to the uncanny repetitions which function as centrifugal trajectories and constantly defer meaning: 'To enter into a work of fiction', Coates suggests, 'is in a sense to transform the Other into a Double: to discover in the apparent foreignness of another person the lineaments of one's own aspirations and hopes'.[42]

MAGICAL HIGHLANDS VS. 'REAL' LOWLANDS? ALISON FELL'S *THE BAD BOX*

Set against the juxtaposed landscapes of the Highlands and the Borders of Scotland, Fell's *The Bad Box* articulates preoccupations about the Scottish schizoid identity in a coming-of-age story intertwined with the supernatural motifs of traditional folktales. Two parallel stories coexist in *The Bad Box*: the realist strand of Isla's story, set in various locations in Scotland in the 1950s and 1960s is interwoven with the hind girl's story, the supernatural tale of a semi-human creature's encounter with the human world. The two strands overlap within the twofold narrative structure: Isla's fractured identity, supported by the Highland/Lowland opposition is also reflected in the hind girl's split self: part human and part deer, the hind girl is also divided between her loyalty towards her mother and father, between the supernatural dimension she belongs to and the human world of her lover.

A divided Scottish landscape underpins the novel's articulation of psychological duality. More than a backdrop to Isla's *Bildungsroman*, the Highland/Lowland opposition is a prominent theme throughout the narrative. To begin with, Isla's deeply emotional bond with the Highland landscape of Dalriach (Gaelic for 'the field strewn with boulders') is set in contrast with her mother's prosaic affiliation to the Borders: 'The shops, the picture-houses maybe: she could see that her mother could miss all that. But compared to Glenalastair? No, she simply couldn't see the sense of it' (Fell, *The Bad Box*, p. 25).[43] Conversely, the Lowland landscape feels alien and devoid of character, a world where Isla is not allowed to negotiate her hybrid identity: Isla's Highland affiliation is significantly endorsed by the awareness that 'by the burn or in the forest you could be boundless and invisible; by the boulders you could be more naming than named' (p. 39), and her choice of the elemental over the social. The Highland world represents the absence of boundaries, freedom from social constraints, the open resistance to categorical identity, while, at the same time, infusing the subject with a powerful sense of self-awareness. The Borders, on the other hand, embody entrapment, enclosure and the claustrophobic boundaries of 'the bad box', an alienating space where communication is tricky: 'Not only her accent was wrong for the south, but also there was much that couldn't be said, for fear that the Lowland children would look at her slant and call her mad' (pp. 39–40). The inability to understand and be understood by the Lowlanders is not just due to a different variety of dialects, as her accent represents; it is rather that her voice reveals, through its *strange* intonation, an *uncanny* way of thinking: 'through Isla's perceptions', Flora Alexander rightly suggests, 'the nature of Scotland as an amalgam of contrasting subcultures is displayed'.[44] The migrant's alienation, then, reinforces the preoccupation, running through most Scottish novels of the double, with the schizoid nature of Scottish identity, where 'self' and 'other' coexist within the same (collective) psyche.[45]

The Highland world is evocatively construed through the magic conjured by the dramatic beauty of its landscape and the cultural layers of its supernatural traditions. Here, Isla and Ray, children of family friends, develop a close relationship, at times reminiscent of the symbiotic bond of Heathcliff and Cathy against the sublime backdrop of the Yorkshire moors in *Wuthering Heights* (1847). As in Brontë's novel, the ambiguity of Isla's friendship with Ray reveals a doppelgänger subtext: 'Ray and Isla, Isla and Ray. A right pair of dreamers, said the Camerons and the Beattys, unable to decipher the bond between them' (p. 8). A hint of a supernatural bond –'But weren't you, if the truth be told, brother and sister, separated at birth?' (p. 8) – also reinforces their Platonic (two bodies/one soul) bond.

Significantly, existential discussions about the boundaries of one's self emerge from the act of story-telling and the sharing of Celtic myths and folktales – 'Tales of Donald Ban's great ships with two-sided sails for the watchers on the shore [. . .] Tales of the Spring Goddess Bride and her bards, green maidens' (pp. 8–9) – and reincarnation is envisaged as a possibility of being 'other' than oneself: 'a knight or a nobody or a newt, [. . .], or even a white cloud someone yearned into the world' (p. 10), or 'Morgan Le Fay' (p. 12). Isla's choice implies the necessity of the 'bad box', intended as a state of mind that perhaps even already at this stage she is longing to share with her alter ego. Tempted by the potential of an evil double, Isla is Jekyll's heir in her subdued anxiety and urge to transgress the stiffness of a stable role and take over a secret identity to guarantee her freedom.

In contrast, the negative response to the Lowlands catalyses the narrative's psychological conflict, with Isla's loyalties oscillating between the paternal world of the Highlands and the maternal space of the Borders. Choosing the Highlands detaches her from her mother's world and, at the same time, from her own womanhood. Unable to reconcile the two sides of her identity, 'Isla of Dalriach' and 'Christine Cameron's girl', Isla seemingly repudiates conventional notions of femininity for a looser sense of identity. In the Lowlands, however, the strong urge to follow the script dictated by her imagination is also a symptom of the escapist desire to find an alternative existence from everyday reality. Trapped in the dullness of the Border village, 'Isla might be bullfighter or ballerina, or master-builder irrigating the whole of India' (p. 55), while 'Wanda would be trapeze artist, or bareback rider, or rancher's wife who under cover of the night rode with outlaws' (p. 55). Moreover, the fantasies shared with Wanda have a much stronger sexual undercurrent, showing that sexuality becomes a pressing issue as the story develops, though Isla 'didn't see what was so good about growing up to be a woman if it meant staying at home like that, and bleeding and having babies' (p. 72). While repressing the first signs of her sexual awareness, Isla finds her only shelter in the memories from her childhood, not only memories of her friendship with Ray, but also of the times when she shared an innocent relationship with her father, 'racing round and round the kitchen table for Daddy, rapturously bathed and naked, round and round' and 'sprinting, sleek as a hind' (p. 64).

The reference to Isla's body, 'sleek as a hind', suggests Isla's self-conscious identification with the hind girl of the parallel story, though this psychological reading is not openly supported by the main narrative. The hind girl's story is both integrated in and detached from the main narrative: while the italicised typeface signals a different narrative level, cross references – Isla features at the beginning of the hind girl's story (p. 31); a white hind (pp. 2, 9) appears in Isla's story; Ray's fatal accident is apparently caused by a 'white animal' (p. 161) – blur the boundaries between the two stories, their characters and worlds. Significantly, the first section of the hind girl's story occurs in 'the bad box', the state of alienation Isla enters through a 'door' after her father's beating (p. 15). Much like Isla, the creature is a schizoid, alienated being: part human and part animal, the hind girl embodies hybrid duality. Mirroring Isla's inability to communicate in the Borders, to begin with, the hind girl 'can't speak a word' (p. 43). Her quest, too, opposing her mother and father, resonates in the psychological split of Isla's story.

The topic of the princess transformed into a deer, classified by Antti Aarne among 'Tales of Magic', is well spread across Europe and the Americas,[46] and the West Highland version of this tale, 'The Weaver's Son', is clearly behind Fell's creation of the hind girl's story. This is the story of a young man who succeeds in breaking the spell cast over the deer princess and eventually marries the princess who is, he discovers at the end, the daughter of the king of the Great Isle. In the last section of the tale, the weaver's son reaches the deer princess's island which lies 'far beyond the edge of the world',[47] where he is wounded and magically healed through the deer princess's indirect help. Several narrative elements link the hind girl's story in *The Bad Box* to the 'The Weaver's Son'. The two female creatures, although seemingly human at the end of the stories, are represented in zoomorphic shape: while the deer princess is herself an animal, the hind girl is born out of one. Both stories focus on the encounter between the two animal girls and their human partners and in both instances this is followed by a quest: after their encounter, the weaver's son travels to find the princess, while Alec pursues the hind girl's quest for revenge against her father.

Significantly, the investigation of problematic notions of female self-determination exposes the split unconscious of the heroine in each story. In the traditional tale the princess appears autonomous in her will to help the weaver's son heal after his flight to the island, perhaps because she knows he was responsible for discharging her from the magic spell; subsequently, however, although she seemingly follows her own will in marrying the weaver's son, the princess's claim to self-determination is overshadowed by the king's authority: as the marriage is celebrated because 'the King was very willing' (p. 407), the Law of the Father seems still unquestioned.

The hind girl's story explores similar conflicts and dilemmas further, creating a more ambiguously psychological narrative, thus reinforcing its links with the realist narrative of *The Bad Box*. Towards the end of the hind girl's story, the inner conflict appears increasingly unresolved, as the heroine is torn between the two poles of her dilemma, unsure whether to keep her loyalty to her mother who sent her on this mission, or to side with her father instead:

> *She looked at her sinewy strong legs and saw they were like his. She clenched her fist and felt the hunter in her own flesh straining to be free. And she raged at her mother for the bonds of blood and tides which held her to the earth, and the loyalty which tied her to her promise.* (p. 117)

The dilemma becomes less clear, as the opposites of mother and father, well defined up until this point, shift in the hind girl's mind: behind the interrogation of the quest for revenge, is the questioning of the maternal bond, and, in turn, the foundations of her identity.

As it investigates the dynamic development of feminine subjectivity based on dialectic conflict, the supernatural strand of *The Bad Box* ultimately reveals a self-reflective layer: as well as being a story about inner conflicts and problematic belonging, this is also a story about the lost language to express a broken self, signified by the hind girl's disembodied voice throughout the interrupted sections of her story, 'that voice [that] echoed out from somewhere, from nowhere' (p. 59). In the climax leading to the end of both stories, Isla's traumatic discovery about Ray's death is juxtaposed to the hind girl's confrontation with her mother, '*a childish babble of words and rhymes* [. . .] *snatches of songs and time-tables and once upon a time princesses* [. . .]. *It was as if some dam had burst, and the words poured out fast and furious*' (pp. 161–2): even on the threshold of their resolution, it is the semiotic, rather than the symbolic, that registers the unutterable conflicts in the lives of the hind girl and Isla.

Rather than conclusive resolutions, the ending generates new beginnings: with her parents '*thinning or blurring*' (p. 165), Alec's '*strong tug at her arm*' helps the hind girl to move beyond the past, '*For ahead his live parents waited impatiently to greet them*' (p. 166); the embracement of the hind girl's earthly existence foreshadow the optimistic – if open-ended – reference to Isla's 'new life' in the Epilogue of the realist story: 'There was a sluggish mist over the rooftops, but later Edinburgh would be sharp and blue' (p. 167).

THE SCHIZOID MATERNAL BODY: SIAN HAYTON'S *THE GOVERNORS*

Published in the same year as *Hidden Daughters* (1992), *The Governors* shares with the second volume of Hayton's trilogy a preoccupation with feminine identity, which emerges as a psychological investigation of the tensions created within the maternal space against the supernatural backdrop of a parallel story: while the supernatural materials of Hester's journey derive partly from Scottish/Celtic superstitions, the existence of a marvellous other world independent from Hester's mind is simultaneously questioned throughout the narrative. In fact, the frequent – and often overt – transtextual references to the psychoanalytical theories of Freud and Jung suggest a psychological reading of the magical journey as a figment of Hester's schizoid imagination, as does the early admission that Hester 'never let anyone know about her boisterous imagination since she thought it made her a bit weird' (Hayton, *The Governors*, p. 12).[48] What links the two narrative strands is a persistent marine theme, as the underwater world pervades both psychological and supernatural dimensions.

As with *The Bad Box*, the textual and narrative structure of *The Governors* is pervasively fragmented. Epigraphs at the beginning of each chapter link the narrative to a wide range of textual precedents, hinting of Oedipal conflicts (*King Lear*) and supernatural quests (*The Tempest*, *Alice in Wonderland*), and revealing the narrative's palimpsestual structure. Additionally, two narrative voices – third- and first-person – alternate within the text. At the start of the narrative, the problematic intrusion of an anonymous first-person narrator disturbs the illusion of narrative reliability set up by the conventional third-person narrator:

> *I knew she was trying to get me going – fooling around in the bath like that – but I managed to even the score at the party. Ronnie, the neighbourhood fat man was making the usual demand for attention. She had parked on a straightbacked chair and was gazing out at the golden triangle of sea glinting between the houses.* (p. 10)

The use of italicised typeface and juxtaposition of personal pronouns (I, she) creates the effect of estrangement and duplication every time the first-person narrator intervenes. The occurrence of these intersections becomes more frequent in the narrative as Hester's mind becomes involved in a world that is separate from the real world, and whose boundaries are not defined: the other voice not only coincides with Hester's hallucinations, but frequently intrudes into the realist plot.

The background to the fragmented plot of *The Governors* reveals complex psychological tensions: Hester's father, a frustrated marine biologist, had named his daughter Hesione after the daughter of King Laomedon of Troy, sacrificed by her father in order to placate a sea monster and eventually rescued by Hercules;[49] the reference to the Greek myth exposes the issue of patriarchal oppression. Hester's rejection of her paternal name reflects her subconscious resistance to the world of patriarchal/parental rule, though the implicit subversion of the Law of the Father leaves an unsolved trauma. The existing psychological tensions increase with pregnancy; this also fails to establish 'the homosexual facet of motherhood, through which a woman is simultaneously closer to her instinctual memory, more open to her own psychosis and consequently, more negatory of the social, symbolic bond', as theorised by Kristeva.[50] Hester's pregnancy erodes instead her relationship with her mother, and, no longer anchored to the symbolic, progressive alienation accentuates and accelerates the sense of abjection within the maternal body:

> Once I was sealed and perfect. Gravity hadn't dragged at my flesh to make it sag and hang – children hadn't stretched my skin beyond its capacity to shrink back to shape – my tissues were intact. But everything has been forced out of place. (p. 103)

The relevance of Hester's psychological dissociation and trauma is complicated by the intrusion of the supernatural story: the plot of *The Governors* thus oscillates between the marvellous and the uncanny of Todorov's fantastic spectrum. The sudden appearance of a mysterious door, frequently the gateway to another world in fantasy literature, on the ground floor of her house signals the start of Hester's schizoid split. Doors are also the subconscious representation of female sexual organs, as explained by Freud, 'rooms represent women and their entrances and exits the openings of the body'.[51] Freud also suggests that 'cupboards, carriages or ovens may represent the uterus'.[52] A psychoanalytical reading of the door becomes even more plausible when the passage hints at a marine environment, as Hester steps beyond the threshold and through the tunnel, 'down a long gentle spiral with tides of whispers washing about her' (p. 69). In the section on water dreams Freud quotes a case study that resembles this first stage of Hester's vision:

> A subterranean channel led direct into the water from a place in the floor of her room (genital canal-amniotic fluid). She raised a trap-door in the floor and a creature dressed in brown fur, very much resembling a seal, promptly appeared.[53]

The identical imagery liaises the first stage of Hester's hallucination with Freud's interpretation of birth-dreams, 'accompanied by anxiety and having as their content such objects as passing through narrow spaces or being in water, [these dreams] are based upon *phantasies of intra-uterine life, of existence in the womb and of the act of birth*' (my emphases).[54] Distinctively identified by the presence of water, according to Freud, these dreams signify desire for renovation, rebirth or maternity. Significantly, in *Concerning Rebirth* (1950) Jung also explains the concept of rebirth in terms of 'subjective transformation',[55] a process of personality change that can originate from the 'loss of a soul',[56] or an identity crisis: Jung's theory of rebirth further cements a psychological reading of Hester's traumatic background in relation to her schizoid fantasy. Specific recurrent motifs – passage through a hole, symbolic death, ablution and name change[57] – in the rebirth rituals listed by Jung confirm this interpretation.

Hayton's self-conscious deployment of psychoanalytical discourse supports a reading of *The Governors* as an investigation of feminine split subjectivity: 'The sea dreams and often disgusting rites of therapeutic passage', Gifford argues, 'mark the beginning of Hester's quest for integrity and wholeness. They represent her necessary subconscious drowning in the past, in her guilts and fears, to cleanse or more appropriately naturalise her'.[58] As her alter ego on the other side of the human world, like the mythical Hesione, Hester is forced to face the monsters of her existence and come to terms with her schizoid identity. In this context, Hester's resistance to the removal of her sex – 'the necessity of sexual intercourse, childbirth and menstruation' (p. 180) – reveals symptoms of reconciliation within the abject female body; similarly, the quirky encounter with Mer Maid (M. M.) has a determining effect on Hester's body/mind split.

Embodying two opposed versions of femininity – the sensual *femme fatale* and 'the greatest little housewife' (p. 189) – the mermaid represents the kind of feminine whole Hester has longed for all along.

Much like Hogg's *Justified Sinner*, Hayton's narrative sustains the possibility of a dual interpretation – psychological and supernatural – throughout the story. Beside its reading as post-traumatic psychosis, the narrative opens itself to a supernatural interpretation. After Nerine's birth, Hester cannot explain, for instance, 'the grains of sand trapped between the sole and the upper' (p. 102). Most importantly, the ambiguous function of the first-person narrator is never fully explained throughout the narrative, its apparent belonging to the marine world also encouraging a supernatural interpretation:

> *I gave Hes a wave of the fin, but she only rippled her fingers in reply and backed out of the doorway like a zombie on speed. She's never seen me in the skin before, so I guess it was no wonder she didn't recognise me.* (pp. 187–8)

The ambivalent supernatural aura surrounding the first-person narrator challenges a view of Hester's hallucination solely as post-traumatic syndrome.

Recurrent hints to Scottish/Celtic selkie lore attach a significant supernatural layer to the psychological reading of the story. Many of these legends refer to the unhappy unions between a human being and a seal, often ending with the seal's escape to the sea, or the human fear of sea mammals in stories reproducing the old fight between man and animal in mythical terms.[59] The selkie's entrapment on dry land – and 'dual' identity dictated by the evocative wearing of the 'skin' – is an important subtext to the story: like the selkie's, Hester's soul feels, in a sense, disembodied. A solid pattern of repetitions weaves the selkie motif into the realist narrative: the reference to the story about a heartbroken fisherman and a selkie woman from a 'really old collection of Scottish short stories' (p. 27), for instance, mirrors the corpse of the dead female seal found on the beach on a family outing to the sea (p. 66) and the image of a battered seal in a television programme (p. 118). These coincidences question the boundaries of Hester's real and imagined selves: to Hester's subconscious there is little difference between the corpse of the 'real' seal and the selkie of the legend; they are both, arguably, projections of her own (battered) self.

The psychological/supernatural ambiguity remains unsolved until the very end. While the nature of Hester's hallucinations is apparently explained, in the last chapter, as the effect of the severe trauma suffered since her father's death, the psychological/supernatural strands of the narrative ambivalently merge in the last scene, marking the final stage in Hester's process of self-rebirth. Built into the third-person narrative is the brief exchange with 'the beast' – the unidentified voice from the first-person narrative? – that erases the boundaries between the two narratives/voices:

'You're doing fine,' said the beast.

'I think so too.'

She wiped her finger on a tissue from the box beside the bath and flicked it down the toilet.

'I can't be absolutely sure.' She continued, 'but I think I like myself – slime and all.'

'Splendid,' came the reply. (pp. 222–3)

'OTHER' SISTERS AND MISSING MOTHERS: KATE ATKINSON'S *BEHIND THE SCENES AT THE MUSEUM*

'I exist! I am conceived to the chimes of midnight on the clock on the mantel-piece in the room across the hall' (Atkinson, *Behind the Scenes at the Museum*, p. 9):[60] Ruby Lennox makes her grand entrance into the world of living things with an opening chapter echoing the magical realist playfulness of Salman Rushdie's *Midnight's Children* and, as noted by Paola Splendore, Laurence Sterne.[61] Atkinson's first novel, *Behind the Scenes at the Museum*, is, in more than one sense, an embryonic narrative, launching as it does into a family saga told by Ruby as a foetus, and later following her life-journey via numerous digressions: 'By starting with the perspective of Ruby as an embryo', Sinead McDermott notes, 'the reader is given an insider/outsider's take on the Lennox family'.[62] As the narrative starts in the womb, Ruby's voice is emblematically self-referential of the Kristevan *chora*, or the 'rhythmic space', the yet undifferentiated state of self which precedes the origin of symbolic language. Yet the paradox within Ruby's voice is that – albeit apparently pre-natal – it displays the experienced tone of a mature story-teller. Her debut, therefore, signifies the beginning of beginnings, simultaneously reflecting on the origin of the story in a metafictional sense, and, in a more metaphysical respect, the origin of existence. Interwoven with these two strands are questions about identity and homeland(s), motherhood and memory, as Ruby's narrative (and existence) starts, significantly, on the cusp of a new day, at midnight.[63]

From the beginning, Ruby's narrative presents an intense interrogation of her identity and belonging, which can only be defined – consciously, as well as sub-consciously – in referential terms. Ruby questions the maternal/uterine space she occupies: '"Bunty" doesn't seem like a very grown-up name to me – would I be better off with a mother with a different name?' (p. 9). Simultaneously she cherishes her foetal status within the safe boundaries of the maternal body: 'I tap my tiny naked heels together three times and think, there's no place like home' (p. 25). Through Bunty, Ruby gains mediated second-hand experiences – 'My first ever cup of tea' (p. 14) – and unravels a family saga spanning three generations of missing mothers and daughters: Ruby's great-grandmother Alice runs away with a French photographer, Monsieur Armand; her daughter Lillian emigrates to Canada; Ruby's own sister Patricia disappears after giving birth to her own baby, and even Bunty deserts – albeit temporarily – husband and children for a week. Such loose maternal bonds prompt Ruby to question the foundations of her fragile existence –'I'm hanging like a pink-glass button by a thread. Help' – and position in relation to her closest family members: 'Where are my sisters? (Asleep.) My father? (Cooking breakfast.) Where's my mother?' (p. 26). Despite the dysfunctional environment of the Lennox household, the enforced exile after the death of her twin, Pearl, reinforces Ruby's assertion of her identity in relation to her family: 'I confirm my existence to myself with a growing sense of panic – my name is Ruby Lennox, I have a mother, a father, sisters' (p. 111).

The nucleus of Ruby's fragmented identity significantly goes back to her embryonic existence as a twin and Pearl's tragic death which results in Ruby's Recovered Memory Trauma, a form of amnesiac behaviour which forces her to forget about Pearl's existence. Spectral references to the missing twin haunt the narrative from its embryonic beginning – 'And why do I have this strange feeling, as if my shadow's stitched to my back, almost as if there's someone else in here with me? Am I being haunted by my own embryonic ghost?' (p. 15) – even though the reader may only appreciate them retrospectively: 'In effect Atkinson manoeuvres the reader into the position of the unknowing subject of repressed memories', Roger Luckhurst argues, 'subject to all the estrangements and dissonances a belated revelation of a hidden secret can produce'.[64] Against the historical background of Coronation Day, Ruby's recollections reveal repressed memories of Pearl:

> I don't know how I move so fast – one moment I'm standing by the television set, the next I'm hurtling through the passage to the kitchen. If you blinked you'd almost think there was two of me. Perhaps I'm on castors like the Chinese doll – but then I'm very advanced for my age. (p. 79)

Likewise, in the same chapter, national symbols are ironically juxtaposed to the photographs of the four siblings – 'Patricia's Union Jack has migrated to the picture-rail where it droops over our framed Polyphotos, thirty-six tiny black and white photographs of Patricia, thirty-six of Gillian and, for some reason, seventy-two of me' (p. 88) – which Ruby's unreliable memory typically invests with the wrong meaning. A similar interpretation is given to Bunty's locket, which, according to Ruby, contains 'two tiny photographs of me' (p. 149).

Duality indeed haunts Ruby and her narrative in the form of repetitions and double patterns; in Emma Parker's words: 'By creating the impression that there are two Rubys, the duality of her voice anticipates this revelation and reflects her unacknowledged status as a twin'.[65] Apparently trivial details establish evocative links through which the past resonates in the present or even the future, as in the reference to forget-me-nots which relates Frank

–'they were all sat around the table, drinking their tea from the best service, the one that had gold rims and little blue forget-me-nots' (p. 57) – to Albert's 'forget-me-not blue'-coloured eyes, but also 'the saucer that Totty got his food in, with the faded forget-me-nots and scratched gold rim' (p. 106) and Lillian's son Edmund –'Cousin Edmund, Frank said, was the spitting image of Nell's brother Albert' (p. 105). Such patterns of repetition form the backbone of Ruby's non-linear narrative: 'Tea-spoons, buttons, a rabbit's foot become fully con-temporal objects', Roger Luckhurst rightly observes, 'hinting at uncanny repetitions across lost time'.[66] The double motif becomes ostensibly intensified immediately after Pearl's death, when Ruby is sent to stay with Auntie Babs and her twin daughters Daisy and Rose. Ruby's traumatic loss generates an acute sense of dislocation that transforms the twins' bedroom, through echoes of the magical-realist setting of Angela Carter's *The Magic Toyshop*, into a surreal Gothic location:

> In the dark, the furniture takes on a *new malevolence* – the bedroom is crowded out with furniture – big, heavy pieces that don't belong in a child's bedroom at all, not just the arctic waste of their *double bed*, but the huge, *double-fronted* wardrobe and matching dressing-table that's big enough to stow a corpse in. In the *blackness* of night, the furniture-shapes possess a profound *ultra-blackness* that hints at *anti-matter*. (p. 113; my emphases)

Following Pearl's death, post-traumatic amnesia casts a shadow on Ruby's identity, who fears annihilation via her assimilation to the alien set of twins – 'Soon no-one will be able to tell the difference between us and they will have achieved their aim of taking over the body of an earthling' (p. 121) – while the previous boldly assertive statement, 'My name is Ruby. I am a precious jewel. I am a drop of blood. I am Ruby Lennox' (p. 44), is replaced by the tenuous 'I'm not sure who "Just Ruby" is' (p. 121).

Whilst reinforcing Ruby's awareness of her marginal status –'thresholds are safe' (p. 115) – such a pervasive sense of dislocation is also linked to the claustrophobic entrapment which Ruby significantly associates with the twins' doll's house:

> I would be frightened – I am frightened – of getting trapped in there and becoming one of the tiny ringletted and pinafored little girls up in the nursery who have to play with teeny-weeny dolls all day long. Or worse – the poor scullery maid, forever consigned to blacking the kitchen range. (p. 114)

Behind Ruby's immediate – albeit apparently unfounded – fears are layers of female entrapment, a subtext which *again* links three generations of women in the family saga, from Alice and Rachel, through Nell and Lillian, to Babs and Bunty, as Ruby does not fail to notice: 'perhaps Bunty is also trapped in a doll's house?' (p. 118): 'One implication of these repetitions seems to be a critique of women's place in patriarchy, as women are repeatedly trapped within an unsatisfying domestic sphere'.[67] Yet, such glimpses of understanding are precarious, as the distance between Bunty and her daughters grows progressively larger, particularly after Gillian's untimely death, ironically set after her performance at the Christmas pantomime. Bunty's maternal emotions seem to be relegated to the vestigial memories of her dead daughters – 'My Gillian, my pearl' (pp. 189 and 207) – whereas, though admittedly more anxious for the lives of her daughters, she opens a wider gap between herself and the surviving daughters: 'she's always at least three feet away in front of me', Ruby notes, 'as if there's an invisible umbilical cord between us that can stretch but never contract' (p. 203).

This is particularly problematic for Ruby who, as the surviving twin, also personifies Pearl's spectral existence: 'She [Bunty] catches sight of my reflection walking past and gives a start as if she's just seen a ghost' (p. 208). Ruby's own subconscious identification with Pearl's revenant emerges in the pervasive references to spectrality in her narrative; references to classic ghost stories from *Dracula* –Lucy-Vida is repeatedly associated with Lucy – to *Rebecca* – Ruby compares Marjorie Morrison, the housekeeper at the Royal Highland Hotel, to Mrs Danvers (p. 353) – and *Wuthering Heights* – Ruby, the 'little ghost child', compares herself to Cathy (p. 318) – frequently pop up in the story, as do references to 'actual' ghosts: the house above the shop is haunted by benign spectral apparitions from the past, whereas malevolent spirits seemingly disturb Ruby's stay at Auntie Babs's: 'The amiable ghosts Above the Shop have been replaced by something that crackles with evil' (p. 114). Though Ruby's fascination with ghosts shares similarities with other spectral narratives, as with Janet in *O Caledonia*, adolescent Ruby fantasises about her own funeral: 'The church is filled, not just with friends and family, but even people I have never known – an admiring Leonard Cohen and a soulful Terence Stamp, for instance' (p. 314); rather than signifying self-destructive fantasies, these references concur to represent Ruby's increasing sense of self-estrangement: proof of this is her increased alienated self-consciousness, which is significantly reflected by her notion of being 'a ruby solitaire' (p. 280) after Patricia's disappearance, as by her self-referential association with the 'huge outsize girl' (p. 287) in Lewis Carroll's *Alice in Wonderland*, 'crammed in amongst smaller ones' (p. 287) at Uncle Ted's wedding.

The novel's structure and overarching scope also reveal dichotomies and bifurcating strands reinforcing the emphatic sense of otherness in Ruby's narrative. As the family saga is told primarily through digressions from the main story, 'footnotes' create an alternative plot, which develops in a non-linear chronological fashion. Such digressions constitute the 'other' text, or the 'other' narrative, much like major historical events become somehow second-ary to the peripheral lives of Ruby's ancestors.[68] In doing so, Ruby's narrative challenges the concept of narrative time – with reference to Proust, Ruby notes 'but how can time be reversible when it gallops forward, clippity-clop and *nobody ever comes back*. Do they?' (p. 210) – and the construction of (histori-cal) past – 'The past is a cupboard full of light and all you have to do is find the key that opens the door' (p. 379), echoing Rushdie's own reflections on the historical references in *Midnight's Children*: 'History is always ambiguous. Facts are hard to establish, and capable of being given many meanings. Reality is built on our prejudices, misconceptions and ignorance as well as on percep-tiveness and knowledge'.[69]

And if Ruby's identity cannot easily be pinned down against a past which seems far from stable, then notions of belonging are also persistently inter-rogated throughout the novel, particularly during the family trip to 'the most foreign location of all – Scotland!' (p. 247). The journey questions stereotypical cultural representations of Scotland; from the moment the Lennoxes and the Porters choose a Scottish farm for their joint holiday, 'their brains are awash with hot bannocks and girdle scones dripping with salty sun-yellow butter and thick porridge in a pond of cream, warm from the cow' (p. 252). North of the border, however, Scotland resists definition and seemingly lacks authenticity: 'Where is Scotland? What is Scotland?', asks Ruby, 'Is it rain solidified into the shapes of houses and hills? Is it mist, carved into roadside cafes with names like The Crofter's Kitchen? [. . .] Who knows?' (p. 252); and these questions remain unanswered until the end of the family trip – 'Somewhere just beyond the mist, there's our real Scottish holiday – and perhaps all the other holidays we never had as well' (p. 266) – though in Ruby's narrative there is also room for a romanticised Scotland of the mind: 'over those hills and far away, at the outer barriers of the von Leibniz property, is where the real Scotland seems to be (I have read *Rob Roy* and *Waverley* and *The Heart of Midlothian* in prepa-ration of this trip)' (p. 256). Even though 'A black cloud, both metaphorical and real, settles above our heads as we enter Glencoe' (p. 257), there is little atmosphere left to Fort William, the heart of the Scottish Highlands: having left their guidebook behind, the party is unable to identify any historical sights of interest, taking refuge at last in the Wee Highland Gift Shop to purchase 'many totally useless objects adorned with thistles and heather' (p. 258). Inconsequential as the journey may appear, it typically foreshadows the most important events to come, including Ruby's recollection of Pearl's death by water – as she stares at Lochness, Ruby notes 'It reminds me of something, but what?' (p. 260) – and Patricia's later disappearance. It is during this trip that Ruby – whose name Patricia changes to 'Shutupruby' – further questions her identity and belonging, as she learns that 'Lennox [. . .] is a Scottish name' (p. 265). This is later echoed by Marjorie Morrison, when Ruby is working as a hotel-maid in Edinburgh: 'You must have Scottish blood in you' (p. 357). And the problematic notion of Scotland, blood, belonging and identity persists until the very end – 'I belong by blood to this foreign country' (p. 381) – as Ruby settles to work as a translator in Shetland, after a failed marriage to an Italian man met in Edinburgh. Ultimately, Ruby concludes, language is the only place where one's whole identity belongs:

> In the end, it is my belief, words are the only things that can construct a world that makes sense. [. . .] I'm in another country, the one called home. I am alive. I am a precious jewel. I am a drop of blood. I am Ruby Lennox. (p. 382)

REWRITING THE SCOTTISH DOPPELGÄNGER: EMMA TENNANT'S *THE BAD SISTER* AND *TWO WOMEN OF LONDON*

Duality pervasively seeps through Tennant's Scottish novels – *The Bad Sister* (1978), *Two Women of London* (1989) and *Wild Nights* (1979)[70] – highlighting her conscious understanding of the binary blueprint of Scottish identity; North/South and Scotland/England polarities form the backbone of the most autobiographical of Tennant's Scottish novels, *Wild Nights*: 'Borders and boundaries are frequent motifs', Alexander emphasises, 'and she is consistently interested in differences between Scotland and England, and the ways in which Scottish people have their own ways of thought and expression'.[71] Division and duality are also behind *The Bad Sister* and *Two Women of London*, hypertextual transpositions of Hogg's *Justified Sinner* and Stevenson's *Dr Jekyll and Mr Hyde* respectively. While exploiting similar narrative strategies to Hogg's and Stevenson's doppelgänger texts, Tennant's schizoid narratives are underpinned by a postcolonial sense of nostalgic separation and 'physical exile' from Scotland and the distinctive preoccupations about the fragmented Scottish female identity in late twentieth-century Britain.[72] The focus on gender is important to all of Tennant's rewritings,[73] and behind Tennant's rewritings of the classic Scottish double tales is the complex articulation of the problematic positioning of women in a consumerist society, the objectification of the female body and its resistance to patriarchal modes of exploitation. Within both narratives the Scottish landscape – more vividly represented in *The Bad Sister* and alluded to in *Two Women of London* – functions aesthetically to accommodate a problematic sense of belonging and dislocation.

At the threshold of *The Bad Sister*, the epigraph from William Wordsworth's 'Yarrow Unvisited' – 'The swan on still St Mary's Lake/Float double, swan and shadow!' – announces the motif of duplication and the partial setting of the novel in the Scottish Borders, home to the Ettrick Shepherd. As with Hogg's text, Tennant's novel is structured around two narratives: the 'Editor's Narrative' introduces and posthumously reflects upon 'Jane's

Journal'; moreover, much like *Justified Sinner*, *The Bad Sister* swings between supernatural and psychological readings of the events, eroding narrative reliability from the beginning. The possibility that the main character, evocatively named Jane Wild, like Wringhim, could have been the victim of a supernatural agent is suggested in the Editor's Narrative: 'I am in no way psychic or superstitious, but the suggestion of my psychiatrist friends, that there had never been any such people as Meg or Gil-martin [. . .] seemed to me more than inadequate' (Tennant, *The Bad Sister*, p. 166). The overt reference to Hogg's devil, along with a plethora of sinister omens, foreshadows Jane's existence and from Hogg's narrative Tennant also borrows the superstitious belief in the demonic kinship of the third child in a line of adultery: 'it was well-known that all such were born half deils [sic] themselves, and nothing was more likely that they should hold intercourse with their fellows', admits the Laird (Hogg, *Justified Sinner*, p. 38).[74] Jane's birth is preceded by a series of superstitious allusions to 'doubles': whilst gambling in London before his wedding, Lord Dalzell, Jane's father, loses because the backgammon dice keep showing only 'twos'; his gambling mates nickname him 'Deuce Dalzell' and warn him: 'You'll be seeing double at the wedding, old boy!' (Tennant, *The Bad Sister*, p. 6). Once born, Jane is held to have devilish connections and, like Wringhim, is ostracised by her father as illegitimate daughter.

While superstition ambiguously encourages and undermines the supernatural authenticity of the story, the text also exposes the power of ideology on a weakened mind: the rigid Calvinist dogmas that haunt Wringhim's memoirs in Hogg's novel are translated into a cryptic form of 'radical feminism' in *The Bad Sister*. The severe effects of continuous brainwashing received during her upbringing in a women's commune seemingly justify Jane's psychotic dissociation, developed from the coexistence of two opposed notions – 'a state of perpetual war with the society they lived in' and the desire for 'peace and harmony' (p. 25). Meg is Tennant's personification of Hogg's Gil-martin, who also appears in the novel as Meg's brother, and superior male agent whose union Jane urgently seeks throughout her memoirs. It is Meg, however, who stirs Jane's hatred of capitalism towards the 'bad sister', the usurper of Jane's place in her father's affection. The root of the conflict is expressed in a sophisticated and esoteric formula, which, Meg argues, summarises the core of the world's major problems, the 'two women-in-one' or 'the suppression of masculinity in women and femininity in men' (p. 27). The idea of woman's impossible search for the male Muse – traditionally a female creature – inspired by Tennant's reading of Virginia Woolf, creates the fundamental basis for the character's schizophrenic development.[75]

Preoccupations with the commodification of the female body surface in Jane's increasingly alienated confessional narrative, which fits uneasily against the patriarchal institutions of marriage and nuclear family: Jane's disaffected relationship with her partner, Tony, and her dismissal of traditional customs such as the Sunday lunch signal her unyielding attitude towards established patriarchal traditions meant 'to be a cementing thing for couples' (p. 47). Jane's rebellion thus unveils a paradigm of resistance against female entrapment behind the apparent security of patriarchal myths of domestic bliss: 'in this godless street' (p. 43), Jane notes in her memoirs, old women's heads resemble 'winter cabbages' (p. 43); even past its closing time 'the ghostly figures of women' remain 'enclosed' in the corner supermarket, 'the compound for the women who are not battered nor dyke' (p. 39); and her own body feels 'ripe, ready for a mouthful to be taken out' (p. 33): 'Imagery of woman as food [. . .] suggests that women are objects packaged for a consumer society'.[76] The consumerist approaches to the female body cause a schizoid split in the female psyche: with no other referents, the female subject cannot but exist as an alienated consumer of its own image.

Descriptions of Jane and even identikit photographs are, the Editor notes, 'all ridiculously dissimilar to each other [. . .]. Her face was curiously blank' (p. 29). Similarly, like Hogg's Gil-martin, Meg is a chameleon, easily confused with other characters, to the point that Stephen, a friend of Jane's, admits to the Editor that 'it all depends on what you believe' (p. 26) and that 'Meg was a kind of embezzlement [. . .] an enravishment' (p. 30). Inconsistency pervades also Jane's ambiguous relationships towards other women, simultaneously eroding liberal feminist notions of sisterly camaraderie. Repulsion and voyeurism replace, instead, Jane's feelings towards the unknown, anonymous fleet of outcast women (the 'battered and the dykes') encountered every day on her wanderings. Torn between the opposed tensions within herself, Jane gradually concentrates her inner struggle on the obsessive love–hate relationship with the three main female characters, Ishbel/Miranda, Meg and Mrs Marten.

In the visionary flashbacks of crucial episodes and childhood memories, the ambiguous nature of the feelings between Jane and Ishbel surfaces in the memoirs: 'I was completely and obsessively jealous of her. I was her shadow and she mine' (p. 74). Forced to be apart from her sister and an unacknowledged daughter of her father, Jane develops a hatred nourished by both her feelings of rejection and her brainwashing by the commune women. Jane's memories and feelings for Ishbel appear confused with her fantasies, in which she either imagines murder or fantasises about a morbid attachment to her, while Ishbel's identity is confused with that of Marie – the servant girl Jane seemingly sleeps with – and Miranda, Tony's former girlfriend. Jane's paranoid fear and desire to get rid of Ishbel are symptomatically expressed by her indiscriminate search for a woman whose name she knows starts with the letter 'M':

M. . . why should she be in under her first name anyway? But I have a feeling she is. M for mother, for murder, for Meg. M for her. She made

> me a shadow, discarded by Tony before he had even met me. I am in Meg
> now, for Meg has my blood, and soon M, you will be. (p. 111)

The superstitious reading of 'M' as ominous, 'thirteenth letter, the centre of
the alphabet' (p. 112), is diffused by the psychological suggestion that 'M' is
also the initial of both of Jane's parents (Mary and Michael) and a reference to
Jane's partner's mother, Mrs Marten. On his visit to Mrs Marten, the Editor
remarks a singular coincidence: 'I don't know why, but I couldn't help remembering Stephen's description of his visit to Meg, and the white petals blowing
in from the window onto her hair' (p. 167). At the end of Jane's memoirs is a
further ambiguous association between the two female characters:

> I glanced from one woman to the other. Mrs Marten was preening herself
> in a compact mirror now, and Meg – or a slice of Meg – was reflected
> alongside her. Why did they seem suddenly so alike – I could hardly tell
> the difference. (p. 143)

The assonance of 'Marten' with 'Gil Martin', allegedly Meg's brother, further
strengthens the identification.

The narrative oscillates between the notion that womanhood is neither
homogenous nor stable and that all modern variations of female subjectivity
paraded in the novel are (literally) travesties of that which, ultimately, resists
representation: the female other. Physical metamorphosis, in itself a symbolic
representation of mental instability, moves increasingly out of Jane's control:
whereas at the beginning she deliberately dyes her hair blonde to resemble her
half sister and then cuts it short, later her body is subject to changes apparently
independent from her will, as her figure appears to grow and shrink uncontrollably. Manifesting the desire to be something other than oneself, such physical
changes also point to the female obsession with images and self-representation:
'Women and mirrors; mirrors and women' (p. 36); Jane's fluid body – like
Cixous's and Clément's 'newly born woman' – challenges categorisation and,
simultaneously, deconstructs the unity of the female subject: 'Jane seems to be
uncertain about her identity', Anderson argues, 'seeking another self through
different clothes'.[77] Particularly significant, in this respect, is Jane's choice of
the denim uniform –'These magic garments, which make you invisible because
everyone wears them, which transcend sex and wealth and individuality'; the
longing for a genderless body follows Jane's rejection of any reductive self-
representations or versions of her femininity:

> In my perfect androgyny, my face round as a mermaid's, my mouth black
> and slit like a wound from a knife, my legs like a stevedore's that tells
> how long I have been under the sea, hair growing upward, sucked by
> the bubbles, waving like weed in the cold green current like a treasure
> long lost at sea, embedded in nacreous green rock, shifted here and there

on the sandy floor by shoals of spotted fish, I am for them the dread of their seafaring days: the siren with a cracked voice who lures them to the bottom of the sea, the forgotten woman and half-man who make up the Angel of Death. (p. 41)

The androgynous, half-animal/half-human mermaid embodies Jane's dream of revenge. In her hallucinatory state, Jane transforms herself into an alluring and bewitching creature but also, paradoxically, an 'angel of death', much like the corpse-like body of Mrs Marten, whose 'white face looks more of a mask than the real ones' (p. 157), in the lugubrious Pierrot outfit for the fancy-dress party; Jane, in turn, is forced to masquerade her body in the clichéd version of graceful femininity, a 'ballerina dress of pink net with a spangled bodice' (p. 147) which, Mrs Marten explains, 'belonged to my poor dead sister' (p. 148): 'a costume as stereotyped', Catherine Spooner notes, 'as those of all other women at the party',[78] either cast as 'witches' or 'courtesans' (p. 153). Ironically, it is with her body dressed in such a conventionally packaged version of feminine elegance that Jane, if we believe her memoirs, murders Miranda, delivering her death in an ambivalent parody of lesbian vampirism:

I close in on her. . . My teeth into her smooth neck. Miranda. . . these are my hours. . . when it's so dark outside that I can fly the streets without dread of the stake, ravenous, insatiable! You knew I was coming! You welcomed me almost. You give me your blood! (p. 158)

Alexander suggests that 'Jane's quest for wholeness is presented in terms that recall, in Kristevan terms, the desire to return to the semiotic state, undivided from the mother, while at the same time an element of destructiveness in their relationship is signalled by a suggestion of vampirism'.[79] Her own death returns Jane to the Scottish Borders, to the plot of land 'formerly part of the Dalzell estate, now Government property' above St Mary's Loch (p. 163), as reported in the fictional extract from *The Scotsman* that Tennant, like Hogg, includes at the end of the Editor's narrative. The report constructs the Scottish setting in supernatural terms: 'the clearing was thought to be haunted' (p. 163), significantly after a 'young woman' (Meg?), described by the locals as 'a walking corpse' (p. 163), vanished after spending a night at the St Mary's Arms in the 1970s. The Editor's repeated references to 'the purple heather' – with its '*stubborn roots*' (my emphasis) – and the 'dark, low clouds', while in line with the Gothic mood of the scene, are strongly evocative of the Romantic sublimity of the Scottish landscape; references to the spectral remains of the Ettrick Forest, which has been replaced by 'the man-made forest' (p. 164), however, juxtapose such nostalgic depictions with the transformations suffered by modern Scotland – commercial exploitation of certain aspects of Scottish culture were previously hinted in the 'bright tartan package' (p. 39) used to allure female consumers in modern supermarkets. In the end, Jane's corpse, which has been stabbed with a stick like that of a vampire, presents the androgyny longed for throughout her troubled existence: 'there was something completely hermaphroditic about it' (p. 165). While the episode of the exhumed corpse has parallels with Hogg's inconsistent descriptions of Wringhim's corpse in different accounts of the burial and evidence produced by the exhumed body (pp. 199–207), the novel, much like Hogg's, resists closure. Impossible to identify, Jane's body is, until the very end, the site of contested conjectures. With the spectre's elusiveness and the vampire's rapaciousness, Jane remains the female other, nothing but the double of her own self:

> I am the bad throw of the dice. I'm the double, now it's me who's become the shadow. Where I was haunted, now I will pursue. And the world will try to stamp me out, as I run like a grey replica of my vanished self-evil, unwanted, voracious in my needs. (p. 111)

A critique of patriarchal structures of oppression also underlies *Two Women of London*, a story that exploits the notion of social pressure in Stevenson's *Jekyll and Hyde* to articulate feminist preoccupations specific to Thatcherite Britain. The narrative frame is provided by an anonymous Editor investigating the mystery behind 'the terrible history of that summer in West London of '88' (p. 177). The use of various narratives and (unreliable) points of view is borrowed from the original *Jekyll and Hyde*; yet Tennant's text moves beyond its Victorian model to expose the simulated quality of the postmodern culture her story refers to: the characters' theatrical introduction under the collective '"cast" of this rather perverse drama' (p. 177) and the emphatic reliance on visual devices used to represent the story both underpin the notion of mediation:

> All day *excitement* will spread. From the police themselves, who have spent so long trying to track this man down. From the press, who will interview past victims; *from TV which takes the victims and sits them blindfold in the studio to make them talk of rape and violence* [. . .] Nobody knew his face; and yet, as the police vans arrive and the *TV cameras beam their hot, white light in the February darkness*, those who run out and catch a glimpse of him as he lies there on the path seem to feel they have lived closely with him for years. (pp. 174–5; my emphases)

The victim of Mrs Hyde's murder referred to in the passage is not the Notting Hill ripper – though Tennant plays with a parody of the Ripper murders that occurred a century earlier at the other end of the city – but the late Jeremy Toller, Eliza Jekyll's former husband. The media's exploitation of the fear-generated collective hysteria is as ruthless to the female victims of rape as to the male victim of Mrs Hyde's murder; whilst it creates an interesting comparison with the proliferation of Ripperologist narratives and conspiracy theories, the scene is also emphatically suggestive of the process of mediation, central to the novel's critical representation of the real. Significantly, Mara's collages are the first clue to the pervasive motif of fragmentation: 'I shoot film of all the women and I intercut the stills so I get the ultimate woman', Mara explains, 'It's the Face of Revenge' (p. 182). At the end of the novel, it is Mara's vision that reveals through the reverse technique how 'the features of Mrs Hyde, cut up and pasted down in so many of her collages, seemed [. . .] to be fleetingly but unmistakably imprinted on the face of Eliza' (p. 257). The fact that Eliza works for the Shade Gallery further implicates the notion that her face and body are part of the commerce of images that a media-obsessed culture thrives on; owned by Sir James Lister along with 'the massive new supermarket' (p. 182), behind its artistic facade the venue ensconces the exploitation of women's beauty: 'I put my hair up high and painted my nails', Eliza recalls, getting the job at the Gallery, 'and went out on high heels' (p. 256). The deep impact of media and consumerism on female beauty form the ideological backbone of the story: 'The novel directs attention to society's emphasis on female youth and beauty', Anderson rightly suggests, 'and explores women's problematic relationship with the visual, especially the objectification of women by film, photography and the media'.[80]

Though temporarily empowering, Eliza's flawless beauty poses questions of authenticity: at the Shade Gallery Eliza's 'manner' is, the Editor notes, 'rather artificial' (p. 184), while her 'impossibly perfect' (p. 245) physical appearance is as unfathomable as that of her alter ego's, 'alarming and repellent in appearance as a ghost' (p. 204). Eliza's conscious exploitation of her drug-enhanced beauty divorces her from other women: 'Eliza is the kind of woman who gives women a bad name' (p. 191), Mara claims, adding that 'Capitalism is the cause of Eliza Jekyll's prosperity' (p. 192). Whereas Eliza's predicament seems at this stage the beneficiary of the consumerist society which she allegedly exploits to her own advantage, at the other end of the spectrum Mrs Hyde's body is construed to signify the 'other' (less glamorous) end of the production line, the reject:

> There was certainly nothing homely about the sight of Mrs Hyde that evening. Disgusted, possibly, by an unwelcome combination of the familiar and the unknown – for the 'thing' wore nothing more alarming than a white mac, one of those plastic, half-transparent coats with a hood that sell in millions. (p. 197)

Packaged in the mass-produced plastic coat, Mrs Hyde's transparent outfit reveals women's perverse predicament that consumes them as images. Simultaneously, far from 'homely', Mrs Hyde's 'apparition' speaks of the uncanny – in the Freudian sense of the word – embodiment of women's unconscious fear of the female enemy *within*, echoing Kristeva's understanding of the female subject that is 'at once the attacker and the victim, the same and other, identical and foreign'.[81] Reduced to her objectified status, Mrs Hyde's abject 'thinginess' is suggestive of repressed drives, because the 'thing' is, in Lacanian terms, 'the cause of the most fundamental human passion'.[82] As such, Mrs Hyde cannot be pinned down to any-thing: her physicality, though rendered in graphic tones, eludes stable definitions, as shown through Mara's footage:

> The lens shows us a face that seems almost to have stopped being a face altogether. It's as if a once wide-boned, generous face, a beautiful face, even, to go by the edge of the high bridge of a slender nose and the curve of the jaw, has in some indescribable way been pulled sideways and downwards – so that an evil, spiteful face, a nose hooked like a witch's in the old pictures, eyes baleful and peering in a cloud of rain that's like the rising mists of a Hell that lies always at her feet – looks back at us in Mara's version. (p. 198)

Though Hyde's face may conceal her past as Jekyll, to the spectators the links remain invisible and ultimately her features resist identification: 'I can't describe it all', Jean Hastie admits, 'It had nothing to distinguish it' (p. 212). Reduced as a mere image, Tennant's Jekyll/Hyde personifies the postmodern hyperreal, depthless surface with no substance. As the Editor laments towards the end of the story: 'perhaps Mara is no more than a presage of a world where the sole survivors are machines; where the *images* of people, imprinted like Fayoum portraits at the neck of ancient Egyptian tombs, speak in *solitude* and *isolation* to each other across time' (p. 258; my emphases); in the consumerist world of the late twentieth century, Tennant seems to suggest, the arrogant power of images has seduced and reduced the female subject to embrace the simulacral reproduction of her disembodied self.

The contentious boundaries of self/other inform the problematic issue of identity in the original *Jekyll*; as in Stevenson's story, whose characters are all incestuously linked to Hyde, so do all characters from *Two Women of London* partake in the fractured identity of Eliza Jekyll. Just before her death, while Dr Crane declares that she is 'in *two* minds about the possibility of the whole thing' (p. 176), Jean Hastie admits being '*doubly* cautious, as a Scot' (p. 203) (my emphases); the Editor's account also reveals Mrs Hyde's disturbing hold on Jean Hastie:

> It occurred to me, slightly uncomfortably, that evil women like Mrs Hyde have a fascination for women such as Jean Hastie: as if a whole buried side to their nature, coming alive for a moment or so at the mention of the crime or whichever wicked deed, stirs pleasurably in them before subsiding again. (p. 238)

Tennant's narrative may suggest that the real outsider, or the 'other' woman, is in fact the Scottish lawyer, Jean Hastie, whose proximity with Mrs Hyde becomes more apparent as the story develops. With her 'provincial manner' (p. 210) and 'Scottish burr' (p. 185), 'Jean's foreignness' (p. 220) is manifestly juxtaposed to the glamorous Eliza, 'a woman in the centre of metropolitan life' (p. 201). In contrast to Jean's native Scotland, London is a disjointed space, a dystopian urban environment with disorienting streets. Elphinstone suggests that 'like Stevenson, she [Tennant] uses a London background that suggests Edinburgh',[83] but much more than Edinburgh, arguably, Tennant's London is portrayed to accommodate the ambivalent postcolonial metropolis. At the end of the twentieth century, the alluring cosmopolitan city attracts single women from all backgrounds (Mara Kaletsky is an 'itinerant' artist (p. 178); Robina Sandel's family are Jewish; Tilda, her niece, has arrived from Austria to learn English). Nevertheless, as Eliza admits, 'life's impossible in London now, for the poor, the single mother' (p. 227): behind its glittery veneer of wealth, much like Jekyll/Hyde, London conceals poverty and corruption. The city feeds off the worst aspects of capitalist society: 'We are surrounded daily by evidence of violence, poverty and misery in this city', the Editor admits, 'The media leave us in no doubt that rapaciousness and a 'loadsomoney' [sic] economy have come to represent the highest value in the land' (p. 177); and the night Mrs Hyde kills Jeremy Toller, it is 'the *false* dawn of a London *night*' (p. 264; my emphases) which accompanies the crime. Against the grime and misery of the capital, Jean's Scotland represents the safe harbour of homeland: 'once safely ensconced in the noon express to Waverley' (p. 230), Jean can distance herself from the metropolitan corruption of the city and later rejoice being past 'the border' (p. 233).

Jean's observations highlight the problematic notion of home as maternal space in relation to modern Scotland. What links Jean to Mrs Hyde ultimately is their role as mothers. Questioning the feminist emphasis on career-driven women, Jean admits 'I prefer to raise my children in the calm, sane atmosphere of the countryside rather than in the frenetic drug-ridden inner cities' (p. 201). London is ultimately, in Jean's mind, to account for the abuse suffered by Mrs Hyde's children, 'so different from her own bairns: so pale and underfed and miserable, such examples of an upbringing in the cruel city' (p. 216). Such notions of the safe Scottish home are nevertheless questioned upon the Editor's visit to Scotland. Surprised 'to find her [. . .] looking straight down the barrel of a gun' (p. 237), the Editor's observations raise doubts about the rural innocence of the Scottish countryside: 'we weren't far [. . .] on this lonely hill, from the scene of many murders in border keeps. . . and tales, too, of doppelgängers and people metamorphosed to beasts or three-legged stools, somewhere in the depths of the woods' (p. 239). Behind Jean's (defensive?) gun is the ultimate fear of the 'maternal' instinct, in the name of which the mother of her foster-children could come back to reclaim them: 'I keep hidden from her children, who stay with me here and breathe the purer air of Scotland, any news stories or headlines that crop up in the search for their mother' (p. 268). And with Mrs Hyde's last words, 'Mother Pride' pencilled at the end of her shopping list, still lingering in the air, the ambiguous ending of *Two Women of London* leaves an unsettling openness. Alive, dangerous and ready to strike again, Mrs Hyde is the subversive 'newly born woman' with her own legacy left behind, in Scotland.

THE REFLECTIVE *TABULA RASA*: ALICE THOMPSON'S *JUSTINE*

Like Tennant's novels, *Justine* reverberates echoes of several literary precedents, reinforcing its engagement with the self-reflectiveness of much Gothic writing.[84] The novel's obsessive repetition of mirror images and blank pages serves thus a dual purpose: on one hand, it articulates a critique of gender definitions; on the other, it self-consciously exposes the complex dynamics of desire that underpin the act of writing/reading.

The novel's engagement with the Gothic is manifested through the legacy of the Scottish doppelgänger: the narrative, as noted by Douglas Gifford, discloses several 'deliberate echoes of Hogg and Stevenson'.[85] As well as playing the psychological/supernatural ambivalence of Hogg's *Justified Sinner* and the Victorian duality of *Dr Jekyll and Mr Hyde*, an emphatic concern with one's own 'mirror' image is also reflected in the veiled references to Oscar Wilde's *The Picture of Dorian Gray* (1891): the narrator, who has an Oedipal love–hatred relationship with his mother, notes that his 'own face seemed to grow younger rather than older as the years passed, while his mother ages inexorably.[86] The link is further reinforced by the modality of his first encounter with Justine: Justine's first appearance is through the medium of a canvas which, much like Dorian's portrait, seems to change with time: 'To my shock a change had come over her expression: the consolatory quality of her beauty had disappeared' (p. 13). Featuring a woman sitting by 'a window whose bars flung their shadows across the left-hand of her face' (p. 10), the description of the painting is also reminiscent of the Arthurian legend of the Lady of Shalott, the subject of Victorian poetry (Tennyson's 'The Lady of Shalott') and many Pre-Raphaelite paintings, including the famous version by John William Waterhouse; as with Tennant's *Two Women of London*, the painting, whilst reinforcing the Victorian foundations of the novel's transtextual palimpsest, announces notions of aesthetic entrapment in relation to female identity. Justine, it will be seen, resists the narrative trap, ultimately dissolving the notion of a monolithic feminine self within the proliferating versions of her represented self.

More than any other precedent text, Thompson's *Justine* echoes Sade's novel *Justine or The Misfortunes of Virtue*, the scandalous novel written by the Marquis de Sade in a fortnight while in jail and published anonymously for the first time in 1791.[87] Several references, beside the title, point to the transtextual relationship between Thompson's and Sade's *Justine*. As noted by Anderson, both Sade's characters and his novels appear in Thompson's *Justine* (pp. 54 and 117).[88] As in Sade's novel, Justine and Juliette are sisters, and in Thompson's novel the binary opposition found in the Sadeian novels is underpinned by the fact that Justine and Juliette are allegedly 'identical' twins. Like Sade's fiction, Thompson's novel presents the reader with a narrative loaded with philosophical questions, a trait which Thompson identifies as being pervasive throughout the Scottish literary tradition:[89] in particular, her self-conscious employment of the doppelgänger supports the novel's interrogation of gender categories and the boundaries of real/fictional worlds.

The transtextual reverberation underpins the narrative deconstruction of the same/other dichotomy. Although the unnamed narrator is often unable to tell the difference between the two sisters' voices and their looks, at other times he is, conversely, asserting his ability to distinguish between them: Juliette's face displays 'child-like movements' and a 'troubled sexuality' (p. 22), but her abrupt mood changes make the narrator suspect 'she is a sorceress' (p. 33); as the plot unravels, the story becomes a complicated maze of identity and role reversals. Significantly, Justine's identity is questioned when, after the alleged publication of her novel, she is being stalked by a mysterious reader obsessed with the character in her novel. This is, in her words, 'A typical case of literary mistaken identity' (p. 57), though Justine also admits that she is 'beginning to wonder who I am' (p. 58), while the narrator's doubts undermine her actual existence: 'The real Justine never existed. Justine was an impostor: she was just an empty shell of living insects. Justine, like her picture, wasn't real at all, she was another fabrication' (p. 61). The inability to tell Justine and Juliette apart triggers, in turn, his own loss of identity: 'I caught sight of myself in the mirror and a stranger stared back' (p. 62). Rather than self-consciousness, the self/other conflict presented by the evocative mirror produces instead a climactic sense of dissociation reminiscent of Wringhim's crisis in Hogg's *Justified Sinner*:[90] 'I then seem to split into two people as I watch, from a position high up in the sky, myself walk inside the house and disappear, the door shutting behind me' (p. 103).

The novel's pervasive use of double imagery is further emphasised by the repetitive use of complex mirror images; as a child, the narrator voyeuristically watches his mother's image: 'She would be sitting, half naked at the mirror, her round full breasts reflected in the glass so that I could feast upon them from any angle' (p. 4); Juliette's enigmatic expression is 'like a cracked mirror, always self-reflecting an image that was deformed' (p. 35); similar patterns of repetition are also visible in the paratext of the novel: in the first edition the front and back covers are reverse mirror images of each other. Likewise, at the very end, when the narrator finally wakes up in the exact 'replica' of his own flat in Kensington Gardens, he is surrounded by his library: 'The shadows are only books. When I hold up their pages to the light, the paper of many of them is so thin that the words on the other side shine backwards, through' (p. 137). The repetitive mirror images, as in *Pharos* and *Pandora's Box*, erode the foundations of any absolute categories of symbolic signification, destabilising the real/fictional, angel/monster, virgin/whore binary patterns of differentiation.

The two women characters epitomising virtue and vice in Sade's novels merge into one ambiguous creature, simultaneously prisoner and victim, prey and pursuer. Unintelligible like a *tabula rasa*, Justine/Juliette has the ability and the potential to embody either whore or angel fantasies. But Thompson's Justine is only apparently the malleable subject of male desire, and her blankness personifies in fact her fluid resistance to stable gender roles: it is impossible to master her drives and to divide the two sides of her character, something that the narrator and Jack, Justine's lover and partner in crime, both try, to their own detriment:

> Did either of you really think you could divide me up that easily? [. . .] The characterizations were so basic. Omnipotent Justine and needy Juliette, virgin and whore. Just enough to titillate the preconceptions. You were both one of a kind, the murderer and the murderee. It was inevitable in the end that you had to cancel each other out. (p. 123)

The hierarchical subversion raises questions about the position of female characters in the light of Sade's characterisation. In *The Sadeian Woman* (1979), Carter highlighted Sade's merit in the endorsement of his controversial stance against female passivity and masochistic tendencies embodied by his Justine. Conversely, Juliette – though less honest – is in control of her own destiny, debunking male authority in the sexual sphere: 'The sisters exist in a complex dialectic with one another', Carter explained, 'the experience of one makes plain the experience of the other'.[91] Although it is true that, in Sade's novels, Justine is virtuous, and dies, while Juliette is dishonest, and thrives, as John Phillips observes, 'the apparent simplicity of this division of women into two stereotyped categories is misleading'.[92] What dictates the two women's destinies is not the external force (Fate), as Maurice Blanchot rightly remarks,[93] but in fact their own internal energies, manifested in their polarised attitudes towards pleasure/pain. Far from being easily categorised, and therefore annihilated, the charming cruelty of Juliette's subversion should be read in line with the complex discourse of feminine transgression, a point developed further in the third philosophical dialogue of Sade's *Philosophy in the Bedroom* (1795).[94] Although Sade's Justine and Juliette are represented in binary fashion, such apparent duality does not simplistically call on the juxtaposition of two clichéd versions of femininity, supporting, instead, Sade's universal discussion of virtue and vice, which Justine and Juliette personify in his stories, as Beauvoir remarks: 'The places he evokes are not of this world, the events which occur in them are *tableaux vivants* rather than adventures'.[95]

The complex ambiguity emerging from the gender politics presented in Sade's novels underlie Thompson's rewriting. The central nucleus of Thompson's *Justine*, as the author claims in interview, is the politics of gender representation: 'I wanted to undermine the virgin-whore archetype of the feminine. By making Justine and Juliette the same woman I was playing with that simple-minded dichotomy that takes place in literature from Adam and Eve onwards'.[96] Rather than against Sade's positions, Thompson's intentions stand in alignment with the disruptive stance against enforced social norms found in Sade's controversial texts. Simultaneously virtuous 'virgin' and 'vicious' whore, Thompson's character escapes identification with categorical signification. Having broken free from binary gender stereotypes, Justine/Juliette remains the embodiment of the undistinguished other, the unfathomable unknown, the enigmatically subversive 'newly born woman'.

Within this power reversal Justine's exploitation of the narrator acts as a reversal of Justine's victimisation in Sade's novels. As Justine explains:

> The real victim of your obsession has not been me. It's been you all along. The prison I have made for you, and what I do to you inside it, is the physical manifestation of what you have been doing to yourself. I have simply transformed your obsession into literal truth. I have made your spiritual prison real. (p. 134)

In a literary sense Justine's resistance to the narrative plot imposed on her by the male narrator reveals the highly self-conscious facade of Thompson's postmodernist text, somehow reminiscent of another sadomasochistic relationship between pseudo-author/narrator Samson Young and his murderee/character Nicola Six in Martin Amis's *London Fields* (1989). While, on one hand, the character seems to exceed the limits imposed by the narrator's imagination, Justine, much like Nicola in *London Fields*, also persistently haunts the narrator and manipulates his story in ways he is no longer able to control. Questions of authorial control and desire are overtly exposed in the recurrent image of the blank book: at the very end, Justine hands over her 'blank book' – just like the uncut pages of the first edition of Thompson's *Justine* – challenging the narrator to find out who she is (p. 136); Justine's authored book, significantly titled *Death is a Woman*, is a collection of blank pages (p. 63), though, at the end, Justine admits that her novel 'never existed'. The final (metafictional) confession points to the memoir, that is Thompson's novel, as the only text: 'I'm talking about the story I have really written, the story of Justine. The story I have got you, my ghost writer, to write for me' (p. 123). Thus the haunted text reverts back to its double, a blank table, 'the tabula rasa, [. . .], that begged me to write all over her' (p. 28).

Eroding the possibility of easy gender categorisation, Thompson's *Justine*, like Tennant's *Two Women of London*, also exposes the simulacral void of postmodern culture which, having lost any sense of authenticity, replaces the real with the mediated images of its spectre. In the late twentieth-century, postmodern context the novels refer to, feminine subjectivity becomes the hub of complex centrifugal and deconstructive drives; duality exposes the problematic coexistence of multiple, dislocated, hybrid roots (*Behind the Scenes at the Museum*), the longing for/dissociation from the maternal (*The Governors*), and the attachment/repulsion of one's homeland (*The Bad Sister*, *The Bad Box*).

NOTES

1. Plato, *Symposium*, trans. Seth Bernardete, ed., with a commentary by Allan Bloom (Chicago: University of Chicago Press, 2001), p. 22.
2. G. Gregory Smith, *Scottish Literature: Character and Influence* (London: Macmillan, 1919), p. 5.
3. Edwin Muir, *Scott and Scotland: The Predicament of the Scottish Writer* [1936] (Edinburgh: Polygon, 1982), p. 8.
4. Karl Miller, *Doubles: Studies in Literary History* [1985] (Oxford: Oxford University Press, 1987), pp. 416–17.
5. See, for example, Narcissus falling in love with his own reflection in a mirror of water; similarly, Persephone's conception of Dionysus occurs whilst looking at her own image reflected in a mirror. For a further discussion of the double in Greek mythology, see Otto Rank, 'The Double as Immortal Self', in *Beyond Psychology* (New York: Dover Publications, 1941), pp. 62–101 (pp. 88, 97); Greek mythology accounts for several versions of the birth of Dionysus: see Timothy Gantz, *Early Greek Myth* (Baltimore and London: Johns Hopkins University Press, 1993), pp. 721–5 and 112–14.
6. See Havelock Ellis, *Sexual Inversion* [1897] (Basingstoke: Macmillan, 2007) and Sigmund Freud, 'On Narcissism: An Introduction' [1914], *SE*, vol. 14, pp. 73–103.
7. See Otto Rank, *Psychology and The Soul* (New York: A. S. Barnes, 1961), p. 13.
8. See John Herdman, *The Double In Nineteenth-Century Fiction* (London: Macmillan, 1990), p. 3.
9. For a more detailed discussion on the role played by twins in the development of double beliefs and superstitions see: C. F. Keppler, *The Literature of The Second Self* (Tucson: University of Arizona, 1972); J. Rendel Harris, *Boanerges* (Cambridge: Cambridge University Press, 1913); E. Sidney Hartland, 'Twins', in *Encyclopaedia of Religion and Ethics* (1911–58), vol. XII, pp. 491–500; Rank, *Beyond Psychology*.
10. Paul Coates, *The Double and the Other: Identity as Ideology in Post-Romantic Fiction* (London: Macmillan, 1988), p. 32. See also Apter, *Fantasy Literature*, p. 51.
11. Herdman, *The Double in Nineteenth-Century Fiction*, p. 2. See also Margaret Bennett, *Scottish Customs From the Cradle to the Grave* [1992] (Edinburgh: Polygon, 2004), pp. 204–17.
12. Sigmund Freud, 'Lecture 31', *SE*, vol. 22, pp. 57–80 (p. 58); see also vol. 18, pp. 105–10.
13. Freud, 'Lecture 31', p. 72.
14. Jacques Lacan, 'The Mirror Stage as Formative of the Function of the I as Revealed in Psychoanalytic Experience', in *Écrits: A Selection*, trans. Alan Sheridan (London: Tavistock Publications, 1977), p. 3.

15. Sean Homer, *Jacques Lacan* (New York: Routledge, 2005), p. 25.
16. Homer, *Jacques Lacan*, p. 25.
17. Coates, *The Double and the Other*, p. 2.
18. Smith, *Scottish Literature*, p. 4.
19. Hugh MacDiarmid, *Aesthetics in Scotland* (Edinburgh: Mainstream Publishing, 1984), p. 90.
20. MacDiarmid, *Aesthetics in Scotland*, p. 90.
21. Hugh MacDiarmid, 'A Plea for Synthetic Scots', *Scots Observer* 6: 310 (1932), p. 10.
22. Muir, *Scott and Scotland*, p. 8.
23. Christopher Whyte, *Modern Scottish Poetry* (Edinburgh: Edinburgh University Press, 2004), p. 52.
24. Olga Kenyon, *Women Writers Talk* (Oxford: Lennard Publishing, 1989), pp. 184–5.
25. Kenyon, *Women Writers Talk*, p. 185.
26. Craig, *The Modern Scottish Novel*, pp. 32–3.
27. Cixous, 'Sorties', in Cixous and Clément, *The Newly Born Woman*, p. 63.
28. Cixous, 'Sorties', p. 64.
29. Cixous, 'Sorties', p. 83.
30. Luce Irigaray, *This Sex Which is Not One* [1977] (Ithaca: Cornell University Press, 1985), p. 28.
31. Irigaray, *This Sex Which Is Not One*, p. 26.
32. Irigaray, *This Sex Which Is Not One*, p. 29.
33. Julia Kristeva, *Julia Kristeva Interviews*, ed. Ross Gubermann (New York: Columbia University Press, 1996), p. 96.
34. Julia Kristeva, *Desire in Language: A Semiotic approach to Literature and Art* [1980], ed. Leon S. Roudiez, trans. Thomas Gora, Alice Jardine and Leon S. Roudiez (Oxford: Basil Blackwell, 1980), p. 239.
35. Miller, *Doubles*, p. 417.
36. Elphinstone, 'The Quest', in Whyte, *Gendering The Nation*, pp. 107–36 (p. 107).
37. Butler, *Bodies That Matter*, p. 214.
38. Margaret Atwood, 'Duplicity: The Jekyll Hand, the Hyde Hand, and the Slippery Double', in *Negotiating with the Dead: A Writer on Writing* (Cambridge: Cambridge University Press, 2002), p. 32.
39. Jonathan Culler, *On Deconstruction: Theory and Criticism after Structuralism* (London: Routledge and Kegan Paul, 1983), p. 182.
40. Nicholas Royle, *The Uncanny* (Manchester: Manchester University Press, 2003), p. 192.
41. Jean Baudrillard, *Simulacra and Simulation* [1981], trans. Sheila Faria Glaser (Ann Arbor: University of Michigan Press, 2006), p. 167.
42. Coates, *The Double and The Other*, p. 1.
43. Alison Fell, *The Bad Box* (London: Virago, 1987), p. 25. Further references to this edition are given after quotations in the text.
44. Flora Alexander, 'Contemporary Fiction III', in Gifford and McMillan, *A History of Scottish Women's Writing*, p. 635.
45. See also Germanà, unpublished interview with Alison Fell, in 'Re-Working the Magic', pp. 341–52 (p. 342), and Alexander, 'Contemporary Fiction III', p. 634.
46. Antti Aarne, *The Types of the Folk Tale: A Classification and Bibliography*, trans. Stith Thompson (Helsinki: Academia Scientiarium Fennica, 1964), p. 131 (folk tale type no. 401). See also John MacKay (ed. and trans.), *More West Highland Tales*, 2 vols (Edinburgh and London: Oliver and Boyd, 1940), vol. 1, pp. 394–409.
47. MacKay, *More West Highlands Tales*, p. 403.

48. Sian Hayton, *The Governors* (Nairn: Balnain Books, 1992), p. 12. Further references to this edition are given after quotations in the text.
49. See Jenny March, *Cassell's Dictionary of Classical Mythology* (London: Cassell & Co., 1999), p. 394. See also Homer, *Iliad* 5.638–51, 20.144–8 and Ovid, *Metamorphoses* 11.211–17.
50. Julia Kristeva, *Desire in Language: A Semiotic Approach to Literature and Art* [1980], ed. Leon S. Roudiez, trans. Thomas Gora, Alice Jardine and Leon S. Roudiez (Oxford: Basil Blackwell, 1980), p. 239.
51. Freud, *On Dreams* [1900–1], in *SE*, vol. 5, pp. 633–85 (p. 683).
52. Freud, *SE*, vol. 5, p. 684.
53. Freud, *SE*, *The Interpretation of Dreams* [1900], (Part II) vol. 5, pp. 339–625 (p. 401).
54. Freud, *SE*, vol. 5, p. 399.
55. C. J. Jung, *Concerning Rebirth* [1950], in *The Collected Works of C. G. Jung*, 20 vols, ed. Herbert Read, Michael Fordham and Gerard Adler (London: Routledge and Kegan Paul, [1953–79] 1969), vol. 9.i, pp. 113–47 (p. 119).
56. Jung, *Collected Works*, vol. 9.i, p. 119.
57. Jung, *Collected Works*, vol. 9.i, p.129.
58. Gifford, 'Contemporary Fiction II', in Gifford and McMillan, *A History of Scottish Women's Writing*, p. 616.
59. See, for instance, Donald MacDougall's 'Maccodrum's Seal Wife' (1968), Mrs Anderson's 'Rescued by a Seal' (1970) and Andrew Hunter's 'The Limpet Pick' (1975) in A. J. Bruford and D. A. MacDonald (eds), *Scottish Traditional Tales* (Edinburgh: Polygon, 1994), pp. 365–70. For an extensive study of selkie lore in Celtic countries see David Thompson, *The People of the Sea: Celtic Tales of the Seal-Folk* (Edinburgh: Canongate, 2000).
60. Kate Atkinson, *Behind the Scenes at the Museum* (London: Black Swan, 1995), p. 9. Further references to this edition are given after quotations in main text.
61. See Paola Splendore, 'Bad Daughters and Unmotherly Mothers: The New Family Plot in the Contemporary English Novel', in Adalgisa Giorgio (ed.), *Writing Mothers and Daughters: Renegotiating the Mother in Western European Narratives by Women* (New York: Bergharn Books, 2002), pp. 185–214 (p. 204).
62. Sinead McDermott, 'Kate Atkinson's Family Romance: Missing Mothers and Hidden Histories in *Behind the Scenes at the Museum*', *Critical Survey* 18: 2 (2006), pp. 67–78 (p. 69).
63. Children born at midnight, according to some Scottish superstitions, are gifted with second sight, that is, the ability to see apparitions and, in particular, wraiths. See Margaret Bennett, *Scottish Customs from the Cradle to the Grave*, p. 208.
64. Roger Luckhurst, 'Memory Recovered/Recovered Memory', in Roger Luckhurst and Peter Marks (eds), *Literature and the Contemporary: Fictions and Theories of the Present* (Harlow: Longman, 1999), pp. 80–93 (p. 88).
65. Emma Parker, *Kate Atkinson's* Behind the Scenes at the Museum (New York: Continuum, 2002), p. 32.
66. Luckhurst, 'Memory Recovered/Recovered Memory', p. 88.
67. McDermott, 'Kate Atkinson's Family Romance', p. 73.
68. See Parker, *Kate Atkinson's* Behind the Scenes at the Museum, p. 44.
69. Salman Rushdie, 'Errata. Or Unreliable Narration in *Midnight's Children*', in *Imaginary Homelands* (London: Granta, 1991), pp. 22–5 (p. 25).
70. Republished in *The Bad Sister: An Emma Tennant Omnibus* (Edinburgh: Canongate, 2000). References to this edition are given after quotations in main text.
71. Flora Alexander, 'Contemporary Fiction III', p. 631.
72. See Alexander, 'Contemporary Fiction III', p. 631, and Carol Anderson 'Listening

to the Women Talk', in Wallace and Stevenson, *The Scottish Novel Since the Seventies*, pp. 170–86 (pp. 171–2).

73. See Steven Connor, *The English Novel in History: 1950–1995* (London: Routledge and Kegan Paul, 1996). See also Carol Anderson, 'Listening to the Women Talk', in Wallace and Stevenson, *The Scottish Novel Since the Seventies*, pp. 170–86.

74. James Hogg, *The Private Memoirs and Confessions of a Justified Sinner* [1824] (Edinburgh: Canongate, 1994), p. 38. Further references to this edition are given after quotations in the text.

75. See Anderson, 'Listening to the Women Talk', p. 178; see also John Haffenden, *Novelists in Interview* (London: Methuen, 1985), p. 289.

76. Anderson 'Listening to the Women Talk', p. 177.

77. Anderson, 'Listening to the Women Talk', p. 177.

78. Catherine Spooner, *Fashioning Gothic Bodies* (Manchester: Manchester University Press, 2004), p. 148.

79. Alexander, 'Contemporary Fiction III', p. 632.

80. Carol Anderson, 'Emma Tennant, Elspeth Barker, Alice Thompson: Gothic Revisited', in Aileen Christianson and Alison Lumsden (eds), *Contemporary Scottish Women Writers* (Edinburgh: Edinburgh University Press, 2000), pp. 117–30 (p. 120).

81. Julia Kristeva, *New Maladies of the Soul* (New York: Columbia University Press, 1995), p. 223.

82. Jacques Lacan, *The Seminar of Jacques Lacan, Book VII: The Ethics of Psychoanalysis 1959–1960* [1986], ed. J.A. Miller, trans. D. Porter (London: Routledge, 1992), p. 97.

83. Elphinstone, 'Contemporary Feminist Fantasy', in Gonda, *Tea and Leg-Irons*, p. 51.

84. See David Punter, *Gothic Pathologies: The Text, The Body and The Law* (Basingstoke: Macmillan, 1998), p. 14.

85. Douglas Gifford, 'Autumn Fiction: Clever Books and Sad People', *Books in Scotland* 59 (Autumn 1996), pp. 1–8 (p. 3).

86. Alice Thompson, *Justine* (Edinburgh: Canongate, 1996), p. 7. Further references to this edition are given in the text after quotations.

87. The novel was later developed and published under the title of *La Nouvelle Justine* in 1797.

88. See Anderson, 'Emma Tennant, Elspeth Barker, Alice Thompson', p. 122.

89. Monica Germanà, unpublished interview with Alice Thompson, in 'Re-working the Magic', pp. 374–88 (p. 387).

90. Compare this to the following passage from Hogg's *Justified Sinner*: 'I generally conceived myself to be two people. When I lay in bed, I deemed there were two of us in it; [. . .] The most perverse part of it was, that I rarely conceived *myself* to be any of the two persons. I thought for the most part that my companion was one of them, and my brother the other' (pp. 125–6).

91. Angela Carter, *The Sadeian Woman: An Exercise in Cultural History* [1979] (London: Virago: 1982), p. 103.

92. John Phillips, *How to Read Sade* (London: Granta, 2005), p. 86.

93. Maurice Blanchot, 'Sade', in Marquis de Sade, *Justine, Philosophy in the Bedroom and Other Writings*, comp. and trans. Austryn Wainhouse and Richard Seaver (New York: Grove Press, 1965), p. 49.

94. Sade, *Justine, Philosophy in the Bedroom and Other Writings* (p. 255).

95. Simone de Beauvoir, 'Must we Burn Sade?', trans. Annette Michelson, in Marquis de Sade, *The 120 Days of Sodom and Other Writings*, comp. and trans. Austryn Wainhouse and Richard Seaver (London: Arrow Books, 1991), pp. 3–64 (p. 37).

96. Germanà, unpublished interview with Alice Thompson, in 'Re-Working the Magic', pp. 374–87 (p. 378).

Chapter 5

GHOSTS: DISSOLVING THE BOUNDARIES

Was it a hallucination? Was it the fever of the brain? Was it the
disordered fancy caused by great bodily weakness? How could I tell?[1]

Margaret Oliphant

The ghost imports a charged strangeness into the place or sphere it is
haunting, thus unsettling the propriety and property lines that delimit a
zone of activity or knowledge.[2]

Avery F. Gordon

GHOSTING THE TEXT

Moody sky. A misty glen. A haunted castle. Conjuring up romantic visions
of ghost-ridden manors against the spectral backdrop of a Scottish Highland
landscape, variations of this formulaic setting are the essence of popular
imaginings of Scotland; though frequently associated with Scotland's folklore,
spectres do not exclusively belong in Scottish culture: blurring the boundaries
between presence and absence, phantoms – both literal and metaphorical –
arguably haunt various discourses, including literature, psychoanalysis and, in
the second half of the twentieth century, postmodernist and post-structuralist
theories.

This chapter explores the pervasive presence of the literal/metaphorical
revenant motif with specific references to four texts – Barker's *O Caledonia*

(1991), Thompson's *Pharos* (2002), Kennedy's *So I Am Glad* (1995) and Smith's *Hotel World* (2001). The four novels establish overt links with Scottish ghost lore: the strong psychological dimension of spectrality and the revenant's symbiotic relationship with the haunted space are the most manifest aspects of such legacy. Simultaneously, the texts blend the distinctively psychological appeal of the Scottish supernatural with the articulation of postmodernist questions about the real and a deconstructive exploration of feminine subjectivity and desire.

What this chapter discusses collectively is in fact a diverse range of supernatural phenomena and beliefs. A linguistic overview of the variety of denominators – 'spirits', 'revenants', 'zombies', 'spectres', 'undead' – attached to the supernatural apparitions of ghosts and vampires reveals, as Ralph Noyes rightly remarks, the semantic richness of ghostly terminology.[3] Some of such cognate terms – 'revenants', for instance – reinforce the suggestion that a prominent feature of the belief in – or fear of – spectres derives from the notion, explored by Freud in *Totem and Taboo* (1913), that the vengeful spirits of the dead may 'return' to visit the living. Propitiating rituals attached to the cult of the dead worldwide are further proof of the established belief in the return/influence of the spirits of the deceased. This, Paul Barber argues in his anthropological study on vampire lore, is a universally accepted belief:

> Our sources, in Europe and elsewhere, show a remarkable unanimity on this point: the dead may bring us death. To prevent this we must lay them to rest properly, propitiate them, and when all else fails, kill them a second time.[4]

If unwanted spectral apparitions may produce a reminder of our mortality, the reverse, Nina Auerbach argues, is also true of vampires: 'Eternally alive, they embody not fear of death, but fear of life: their power and their curse is their undying vitality'.[5] At the end of the twentieth century, ghosts pullulate in high and low culture, literature, film and TV:[6] haunting the atheist, materialist, disaffected societies of the millennium, 'ghosts are still invoked when there is some uncertainty about the believability or authenticity of an event or experience in the material world – hence phantom pregnancies, limbs, and phone calls, ghost-writers'.[7] In its various manifestations spectrality unveils postmodernist preoccupations about ontological and metaphysical boundaries; commenting on the origin of vampire lore, Catherine Belsey sharply emphasises its cultural relevance to modern culture: 'Vampires have a material existence and they bring about material effects, but at the same time they cast no shadow and are not reflected in mirrors: they exceed the alternatives of presence and absence'.[8] What ghostly apparitions and vampires equally articulate are questions about the other side of life, the authenticity of the real, desire and the corporeality of text:

it is precisely the experience of being haunted in the 'world of common reality' [. . .] that troubles or even ruins our ability to distinguish reality and fiction, magic and science, savage and civilized, self and other, and in those ways gives to reality a different coloring.[9]

The interrogation of the real begins with specific locations privileged by revenants in folklore as in literature. In pre-Christian Scotland, many a cave, hill, glen and loch would gather a plethora of spirits and superstitions tied to its name:[10] the extensive catalogue of traditionally haunted locations is possibly derived from a Celtic notion of an immanent other world.[11] Anthropological speculations about such beliefs also point to the features of distinctive landscapes as the intellectual foundations to the relationship between locality and culture, which John Berger calls 'address to the landscape': 'The address of western Ireland or Scotland is tidal, recurring, ghost-filled'.[12] Popular traditions in Scotland report sightings often occurring in the proximity of caves, misty glens or loch shores. In the Ettrick Shepherd's 'Mary Burnet', for instance, the first apparition of the demon lover is foreshadowed by the setting chosen for the lovers' rendezvous: the 'little green sequestered spot' alerts the reader familiar with Scottish lore to the imminently supernatural turn of the events (Hogg, *The Shepherd's Calendar*, p. 200):[13] being both 'green' – the colour generally associated with fairies – and 'sequestered' – the preferred setting for supernatural events – the environment foreshadows the fantastic events to come. Although, as Manlove remarks, modern Scottish texts may no longer share the seamless union of supernatural beings and landscape, 'they are all, directly or indirectly, fed by a sense of it';[14] the continuity of such narrative strategies is visible in Margaret Oliphant's 'The Open Door' (1882), where ghostly apparitions occur within the gloomy boundaries of a haunted, mist-clad park, as in George Mackay Brown's 'Andrina' (1983): here hauntings occur 'just before dark'.[15] Blurring the boundaries between the seen and unseen, Royle notes, darkness is a fundamental ingredient of the uncanny atmosphere, that belongs to spectrality:[16] the Scottish origin of the word 'uncanny' underpins such propensities for the obscure and undefined side of things within Scottish culture. Scotland has, in a sense, always been the 'other', both to itself and to its hegemonic neighbouring nation: 'The "uncanny" comes from Scotland, from that "auld country" that has so often been represented as "beyond the borders", liminal, an English foreign body'.[17]

The emphasis on locations suggestive of spatial and/or temporal thresholds facilitates the narrative tension articulated by ghosts: rather than presenting the reader with an overtly supernatural story, ghost stories – and particularly so in the Scottish tradition – leave matters unsolved, sometimes until the very end. The indeterminacy conveyed by the semi-dark, misty, shady quality of haunted locations foregrounds the ambiguity embodied by the ghostly apparition in the text. In this respect, the ghost-ridden island of *Pharos*, directly inspired by the tidal landscape of the Scottish isles, exemplifies the seamless continuity between the seen and the unseen, while the unclear identity of the narrative's ghosts interrogates their authenticity; these are the principal functions of the phantom within any text: insinuating doubt, dismantling certainties, defeating the illusion of objectivity.

In his study, Royle remembers Freud's argument that what is uncanny is 'inextricably bound up with thoughts of home and dispossession, the homely and unhomely, property and alienation'.[18] Although spirit-haunted forests and glens frequently feature as natural backdrops to supernatural apparitions, it is the enclosed, seemingly 'domestic' spaces that best accommodate spectrality. The notion of a haunted house is, in some sense, as David Ratmoko suggests, a tautology: to 'haunt' originally is to 'inhabit'.[19] The Gothic castle is the haunted house par excellence; labyrinthine in plan and multi-layered in height, the castle is a complex space, articulating the crucial questions that permeate Gothic writing: the perpetuation of power and dynasty, the security of heredity and the patriarchal structure of the family are all bound to the fortified walls of the castle;[20] since the publication of Horace Walpole's *The Castle of Otranto* (1764), Gothic writing has become obsessively concerned with the narrative strategies offered by the haunted house, reiterating the *leitmotif* through 'the repetition of other forms of this house, as well as its contents: its villains, incestuous relationships, disembodied parts, and above all, the buried secrets of its origins'.[21] From Bram Stoker's *Dracula* (1897) to Daphne Du Maurier's *Rebecca* (1938), fortresses and manor houses stand for the stronghold of power whose legitimacy is also simultaneously challenged by the dark secrets concealed within their walls.[22] In these contexts, the revenant returns from the grave to haunt the castle with some kind of secretive knowledge: the term 'revenant', Jodey Castricano remarks, is explicitly linked to the notion of 'revenue':[23] 'What returns [. . .] is always linked with desire'.[24] Such desires, from the revenant's point of view, are often tied with the politics of space repossession. In Emily Brontë's *Wuthering Heights* (1847) Cathy's apparition corresponds to a plea for help, interestingly articulated in terms of a request for access into a space that has allegedly been denied to her.[25] Likewise, in Oliphant's 'The Open Door' Willie's ghost haunting visits echo the incessant request: 'oh mother, let me in! oh mother, let me in!' (p. 64). In *Wuthering Heights*, Cathy's ghost enunciates an identical request.[26] The haunted house becomes thus a contested space, staging the demand for power/ knowledge reclaimed by the revenant: such struggles for empowerment emerge vividly against the haunted background of the Scottish mansion house in *O Caledonia*; likewise, in *Pharos*, the claustrophobic spaces of the lighthouse and the crypt expose the subversive subtext of patriarchal and colonial authority. Turning the home into an alien space, the haunted castle becomes the prime site of indeterminacy, the quintessential backdrop to the disembodied self of Gothic literature, 'a fiction of exile, of bodies separated from minds, of minds without a physical place to inhabit, cast adrift on seas of space and time which appear to bear no relation to the moral life'.[27]

When entering a space whose legitimacy the revenant challenges, temporal and spatial disruptions brought in by ghostly apparitions amplify the sense of unsettling indeterminacy produced by spectrality in the first place. In Derrida's words, the ghostly apparition 'de-synchronizes. It recalls us to anachrony'.[28] By returning to haunt the living from the past, the revenant defies the laws of time, disrupting the chronotopic linearity of the ghost story. Such temporal disruption emerges in *Hotel World* and *So I Am Glad*. In both novels the revenants of Sara and Cyrano respectively produce chronological chaos to the narrative worlds they return to visit, undermining, in turn, the ontological foundations of the real: 'the quality of indeterminacy [. . .], the stock in trade of the Gothic mode', Allan Lloyd Smith reminds us, 'is surely the very *raison d'être* of the postmodern'.[29] Such preoccupations constitute the most manifest link between postmodernism and spectrality; not only does the deferral implicit in all ghostly apparitions reflect deconstructive challenges to time and space, but also the notion of spectrality contains questions about the impossibility of knowing the real. Ghosts are illusions, simulacra of that real that we are no longer allowed to know, control or possess: 'Simulacra are like false pretenders' Deleuze explains, 'built upon a dissimilarity, implying an essential perversion or a deviation'.[30] In a postmodern context, simulation replaces representation as the only form of aesthetic and epistemological response to the hyperreal, as Baudrillard designates 'the generation by models of a real without origin or reality'.[31] As 'simulation threatens the difference between the "true" and the "false", between the "real" and the "imaginary"',[32] objective knowledge is a mere illusion, as the only object of knowledge is but a phantom of the real.

The ambiguous circumstances of spectral phenomena undermine their supernatural 'authenticity' and the engendered tension between two possible explanations, a supernatural and a psychological one, underpins much Scottish fantasy. In a letter to J. G. Lockhart, Scott discusses the possibility that revenants' apparitions also stem from their witnesses' own imaginations: 'Who shall doubt that imagination, favoured by circumstances, has power to summon up to the organ of sight, spectres which only exist in the mind of those by who their apparition seems to be witnessed?'[33] Although, on one hand, spectrality forces the spectator – and the reader of a ghost story – to question their own rational strongholds, on the other, ghostly apparitions may reveal spectators' own desires and fantasies. In this sense, the apparitions, projected from traumatised/deluded/bereaved consciousness, conjure up a vision of the recently deceased beloved. In *Totem and Taboo* (1913) Freud explains ghost-belief as the result of the subconscious fear that the souls of recently departed may return to take revenge upon the living. What underpins taboos about the dead – including the prohibition to utter the dead's name – is what Freud defines as 'projection': upon death the souls of the departed are turned into hostile demons, because the surviving relatives transfer their own repressed hostility onto the souls of the deceased.[34] Ghosts are, consequently, feared because of the potential threat they represent for the living: 'More often than not, the dead do not return to rejoin the living', Nicholas Abraham notes, 'but rather to lead them into some dreadful snare, entrapping them with disastrous consequences'.[35]

This is particularly evident in feminist ghost stories, such as Charlotte Perkins Gilman's *The Yellow Wallpaper* (1892), which deploys the ghost trope to articulate a critique of patriarchal oppression. Similar strategies, Armitt notes, underpin explorations of repressed feminine subjectivity in Edith Wharton's short stories, du Maurier's *Rebecca* and Atwood's *The Robber Bride* (1992).[36] The ghost's paradoxical 'absent presence' allows ghost stories to investigate, question and challenge the boundaries of female consciousness, stuck between two coexisting, albeit apparently opposite, positions: alienation from/and entrapment within the female body. Exploiting the simultaneously corporal/ethereal dimension the spectre/vampire may embody, as metaphors, ghosts may also articulate preoccupations with female body/mind dichotomies. The four texts explored in this chapter share distinctive preoccupations with issues of entrapment tied to the ghostly apparitions in the texts: delving into characters' consciousnesses, the narratives blend the fantastic, Gothic and magical-realist contours of the stories with psychological investigations; trapped inside the prosaic world circumscribed by the crumbling walls of the mansion house at Auchnasaugh, Janet's self-destructive romantic fantasies epitomise the character's alienated condition in *O Caledonia*; likewise, the premortal ghostly condition, it will be argued, reflects on the unrepresentability of lesbian sexuality/desire as well as a universal postmodern vacuity in Smith's *Hotel World*; in Thompson's *Pharos*, the main (ghost) character's captive condition within the patriarchal structure of the lighthouse is underpinned by the claustrophobic setting and slavery subplot of the novel; in *So I Am Glad* Jennifer's disjointed narrative is set against a constraining world of alienated emotions and self-fabricated lies.

Ghostly apparitions are not always feared. The return of the dead can in fact be the consequence of another, equally powerful death-related drive: desire. The homecoming of demon lovers and revenants is frequently foreshadowed by the expectation that these appearances will in fact take place. In Hogg's 'Mary Burnet' Mary's initial and final apparitions could be interpreted as the result of her lover's and her parent's strained imaginations; prior to the alleged apparition of his demon lover, Allanson is 'palpitating with agitation'

(Hogg, *The Shepherd's Calendar*, p. 201); at the end of the story, too, the final appearance of Mary's 'gilded chariot' also suggests that the apparition may be fuelled by the parents' own projected desires and 'strained eyes' (p. 221).[37] This ambiguous treatment of the revenant as the embodiment of subconscious desire continues in the twentieth-century ghost story: in Mackay Brown's 'Andrina', the ghost of a recently deceased, far-away granddaughter, Andrina, visits her elderly grandfather, Torvald, months after her death. In Mackay Brown's short story, as in Hogg's 'Mary Burnet', the spectral apparition feeds off their witnesses' subconscious desires, as they do also in many Scottish ballads. In 'Sweet William's Ghost', the death of William is followed by his lover's 'marriage' to his corpse. While the encounter with the phantom lover reveals notes of sexual desire, the consummation of their marriage ultimately signifies Margaret's (self-inflicted?) loss of corporeality.

Violating the boundaries between life and death, necrophilia, the love of the dead, is the extreme manifestation of the close link relating erotic desire to death. The representation of demon lovers in literature revolves around psychoanalytical discourses of desire, in Belsey's words: 'the unaccountable, irrational, destabilizing character of desire is projected onto the figure who stands for its cause, and each time this figure is represented as dangerous, nonhuman, demonic'.[38] All texts dealing with demon lovers point to the sinister closeness of the two principles governing the human mind: in Freud's words, the 'pleasure principle' and the 'death instinct', defined as 'a kind of organic elasticity, or [. . .] the expression of the inertia inherent in organic life'.[39] As the longing to return to an inanimate state inherent in all living organisms, death-drive is the powerful counterbalance of the 'pleasure principle'; as Freud explains, 'the pleasure principle seems actually to serve the death instinct'.[40] While desire becomes the contested space between two opposing forces, progressive pleasure and regressive 'death', it also denotes a gap: in relation to the Lacanian linguistic system, Belsey notes, 'desire is the effect of the lost needs: loss returns and presents itself as desire'.[41] Such notion of desire as result of loss and subsequent return underpins the spectral qualities of desire in Lacan's theory:

> desire is also hollowed within the demand, in that, as an unconditional demand of presence and absence, demand evokes the want-to-be under the three figures of the nothing that constitutes the basis of the demand for love, of the hate that even denies the other's being, and of the unspeakable element in that which is ignored in its request.[42]

In its spectral dimension, therefore, 'desire [. . .] deconstructs the opposition between mind and body', addressing the post-structuralist dismantling of binary patterns of differentiation.[43] In the texts considered in this chapter, ghostliness is strongly interlinked with the dynamics of desire, oscillating between the erotic carnality of vampires and the ethereal condition of spirits. The ghost becomes a psychological dimension which feeds off its witnesses' repressed desires, hopes and expectations: the ghost of Savinien in *So I Am Glad* derives from the narrator's post-traumatic neurotic mind, but is also the instigator of a new emotional existence for Jennifer. In *O Caledonia*, while Janet's pre-spectral body longs for a non-corporeal existence, the body/mind conflict is never solved. In *Pharos* and *Hotel World*, the emphasis placed on the ghosts' problematic spectral bodies poses further questions about the objects of their desire.

Challenging the boundaries between real and imagined, flesh and soul, life and death, in its various manifestations the ambivalent spectral body ultimately represents the unknowable, that which simultaneously is and is not. In all its manifestations, spectrality is simultaneously a reminder of the limits and loss of corporeality and a challenge to the debatable thresholds of the body; as Punter puts it: 'The ghost comes to menace the bodily with its limitations; but it also comes to celebrate the loss of the body'.[44] Revenants, literal or metaphorical, possess all narratives, conjuring up, Elisabeth Bronfen argues, the simultaneous absent/present corporeality of texts:

> Their [storytellers'] power of imagination is like a vampire, feeding off this exchange, for they rely on a preservation and production of 'dead' figures – the teller's and the listener's temporary social death and the uncanny presence as absence that fictions embody. Or, to reverse the analogy, storytellers are like revenants in that the liminal realm between life and death inspires and produces fictions.[45]

Spectrality belongs in all layers of textuality: suspended between absence and presence, texts are always ghosted, while both narrators and readers become involved in a vampiric relationship, which revolves around mutual desire and search for pleasure. As Peter Buse and Andrew Stott note, 'fiction [. . .] shares their simulacral qualities: like writing, ghosts are associated with a certain secondariness or belatedness'.[46] As transtextual palimpsests, the transtextual engagement with previous Gothic texts becomes the most overt manifestation of such spectral anachronies. This becomes apparent in *O Caledonia*; Barker's text is haunted by Gothic narratives overtly or subtly embedded in the narrative, amplifying the parodic scope of the novel: the 'Goblin Teasmaid' echoes the goblins of Scott's *Lay of the Last Minstrel*, which lends Barker's novel its title;[47] *Hotel World* reverberates the playful manipulation of the title of Muriel Spark's *Memento Mori*, which functions as an uncanny *leitmotif* throughout the novel; references to precedent literary and philosophical texts underpin *Pharos*'s engagement with the shadow/light dichotomy running through the narrative; literary phantoms, including that of Cyrano de Bergerac, literally possess *So I Am Glad*.

Haunting the layered texts, transtextual references thus arguably highlight the textual vacuums, the narrative black holes the reader is (subconsciously) exposed to. Like a ghostly apparition, Julian Wolfreys argues, the act of reading unsettles secure definitions of the real and the 'imagined'.[48] Occupying the interstitial spaces between categories, the ghost metaphor, then, effectively underpins the interrogation of all binary oppositions, as Derrida argues in *Spectres of Marx* (1993):

> What happens between two, and between all the 'two's' one likes, such as between life and death, can only maintain itself with some ghost, can only *talk with or about* some ghost [s'entretenir *de quelque fantome*]. So it would be necessary to learn spirits. Even and especially if this, the spectral, *is not*. Even and especially if this, which is neither substance, nor essence, nor existence, is never present as such.[49]

Occupying the undefined, though contested, space 'between two', the ghost signifies the overcoming of binary oppositions of structuralism, disrupting the systematic understanding of literature in patterns of binary differentiation. In more than one way, the ghost represents the metaphor central to deconstruction.[50] If ghosts represent the fear of the unknown when viewed in conjunction with Freudian notions of the uncanny, with deconstruction they embody the grey spaces left between what can and cannot be explained. Cixous underlines these spectral ambiguities, in her discussion of Freud's study of the 'Uncanny': 'What is intolerable is that the Ghost erases the limit which exists between states, neither alive nor dead'.[51] Such challenges to the thresholds of the real, Cixous argues, speak of the liminal essence of all fiction:

> Neither real nor fictitious, 'fiction' is a secretion of death, an anticipation of nonrepresentation [sic], a doll, a hybrid body composed of language and silence that, in the movement which turns it and which it turns, invents doubles, and death.[52]

Lingering between life and death and embodying both fear and longing for a self-destructive return to the whole, ghosts occupy the contested space between death and pleasure. Texts, too, oscillate exactly between these two polar instincts: 'The work of writing', Andre Green notes, 'presupposes a wound and a loss, a work of mourning, of which the text is the transformation into a fictitious positivity.[53] Desire-driven, 'writing is [. . .] the place where the subject appears' and, 'paradoxically, the subject *dis*appears, undergoes the death, precisely, of the author':[54] in the text's presence/absence converge the pleasure/death drives of both author and reader; this love/death tension emerges suggestively in the metaleptic drives of postmodernist texts. McHale discusses the use of the pronoun 'you', for instance, as a narrative/textual strategy that erases the barriers separating author/narrator/character/reader.[55] Both *So I Am Glad* and *Hotel World* establish an intimate relationship with the reader through the strategic use of second-person pronoun 'you': by addressing the 'other' in the text, both novels display their self-referential articulation of the spectral, blurring the boundaries that separate text and reader.

LONGING TO DISAPPEAR: ELSPETH BARKER'S *O CALEDONIA*

Cast as a Gothic parody, *O Caledonia* engages with ghostliness both literally and metaphorically, as the plot begins where the story ends: Janet, the novel's main character and point of view, is dead. Her spectre, however, haunts the text before and after her untimely death, and, as the narrative unfolds, ghostliness articulates issues of desire and alienation interwoven with the search for clues to Janet's mysterious demise.

Gothic references are scattered through the transtextual body of *O Caledonia*, whose title derives from Scott's *The Lay of the Last Minstrel* (1804). The supernatural world of the ballad and the sentimental address to the Scottish landscape – 'O Caledonia' – are juxtaposed to the novel's anti-kailyard approach to the Scottish land. More significantly, the setting of the novel echoes Gothic (literary) references, building up the parody upon layers of transtextual echoes: other literary references include ballads – 'Thomas the Rhymer' and John Keats's 'La Belle Dame sans Merci' (Barker, *O Caledonia*, p. 52) – and, repeatedly, William Shakespeare's *Macbeth* (pp. 19, 61), which Janet firmly believes must be set at Auchnasaugh, her family house.[56] Gothic narratives 'about isolated, misunderstood young girls' (p. 45) feature among Janet's favourite readings: as Anderson has noted, 'Janet's own attraction to Gothic, suggesting her youthful taste for the extreme, illustrates the novel's playful self-consciousness'.[57] The Gothic reverberation articulates the spectral and bodily discourses underlying the text of *O Caledonia*. Within this context the background to Janet's story becomes – as often in Gothic fiction – the foreground: the unforgiving sublimity of the Scottish landscape and ancient mansion, with its resident madwoman and depraved gardener, occupy a prominent position and perform a crucial role in the unfolding of the plot. The Gothic setting appropriately serves the purpose of facilitating problematic questions of female emancipation, set, as Gifford observes, against the 'northern landscapes working towards the annihilation of its lonely and sensitive adolescent Janet of Auchnasaugh'.[58]

To begin with, the plot launches the issue of the problematic disposal of Janet's body after her death: her corpse and the ghost of her memory are equally unwanted. Her difficult childhood and adolescence having made her into a misfit, Janet's death seals the ultimate closure her parents have subconsciously longed for since her birth, set against a rather Gothic background, 'in wartime on a fog-bound winter night in Edinburgh' (p. 5). Reduced to taboo, as theorised by Freud, traces of the recently dead Janet are quickly erased, as her ghost is relegated to a peripheral position, captured at the threshold of the main text:

> Her restless spirit might wish to engage with theirs in eternal self-justifying conversation or, worse still, accusation. She had blighted their lives; let her not also blight their deaths. And so, after her murderer had been consigned to a place of safety for the rest of his days, and grass had grown over the grave, Janet's name was no longer mentioned by those who had known her best. She was to be forgotten. (p. 2)

The death of the young heroine – a stock Gothic *topos* – is here deprived of its sublime potential, as the body of the recently murdered Janet, 'oddly attired in her mother's black lace evening dress' (p. 1), lies in the Gothic surrounding of the mansion house at Auchnasaugh. Captured at dusk, the sombre architecture of the mansion house – with its 'vaulting hall', 'tall stained-glass window', 'Gothic arch' and 'circular panel, where a white cockatoo, his breast transfixed by an arrow, is swooning in death' (p. 1) – points to the spectral atmosphere familiar to Gothic narrative conventions, whilst simultaneously uncovering its parodying intentions. Janet's lifeless body is significantly subject to the light with which it is infused. It is the ghost of her recently terminated life, and implicitly conjured up by the uncanny light cast by a setting sun or full moon through the stained-glass window, that captures the reader's attention. As 'atoms of dust' launch hers as spectral existence, the bloody red drops of ruby light masquerade, however, Janet's violent death with vampiric glamour: the convergence of ethereal spectrality and aggressive vamp sexuality foreshadows the novel's ambiguous discourse on the female body. As Dorothy McMillan notes, the opening section of the novel marks Janet as a 'sacrificial victim', capturing her body in the liminal position traditionally occupied by the female corpse in literature and art: still images simultaneously embodying beauty and corruption at the same time.[59]

That this is a complex parody of the death of a beautiful woman is reinforced by the modality of Janet's death, killed, for no apparent reason, by the hunchbacked gardener. Long before her mysterious murder, 'Janet and her needs have been dead things to those around her for most of her life';[60] As with the ghostly Miss Havisham of Charles Dickens's *Great Expectations* (1861), Janet is 'absent, because socially dead'.[61] From the earliest stages of her life, Janet is crafted as a misfit: as a baby, her body foreshadows a budding monstrosity signified by her expressionistically 'black gaping mouth', in its Munchian quality perhaps the most suggestive of her features, hinting at her dark self. Yet, Janet's open mouth signifies also her desire to transcend the limits of her condition and the constraints experienced by the motionless body of a newborn baby. Her struggle – which echoes Lacan's observations about the 'mirror stage' referred to later – authenticates the notion of entrapment and longing for autonomy that accompany her throughout her story.

That Janet may feel imprisoned in her body becomes particularly manifest throughout her adolescence, a phase in human life, Punter notes, associated with the body politics articulated by the Gothic: 'we exist on a terrain where what is inside finds itself outside (acne, menstrual blood, rage) and what we think should be visible outside (heroic dreams, attractiveness, sexual organs) remain resolutely inside and hidden'.[62] The bodily transformations and – in particular – the appearance of secondary sexual attributes, in this context, frustrate Janet's longing for an otherwise bodiless existence. The physical reality of her womanly shape, instead, becomes the prime obstacle for the world of ethereal shadows Janet desires: 'During the next few months a dreadful thing happened. Knobby protrusions appeared on Janet's chest' (p. 59). The unavoidable transformations result in the utmost self-conscious resistance to biological and social norms attached to female anatomy, stressed by Janet's determination to keep her life free of any sexual involvement:

> She would live out her days at Auchnasaugh, a bookish spinster attended by cats and parrots, until that time when she might become ethereal, pure spirit untainted by the woes of flesh, a phantom drifting with the winds. What fun she would have as a ghost.
> She could hardly wait. (p. 60)

Significantly, the only escape route Janet can carve for herself – in her fantasies, if nowhere else – is that of embracing spinsterhood: without sex, life as a single woman becomes the way of life closest to the purely bodiless condition of a spectre.

The novel builds up Janet's longing for a spiritual life against the grim setting of a Scottish Calvinist upbringing within the gloomy premises of Auchnasaugh. The mansion embodies the entirely suitable setting for a Gothic parody; its crumbling walls and archaic decor underpin the timeless dimension of O Caledonia, and such anachronisms add to the spectral quality of the narrative, as do the sinister hogweed branches, 'withdrawn and spectral, parched skeletons drained of their venom' (p. 41). In its hauntedness, the house becomes the site of the conflicting discourses on corporeality and sexuality central to O Caledonia. Against the 'unrelenting chill of a Calvinist world' (p. 6), the mansion offers the promises of a less material world in which secretive fantasies may take place: though 'in many ways unwelcoming', McMillan notes, Auchnasaugh is the place where 'Janet imagines her spirit free'.[63] As well as being the stronghold of Scottish Calvinist principles, Auchnasaugh encloses many 'forbidden and empty rooms' (p. 67), archetypal places of female transgression from the patriarchal chains represented by the haunted fortresses of Gothic tales from Bluebeard to Dracula. The house, therefore, becomes the site of both patriarchal oppression and female resistance to it, the symbol of an ethereal existence free from any kind of social constraints and conventions which force a negotiation out of its boundaries. The grandfather's room at Auchnasaugh, in this context, opens up a world of possibilities exceeding the strictly regulated daily routines of the household. It is here – as well as in her bookish boudoir – that Janet seeks refuge from the prosaic reality of her mother's domestic Eden:

> In this room was a genial liberality absent from the outer household with its routine, its timetable of rests and walks and meals, its grim insistence on self-control and cleanliness, scratchy vests and liberty bodices, tweed coats buttoned tight around the neck, hair brushed until the scalp stung, then dragged back into pigtails. (p. 16)

Auchnasaugh is therefore the ambivalent site where oppression and freedom coexist, where the rigid Calvinist structure of the patriarchal house adjoins Janet's transcendent desires. As the site of patriarchal legitimisation, the house accommodates conservative gender roles, whilst simultaneously deconstructing them through the intrinsic dark spots it conceals. Janet's mother, Vera, represents the carrier of the feminine principle, embodying the spirit of conformity to traditional gender roles. In the name of such established principles of femininity, Vera's attempts to 'feminise' the house, significantly set against 'all that was uncouth, barbaric and disruptive (well, masculine) at Auchnasaugh' (p. 120) are nevertheless doomed to fail, as are her efforts to instil the required attributes of femininity in her eldest daughter. The 'revamping' of Janet's bedroom at Vera's hand simultaneously discloses the mother's effort to camouflage her daughter's odd personality and Janet's own increasing sense of alienation. A (Lacanian) mirror sits on 'a dressing table, bridally veiled in swags and festoons of net' (p. 127); to Janet, however, the mirror opens up the possibility of an 'other' self, subverting her mother's new hopes:

> She had discovered that if she gazed into her own eyes in the mirror for long enough her features would alter and resolve into those of another person, and she feared that she might one day find a manatee staring back at her. (p. 128)

Dualistically juxtaposed to Vera stands the other female principle functioning within the Gothic world of Auchnasaugh: the eccentric, fossil-collecting, reclusive, but sexually active, Aunt Lila is the 'madwoman in the attic', the transgressor of established authority.[64] When Lila is forced to leave the house because of her unacceptable behaviour and alleged liaison with the gardener, her theatrical exit – 'attired in twinset, pearls, and a lovat-green Hebe Sports suit', 'tattered black stockings and stained velvet slippers', and wearing 'liberal quantities of mascara, rouge, powder and lipstick' (p. 84) – reinforces the text's articulation of a Gothic parody.

Although Lila's departure partially erodes Auchnasaugh's subversive inner core, the mansion itself continues to retain its northern austerity, against Vera's mundane attempts at southern civilisation. Moreover, beyond its solid walls, the fortress reveals its contiguity with the aerial world of a bodiless spirituality. The silhouette of its elevated towers and upper storeys reveals the pervasive urge to transcend the imposed limits of an otherwise conventional existence:

> Auchnasaugh was a place of delight and absolute beauty, all her soul had ever yearned for, so although she could understand that many a spirit might wish to return to it, and she hoped that in time she too might do so, she felt the circumstances and mood of such visitations could only be joyous. (p. 35)

It is in fact within the uncanny boundaries of Auchnasaugh that the process of Janet's progressive bodily dissolution starts. To begin with, her fantasies merely involve the creation of a parallel otherworld in which Janet, who is otherwise the plain and introverted girl of a remote Scottish village, metamorphoses into an extraordinary fairy-tale heroine. Such fantasies, interestingly, pivot on fashion discourses illustrating Janet's ambivalent attitudes towards her bodily dimension. Recurrent detailed references to pristine princess-style gowns 'with a tiny waist and ruffles and trains of swirling silken skirts' (p. 17) clash with Janet's own appearance, betraying a schizoid view of her physicality. Against the glittering dream of aristocratic glamour is the prosaic world of a strictly conventional and orderly upbringing: unable to turn into a princess, Janet's scruffy negligence stands out as the only act of subversive resistance against conformity −'Janet had no hope of ever being tidy: her hair grew wilder and frizzier, escaping from pigtails, tangling in everything it touched' (p. 27); these bold statements of self-authentication clash with the knowledge that 'she was an outcast, a tragic dwindling figure soon to be seen no more' and the wish, expressed during a family outing to the sea, that 'the darkness would take her. This would be her revenge' (p. 30). To her family's accusations of 'the crime of self-centredness' (p. 54), Janet responds with the vengeful and wishful fantasy of a vanishing body that simultaneously vindicates her marginal position of 'outcast' whilst freeing her from the mundane restrictions suffered by (all) female bodies.

The complex ambiguities underlying the bodily discourses of O Caledonia are underpinned by the Scottish landscape (and the Scottish home), revealing Janet's problematic relationship with her native land and, Anderson remarks, 'mixed responses to Caledonia' ('Gothic Revisited', p. 126). Janet's self-destructive urges become particularly prominent when she returns from St Uncumba: her exile reveals the problematic fallacy of her affiliation to Auchnasaugh as, upon her return, Janet realises that 'inconceivable as it seemed to her, life at Auchnasaugh had moved on without her. Her absence had made no difference. Away from Auchnasaugh, however, she has been maimed, deprived of her identity, living in two dimensions only' (p. 79). When even her belonging to the ancestral space at Auchnasaugh is questioned,

Janet's descent into a self-destructive abyss seems inevitable. Death becomes an increasingly popular fantasy, ominously anticipating her tragic destiny, though signalling, at the same time, Janet's own desire to fulfil a tragic destiny. Death-drive blends in with decadent pleasures, such as the detailed 'arrangements for her funeral which she had for a long time now been inscribing in the back of her special notebook' (p. 124) or the list of imaginary visitors paying homage to her grave.

Against her fantasies of incorporeality, other forces seem to pin Janet's body down to the prosaic real world and the rigid gender role she should be impersonating. Once again, these appear particularly manifest in the novel's sartorial discourse. When Janet wears her first school uniform, she does so 'with pride and excitement', because 'in her brown felt hat and oatmeal tweed coat she felt that she was refashioned, a different person, vibrant with pos-sibilities' (p. 71). Attempts to crystallise Janet's body into Vera's ideal model of 'the grown Scottish female' (p. 129) are, however, unsuccessful: 'Janet wore her new tweed suit. It prickled incessantly [. . .]. Her legs felt strange and suf-focated in their wrappings of twenty-denier nylon' (p. 130). On the contrary, when invited to the local ball, Janet's determination to wear 'deadly purple rather than virginal white' (p. 137) signals her desire to separate her body from those of the other young women – including her sister Rhona – willing to conform to the required criteria of beauty and (sexual) desirability. Far from being marginalised – and in line with the contradictory spectral discourse running through the text – it is with secretive pleasure that Janet notes that 'her dress had been, as she had hoped, distinctive' (p. 142).

Janet's split between the two opposed urges – to occupy a central position in her world, and, conversely, to abandon her corporeal dimension – reaches a climactic end just before her violent death at the hand of Jim, not before the heroine has suitably adorned her body for one last *coup de théâtre*. Having refused to participate in the family holiday, Janet undergoes one last physi-cal metamorphosis, in the extreme attempt to become something 'other' than herself:

> She rummaged about in Vera's dressing table; she found lipstick and rouge and mascara. Peering into the mirror, she applied them liberally. Then she hung her head upside down and was pleased to see the electric sparks like fireflies dancing around it. She felt strong and bright and beau-tiful. Perhaps it was worth being female after all. [. . .] At last she went to her own room and looked at her reflection in the submarine murk of her new mirror. She was amazed; she was unrecognizable. (p. 150)

The deadly strike terminates Janet's life at this highly ambivalent moment of self-definition. Paradoxically, it is her bodily transformation that, reflecting a 'different' version of herself – echoing Lacan's theorisation of the 'mirror stage'

– simultaneously articulates the most powerful manifestation of self-assertion. Janet, now the truly 'dangerous woman' of the Gothic text, is about to be executed by the representative of the hypocritical Calvinist masculine power still ruling the Caledonian world at Auchnasaugh. The ending of O *Caledonia* echoes its beginning and, as Anderson rightly notes, 'refusing closure, is highly self-conscious':[65] mirroring the opening section, the text performs yet another act of conscious repetition, echoing, as it does, the text's elusiveness and the resistance to conclusive endings to the spectral motif.

GHOSTS AS SIMULACRA: ALICE THOMPSON'S *PHAROS*

As with O *Caledonia*, *Pharos: A Ghost Story* blends elements from the Scottish tradition with a self-conscious treatment of spectrality in a highly evocative historical narrative. Set in the early nineteenth century, on a fictional island, Jacob's Rock, situated twenty-seven miles off the west coast of Scotland, the setting and the lighthouse that dominates the landscape of the story support the multilayered symbolism of the text. Despite the self-conscious subtitle, the novel's ambiguous engagement with generic conventions interrogates 'who is real and what is imaginary'.[66] In fact, much of the novel's narrative strength relies on the postmodernist questioning of its own genre; as noted by Roz Kaveney, '*Pharos* rejects the classic ghost story for an impressively disorienting opening out of its generic rules'.[67] The plot is interwoven with intricate patterns of archetypal dichotomies (God/man, life/death, man/woman, light/darkness, real/imagined, true/false) and challenges the absolute hierarchical structure of the pairs to purport a deconstructive view of such binary oppositions. Asking ontological questions about the 'real' and raising epistemological doubts about the possibility of knowing (and telling) the truth, the text oscillates between the philosophical positions of Platonic transcendent dualism and Baudrillardian simulated hyperreality.

Jacob's Rock discloses references to the Scottish geographical and literary landscapes. The scenery of different sets of Scottish isles creates the first layer of this imagined territory; while the story was first conceived during a trip to Ardnamurchan and a visit to a lighthouse museum,[68] Jacob's Rock also echoes the 'openness and spiritual face of Shetland',[69] which Thompson experienced as a writer in residence. The title of the novel reveals further references to the history of the Scottish islands and their lighthouses: *Pharos* takes its title from the name of the Lighthouse Yacht Walter Scott travelled on 'as a guest of the Commissioners of the Northern Lights' in the summer of 1814.[70] Members of the crew included Robert Stevenson, grandfather of Robert Louis Stevenson:[71] the drawing of the island's map found at the beginning of *Pharos* is in turn borrowed from that of Stevenson's *Treasure Island* (1883), a pictorial reference which underpins, through the transtextual link to Stevenson's classic adventure novel, the story's roots in the Scottish romance tradition.

The map also foreshadows the ghostly plot of *Pharos*, as the illustration reveals the morphology of the ghost-haunted coastline. It is not just that the island is subject to the ghostly cycles of tidal waves, but also that the inhospitable rock formations along its coastline have made it into a death-trap:

> Jacob's Rock stood at a point where three strong currents met over an *invisible* reef. [. . .] Jacob's Rock's lighthouse was built on the place of maximum *danger*, where most people's lives had been lost, most ships wrecked. At the point where boat met stone and the sea swallowed the *corpses* left behind on the rocks. [. . .] on a rough day, these rocks became *invisibly* submerged.[72] (Thompson, *Pharos*, p. 5; my emphases)

The landscape is defined by the treacherous nature of its ghostly geomorphology: the 'invisible reef' is a doubly spectral component of this landscape, representing, on a literal level, the disappearing coastline responsible for the shipwrecks, and on a figurative level – as the text clearly suggests – the ghosts of all bodies perished at sea. The island embodies the ghost-haunted land of all Scottish fantasy writing, a territory whose ambiguity allows for an ambivalent supernatural/psychological reading of inexplicable sightings. As with Auchnasaugh in *O Caledonia*, placing and landscape perform a paramount function in the development of the ghost story, the island's geological appearance articulating the sublime marriage of eternity and mortality. Contemplating the scenery of Jacob's Rock, Lucia, newly arrived on the island, believes that 'this would be a good place in which to meet death. [. . .] This island was not a place for mortals' (p. 45). Jacob's Rock is a ghost-land, a place where death constantly interrogates the legitimacy of life.

Presented as a liminal sort of landscape, the name of the island bears also a strong masculine connotation; Jacob's Rock takes its name from one of the Biblical patriarchs, suggesting the notion that the place is also the site of absolute masculine authority, and anticipating the novel's gender conflict. Standing as a stronghold of human power over the combined natural force of the island reef and the sea, the lighthouse – eminently phallic in its basic erected structure – represents (patriarchal) authority, performing a role similar to other Gothic buildings.[73] In all its architectural variations, the haunted house articulates a complex struggle for power, often explored through the recurrent motifs of female captivity within/male exile from the 'contested' fortress. In *Pharos*, too, the lighthouse incarnates the heroine's psychological and literal entrapment: halfway through the narrative, Lucia admits that 'it is like a prison here' (p. 70); moreover, the captive condition seems linked with the hierarchical structure of the lighthouse itself: 'These people if they wish can give me orders. If necessary, perhaps, lock me up' (p. 70), and to larger questions about the real and knowledge of the truth: 'I don't know who they really are. They could be phantoms. [. . .] I am powerless over their secret desires' (p. 70).

Crucial to obtain freedom from the confined enclosure within the fortified jail in Gothic writing is the discovery of the truth, often obtained through the revelation of a vital secret; 'as the Gothic convention par excellence', Leona Sherman admits, 'its [the castle's] very structure exemplifies the stout, external form, yet it conceals some hidden secret, knowledge of which will ultimately prove more important than the strength of stone and iron'.[74] Much like Dracula's dwelling in Transylvania, or, perhaps more aptly, Bluebeard's Castle, the lighthouse conceals a secret room behind a door 'almost invisible, cut into the side of the wall' (p. 50). That the lighthouse's inner sanctum is somehow connected to the established male authority is sanctioned by its inaccessibility: the door cannot be opened because, Charlotte explains, 'Cameron forbids it' (p. 50). Later, when the door is finally opened, the secret room reveals further affiliations to Bluebeard's torture chamber:

> There was a chain attached to the wall and a chain next to the bed. Dust covered all surfaces. It smelt like mausoleum.
>
> Iron instruments lay by the basin. Knives and forceps. Soiled napkins were piled up in a bucket. On closer examination of the unmade bed she saw the sheets were rust-stained badly with dried blood. (p. 116)

This 'dark ominous place' (p. 116) reverberates with echoes of Carter's rewriting of Bluebeard in 'The Bloody Chamber': here, as in Carter's parody of Perrault's fairy tale, the archetypal forbidden room conceals within its impenetrable boundaries – the room is 'windowless' – the darkest secret of the lighthouse: Grace. The mulatto girl who appears to have been haunting the island, Grace, is not in fact a ghost, but the sole descendant of a group of African slaves perished in a shipwreck off the coast of Jacob's Rock ten years before the beginning of the story. Daughter to the only survivor of the wreck, an African priestess, and Cameron, the girl is the living testimony of Cameron's past sins: deceit and greed. After her mother's death in childbirth, evidence of which is testified by the forceps and blood-stained sheets kept in the secret room, Grace, ejected from the lighthouse, haunts the island, a 'real' phantom of repressed guilt.

Towards the end of the story, the room becomes the setting of one of Lucia's raving dreams:

> the secret room had disappeared, to be replaced by a much larger room, a room whose size would have been impossible for the lighthouse to contain. A throng of bodies filled it. They were standing in front of a raised platform draped with a red and white cloth. (p. 132)

The vision mirrors an apparently disjointed scene placed at the beginning of the narrative, which, significantly, takes place in the only other building (with the exclusion of the 'ruined chapel') on Jacob's Rock: the crypt. As Castricano, among others, notes, the crypt stands for the unsaid, the 'cryptic' secret at the core of any Gothic revenant.[75] In *Pharos*, the crypt reflects this semantic ambiguity. The scene, seemingly the unfiltered projection of the omniscient narrator, raises questions about the identity of the unidentified mulatto girl, later known as Grace, and the authenticity of her existence. The girl's ominous words disclose her relationship with the mystery about the recent history of the island: 'I could hear the other bodies lying beside me, breathing. I could hear the words spoken in their sleep, the names of daughters, husbands and sons. Names which they would never speak again, except in their sleep' (p. 9). The text is deliberately ambiguous about the identity of the speaking voice. At the beginning, the girl's lips 'made no sound', then 'words came out [. . .] as if they were made of solid matter' (p. 9). As becomes apparent, the speech is ventriloquised by the girl's voice, but her trance retells the past story of the wreck of a ship carrying slaves, including her mother. As with all visions in *Pharos*, the boundaries between dream and 'reality' are unclearly marked, revealing the text's interrogation of the real.

Linked to the sea, the origin of Lucia's body also raises questions of authenticity. When she is rescued from the haunted waters of Jacob's Rock, camouflaged by the waves and misleadingly taken for a ship's figurehead, her body is initially unidentified (p. 18). Much like the water that seemingly bears it, the contours of Lucia's body appear to be fluid and consequently placed in ideological opposition to the structured fixity of the masculine body of the lighthouse. The circumstances of her recovery stress her uncanny affiliation with the wrecked ship: her flesh feels like wood and her hair is interwoven with seaweed (p. 17). Moreover, Lucia bears all the ambiguous traits of the vampire: her lifeless body, cadaverous complexion and haemorrhaging wounds evoke the unsettling physiognomy of an 'undead': 'Carrying her up the steps to the lighthouse her naked legs became covered in his blood. The warm red lines trickling and spotting over her white skin as if drawing a pattern of life over its dead white pallor' (p. 18). Once within the confining boundaries of the lighthouse, Lucia's body performs a disrupting function, exposing, as it does, the bogus foundations of its moral structure, resting on the simulated normality its inhabitants act out. Moreover, as an outsider, Lucia's body epitomises the unfamiliar other:

> She was like a wild creature they had captured from the water. Her haunted grey eyes looked alert but fugitive. She skulked behind furniture and they could hear her running up the steps at night like an animal uncaged, its energy set loose. [. . .] Even her skin and facial features seemed evasive, hidden behind her dark cloud of thick, unkempt hair. (pp. 18–19)

As the narrative unfolds, Lucia's point of view becomes the story's principal focaliser, revealing that, as well as being a mystery to the others, Lucia is an enigma to herself. With no memory left of her existence before her rescue from the inhospitable shores of Jacob's Rock, Lucia is a *tabula rasa* and consequently enacts an identity quest during her captivity on the island. Haunted by her missing history and initially nameless, Lucia cannot trace her origin. Preoccupations about the authenticity of her self are overtly disclosed in the (Lacanian) mirror scene, which significantly, occurs before Cameron, in the patriarchal act of naming, chooses to name her Lucia. At this stage, however, Lucia is an undefined body: 'She could not connect herself with what she saw; her face could have belonged to a stranger. It was as if she were wearing a mask, for her features could offer her no sense of self' (p. 21). The shapelessness of Lucia's body here reveals the text's persistent engagement with and, simultaneously, resistance to Platonic duality: matter without form, her body has no essence, no meaning attached to it. But rather than bearing any manifest connections with the real, Lucia's body is in fact a simulacrum, an image without any referential bond to the real.[76] Her 'nebulous spirit' is alienated from the corporeal structure it seems imprisoned in, while the elusive fluidity of her body facilitates her disruptive function within the fixed boundaries of the lighthouse. Her alienation, too, reinforces the notion of her unstable body, while the problematic schizoid approach to her corporeal identity raises further questions about the truth of her origin: 'She could not seem to make her body hers; *it was like touching wood*' (p. 25; my emphasis). What makes Lucia's identity is neither flesh nor spirit, but the wood of a figurehead: neither dead nor alive, the text seems to suggest, Lucia is just a simulacrum. Until the very end, the narrative, however, sustains an unsolved tension between a psychological interpretation (Lucia as a projection of Cameron's own guilt) and a supernatural one (Lucia as a vengeful revenant, risen to avenge the deaths of the African slaves). Paradoxically, the critical interpretative dilemma is exposed by Lucia, when, towards the end of the novel, she raises the crucial question of her identity: 'I cannot live for much longer in this gossamer world of tenuous relationships between shadowy figures where I am the most ghost-like of them all' (p. 113).

True/false, real/imagined binary oppositions overarch the spectral narrative of *Pharos*. Questions about the truth are investigated through the extensive use of symbolism: from the very beginning, *Pharos* – Greek for 'light' – reveals the narrative's pervasive engagement with the light/darkness dichotomy. In the opening paragraph, the opposition is introduced with reference to the lighthouse, which sets the symbolic foundations of the story: 'THE LIGHT during darkness must never go out: it was the one cardinal rule of the lighthouse. Whatever happened, the lighthouse's lantern was not allowed to stop shining. It made Cameron preternaturally sensitive to light' (p. 1). The metaphysical connotation attributed to the lighthouse is further emphasised by the ensuing statement that 'he felt that he was like the lighthouse: without light there would be no point to him' (p. 2). Cameron's self-identification with the light

(-house) exposes the narrative's light/darkness binary opposition. The hierarchical structure of the opposition is, however, far from unproblematic. Though in charge of the lighthouse, the power of Cameron – whose surname, Black, reveals further symbolic ambiguities – is threatened by Lucia (Latin for 'light') – who is also ambiguously associated to the lighthouse, because she goes 'dark intermittently' (p. 32). The lighthouse, therefore, epitomises simultaneously light and its absence, darkness; much like the island on which it is located, it is a reminder of death as well as instrumental in saving lives. Rather than being placed in dialectical opposition to darkness, throughout the narrative, light belongs in an unstable juxtaposition in which the symbolic connotations of the two terms appear interchangeable, as ominously expressed in the epigraph to the novel taken from Thomas Browne's *The Garden of Cyrus* (1658): 'Life itself is but the shadow of death, and souls departed but the shadows of the living: all things fall under this name. The sun itself is but the dark simulacrum, and light but the shadow of God'. Placed before the beginning of the story, the ontological inversion operated by Browne's words foreshadows the spectral motif central in *Pharos*; life, Browne argues, is nothing but a mere shadow of death, while in chiasmic opposition, the souls of the deceased are themselves reflections of the living. The epigraph signals the complex spectral discourses which are interwoven with the ghost narrative of *Pharos*.

The narrative appears to be constantly questioning its own storyline; though the sense of haunting is pervasive, it becomes increasingly difficult to discern who or what is haunting it: 'which of the characters exists on each side of the life and death divide', one of the novel's reviews suggests, 'is in fact one of the central intrigues of the tale'.[77] The lighthouse and all its residents display distinctive affiliations to a supernatural order of things and all partake of the uncanny environment of the haunted site. Behind the facade of a disciplined and regulated approach to life in the lighthouse, Cameron's elusiveness is suggestive of his involvement in the mystery underlying the ghostly sightings on Jacob's Rock. His face, Lucia notes, is 'always [. . .] unreadable', and he appears 'in two places at the same time', 'like a ghost' (p. 67). The incomers – Simon, the assistant keeper, and Charlotte – both display signs of the mysterious forces at work on the island and in the lighthouse. Simon's animistic beliefs and his magical practices enhance the supernatural aura surrounding the lighthouse; moreover, while his teeth are, Cameron notes, 'supernaturally white', Lucia's response suggests that Simon 'looked like a sea spirit in human form' (p. 34). His magical tricks further challenge Lucia's perceptions, posing overt questions about the nature of subjective knowledge and the boundaries between real and magical worlds: 'Perhaps, she thought, it had all been an illusion and she had mistaken the rays of the sun coming through the window for flames' (p. 28). It is his ability to seemingly animate the inanimate (one of his doll-puppets resembles Lucia) that mystifies, one suspects, Simon's creative powers. Similarly, Charlotte, despite her apparent domesticity, shares the uncanny features of a spectral body. By the author's admission, *Pharos*'s governess is a tribute to Henry James's *The Turn of the Screw* (1898),[78] a story which questions characters' perceptions throughout. As with the other characters in the novel, Charlotte's physical features display an amorphous quality: her 'face looked slightly smeared, as if God had finished his creation and then decided to smudge it slightly with his fingertips' (p. 48), but her looks seem to change with time too, 'as if various faces fell off her one by one to reveal the truly beautiful one, like a snake shedding its skin' (p. 48). Like Cameron, whose 'sensual mouth' is highly evocative of the vampire's lips, Charlotte's 'pale face as white as the lighthouse' and 'wide lips' reveal ambivalent affiliations to the undead (pp. 48–9).

While the narrative undermines any secure sense of the real, all characters appear actively involved in the creation of their own fictitious worlds. Charlotte's handmade candles, for instance, bearing 'faces of strange monster-like creatures, sphinxes, goblins, centaurs', reveal her disturbing creativity and highlight the notion that, behind the facade of normality that Charlotte misleadingly represents, lurk the marvellous shapes of a simulated reality. Simon's animated puppets and dolls equally speak of the manipulative power Simon, as an archetypal magician, exercises in order to control reality. Similarly, when Lucia makes 'a small model of a ship, a galley ship' (p. 66) from scraps of wood, her artefact discloses the desire to negotiate reality through the fabrication of her own narrative. Significantly, the subconscious desire seems to surface at the end of the passage when she admits that 'it was her memory trying to get out [. . .] through her hands' (p. 66).

The stories each character fabricates are all, in a sense, self-reflective ghosted texts. Lucia's memoir is titled 'Book of False Memories', emphasising its explicitly unreliable content, deriving, as it does, from the reconstructed memory of an amnesiac mind. The notebook resembles Lucia's own self, seemingly identified with its 'blankness': the ripping of its sheets, a symbolic act of self-harming, is suggestive of the novel's complex approaches to the truth. The lighthouse's secrets are partially revealed by Charlotte's own confession, written because 'If I am not allowed to speak the words out loud I must put them down on paper' (p. 122). Finally, Cameron's own diary reveals the haunted status that pervades the island and affects all characters: 'We are all possessed on this island. Lucia by her forgotten history, Grace by the death of her mother, Charlotte by her secret knowledge, Simon by his animism and me by my God' (p. 135); towards the end of the narrative, Cameron's diary entries become the site of his inner faith crisis, the struggle between his Gnostic beliefs and African Voodoo, which eventually culminates in his mental breakdown. Before the ultimate failure of his rational faculties, Lucia *ghost-writes* his final thoughts, significantly derived from his reading of the *Book of Revelations*: 'All these words, they form part of the chains to this material world. Words are part of the world's huge unreality. There is only Logos: the divine word. All other words are trinkets' (p. 144). To Cameron, 'unreal' words are juxtaposed to divine wisdom (Logos): weighed down by its (corpo)reality and unable to integrate the transcendent to accommodate the divine, the symbolic is ultimately stripped of its signifying function.

Reviewers of *Pharos* have frequently noted that Thompson ties the loose ends of her intricate plot too swiftly.[79] The ending restores order to the chaotic world of Jacob's Rock and even hints at a happy ending for Grace and Simon, who adopts her; with Charlotte dead and Cameron locked up in a lunatic asylum, the real seems to be restored to a stable, structured order. The last passage in the novel, however, returns to Lucia, whose existence will continue on the island, endlessly wandering between real and 'imagined' visions: 'The ghostly spirit still did not know who she was or where she had come from. But she roamed the lighthouse now waiting for someone to claim her, to tell her who she was and why she was there' (p. 150).

Schizoid Projections of the Self: A. L. Kennedy's *So I Am Glad*

In the last decade of the twentieth century, the revenant of a seventeenth-century French writer returns to haunt a Glaswegian radio announcer: that in itself seemingly breaks the convention of the Scottish ghost story: by placing her revenant in the prosaic urban environment of the largest city in Scotland – instead of, for instance, an isolated, crumbling mansion house or a remote, fog-ridden island – Kennedy operates a self-conscious disruption of certain codes; 'a new kind of treatment of fantasy and supernatural', Gifford comments, 'accepts few or no limitations to its scope, and is no longer contained by traditional folk and Gothic rules'.[80] The setting does not simply function as a background to this modern-day ghost story, but occupies a prominent position in the narrative: as the narrative digresses from the main plot to make statements about the state of contemporary Scotland, spectrality assumes a global, rather than personal dimension, reflecting on the nation's simulacral culture.

Simultaneously, Kennedy draws attention to the psychological dimension of the Scottish ghost story, encouraging the notion that the revenant is not a 'real' ghost, but a figment of Jennifer's imagination; as Gifford notes, 'Kennedy keeps the reader guessing for long as to the legitimacy of Cyrano, in the tradition of ambivalence which is the hallmark of the Scottish novel from Hogg and Stevenson to Spark and Gray'.[81] The eminently psychological reading of the revenant motif reverberates the ambiguities of the Freudian uncanny, reflecting subconscious repressed anxieties in the unsettling coexistence of the unfamiliar (the apparition of the flame-oozing revenant of Cyrano) within the familiar world of the character's experience (late twentieth-century Glasgow). Throughout *So I Am Glad* the reader suspects that Cyrano is not an actual revenant as such, but a projection of Jennifer's own unconscious. This is made plausible both by the self-conscious confessional tone of the narrative, where the narrator ultimately admits to deliberately lying – 'Sometimes the best beginning is a lie' (Kennedy, *So I Am Glad*, p. 280)[82] – and by the reader's gradual understanding of Jennifer as a schizoid subject. Alienated from her body, her voice is, at the beginning of the story, literally 'toneless', whilst her inability to feel seemingly derives from the enforced voyeuristic experiences she suffered as a child: 'at the root of her heroine's emotional blankness', Punter explains, 'lies [. . .] the forced watching of parental sex' (p. 112). Though the narrative structure of the novel deliberately sets out to annihilate the chronological linearity of the story, it is *before* the appearance of Cyrano, or Savinien, as Jennifer intimately addresses the ghost of the French author, that Jennifer's sexuality shows signs of her psychological/bodily dissociation.

The opening passage from *So I Am Glad* indicates the psychological preoccupations the narrative unravels. Here the narrator discloses the existentialist problem that haunts her life: 'I don't understand things sometimes' (p. 1). The issue, the reader gathers in the following paragraphs, is deeply rooted in the narrator's bodily alienation. While she masturbates, Jennifer does indeed show a complete detachment from her own body: 'I am a partner, I am one half of a larger, insane thing that flails and twists and flops itself together in ways far too ridiculous for daylight' (p. 1). Such alienating tendencies become more manifest in her sexual relationships with other partners. Confronted with that of another, her body is incapable of feeling, falling into a nihilistic state to which she reacts with apathy, reflected, for instance, when she ironically recalls the loss of her virginity (p. 122). The post-traumatic behaviour manifestly displays the character's emotional distance as a defence mechanism to reinstate control over emotions; hence her mind/body alienation and power-lust, symptoms which emerge vividly highlighted in the sadomasochistic rituals she performs with her partner Steven, where she impersonates the dominatrix 'Captain Bligh', admittedly her 'alter-ego' (p. 123). In this game of sexual fantasies and repressed memories, Jennifer's body appears progressively detached from her mind, while, at the same time, searching for the missing bond by way of the physical/psychological harm she inflicts/suffers. The detachment from the body of her lover – 'I untied his mouth last. I didn't want to hear what he'd try and say' (p. 128) – confirms Jennifer's alienated state. As Christie L. March notes, the ritual is reminiscent of Jennifer's repressed traumas: 'The sight of Steven enjoying the pain she inflicts on his bound body enrages her because it relegates her to the role of voyeur much as her parents' sexual involvement required her to fulfil a similar function'.[83] At the same time, however, such an overt control manoeuvre over Steven's voice discloses clues to the main theme of this apparently disjointed plot: the disembodied voice is the haunting subtext of *So I Am Glad*.

Viewed from a psychoanalytical perspective, it seems fair then to imagine the existence of the ghost within the boundaries of Jennifer's wounded self, as she admits early on: 'Without thinking, I assumed that, in this point, Savinien and I were the same' (p. 102). The revenant, however, appears to keep a certain degree of autonomy, too, within the narrative, occupying a space and performing actions which do not seem to be dictated directly by Jennifer's unconscious. In this sense, their relationship articulates the ambiguous sameness/otherness bond which links Jekyll with Hyde and Wringhim with Gil-Martin, with whom Savinien also shares his false identity: Martin is the name of the new flatmate Savinien is believed to have replaced at the beginning of the story.

While self-consciously playing with the psychological quality of the Scottish alter ego, the novel's use of the ghost trope portrays ghostly alienation as a national state of being; thus, the city of Glasgow becomes the simulacral incarnation of the postmodern city, elusive, centreless and haunted by the spectres of its 'Streetpeople': 'Disinterested pedestrians have always glanced at them from time to time and known in their secret hearts that Streetpeople can never have been young, at school, indoors, in love' (p. 188). Like Jennifer, the city is disaffected, its inhabitants cocooned against their demons and, simultaneously, haunted by them. Throughout her confessional narrative, Scotland appears as an unknowable space, a place which mirrors Jennifer's disturbed past: 'I didn't understand my father or my mother. I didn't understand my country, its past, its present, its future, its means of government or the sense of its national anthem and flag' (p. 65). The collective psyche of Scotland, a nation possessed by the ghosts of its repressed traumas, is eminently affected by a profound, endemic guilt feeling: 'Guilt is of course not an emotion in the Celtic countries, it is simply a way of life – a kind of gleefully painful social anaesthetic' (p. 36). Scotland's is a numbed culture, Kennedy seems to suggest, disaffected and self-enclosed at the same time. Jennifer's attitude towards this diseased nation/world initially displays the signs of an apparent passive acceptance: 'I tried to keep myself separated from images of the news I had to broadcast' (p. 132). As a broadcaster, Jennifer mediates information, exposing the simulacral essence of the real and 'truth' of the globalised community she addresses. Although the story seemingly dismantles the notion of a coherent narrative, as the plot progresses, Jennifer's disaffected fabrication of lies fades away to make room for an increasingly involved critique of British politics:

> My government continues to smile upon the manufacture and export of manacles and anti-personnel – that is anti-people – explosive devices. My government continues to smile upon the manufacture and export of many further types of sophisticated armament to forces engaged in campaigns of systematic genocide. My government continues to smile upon the manufacture and export of ball squeezers, houses of electric fun and other instruments of torture not presently legal in my country.
> Sounds good doesn't it? (p. 219)

Jennifer's progressive understanding of the corrupt structures of global exploitation reveals the early symptoms of her recovery: unable to experience pain or pleasure, her personal statements about illegal torture practices suggest the awakening of her political self-awareness: the development of a 'tone' – 'An unnecessary colour in the voice, an air of negative comment' (p. 218) – points to such redemption. The self-conscious reference to the 'tone' has two functions here: on one hand, it draws attention to the novel's metafictional subtext; on the other, it signals the subversive role played by spectrality in the novel: by developing an inflection in her voice, Jennifer demonstrates her sudden acquisition of a conscience, the recuperation of her damaged self. Paradoxically, it is the ghost that comes to shake the hyperreal world by violating the norms of such simulated dimension, because this particular ghost can, unlike Jennifer, talk about pain: 'Today I know that pain is infectious, or to be more exact, contagious' (p. 174). It is the revenant that restores Jennifer's lost self and world: the ghost story therefore becomes the space in which loss is both mourned and celebrated.

In *So I Am Glad* the ghost articulates bodily discourses in relation to the character's sexuality and the corporeal nature of text. Wrapped in her own spectral armour (or simulacrum), it is paradoxically through the encounter with the revenant, Savinien, that Jennifer seemingly regains physical and emotional pleasure, experiencing what would appear a longed-for moment of self-recognition: 'I am, in myself, proof that there is something beyond matter. There is a soul. He was sure there was a soul. And here, he must have convinced me so much that I had to have one for myself' (p. 265). As Punter suggests, 'the passional delight he [Savinien] brings derives partly from his very inability to bring knowledge, and thus to exercise power, in the context of the petty present'.[84] Thus, though the ghost is the reminder of death and the absence of rational knowledge, in the simulacral context of Jennifer's existence, it becomes, paradoxically, the enlightening carrier of a life-assertive message. Before her encounter with the revenant, Jennifer's emotional numbness reflects the disengaged condition of the postmodern consciousness; in Dunnigan's words, 'This sense of herself as a *tabula rasa*, a blank sheet or canvas on which to be written, works with the text's underlying idea about the redemptive grace of love':[85] it is the love of a ghost, or perhaps the ghost of love, which heals Jennifer's emotional necrosis.

The ghost's simultaneous incarnation of death/desire performs a crucial function in the self-reflective structure of the novel. To Savinien, a French speaker, there is little difference, as he admits, between love and death, 'la mors' et 'l'amour' (p. 235). Such tensions point to the spectral nature of textuality, simultaneously present and absent before its addressee, as Dunnigan rightly notes of Jennifer's letter, never read by Savinien and yet laid 'bare upon the page for her voyeuristic readers or witnesses'.[86] Jennifer's story of emotional resurrection is also a story about the text, its birth, its death and its return in a revenant form:

'Writing is the attempt to find presence, to restore an absence or, in Jennifer's words, an emptiness'.[87] It is also a story she chooses – as she continually reminds us – to tell her implied audience. The frequent direct addresses to the reader – 'You should know that about me' (p. 4); 'Now I want to show you someone else' (p. 8); 'I'm trying to give you as much of the truth as I can and part of any truth will be the order in which it arrives' (p. 19); 'I HATE SECRETS. No, that's a lie, and here I was hoping to tell you the truth' (p. 22); 'AND NOW WE'LL leave me there for a while' (p. 68); 'So you have the full picture now. . .' (p. 102); 'DON'T WORRY. He comes back' (p. 110); 'You can have your own guess on the rest' (p. 120) – have a dual effect, because 'Jennifer's calculated quiescence', Dunnigan argues, 'is paradoxical; as a narrator she strikes an extraordinary intimacy with the reader of her "testament"'.[88] As McHale points out, the use of the pronoun 'you' articulates the text's metalepsis, 'the violation of ontological boundaries',[89] lowering the barrier between author and reader, a strategy through which the postmodernist narrator 'openly' seduces the reader into its creative workshop: 'If authors love their characters, and if texts seduce their readers, then these relations involve violations of ontological boundaries'.[90]

As a result of such demonic textual wooing, as well as being seduced into the text, the reader is also continually exposed to the artificiality of fiction: as Jennifer/Kennedy playfully reminds us: 'If you find what I tell you now rather difficult to believe, please treat it as fiction. I won't be offended' (p. 12). Thus the ghost story reveals its self-reflective essence, highlighting the spectral quality of desire in the economy of the text, which is parallel to Jennifer's own discovery of empathic love: 'The speaker and the listener, the writer and the reader, the man who bleeds and the man who makes him, they are the same thing. We are the same thing' (p. 78).

The text attempts to erase the formal barriers between narrator and reader. In a world where the authenticity of human relationships and emotions is on the verge of virtual extinction, a similar crisis may affect the ways in which we approach literature and the ways in which literature reaches its audience. In doing so, Kennedy's ghosted text draws attention to its fictional status, playfully undermining the foundations of writing and ultimately questioning the purpose of writing:

> In fact, if I was you, that whole *writing a book* thing might make me wonder just what kind of person I could be – spending so much of my time on this, to the exclusion of other, healthier and perhaps even outdoor pursuits. There's something a little bit wrong about doing such things. I should get a life. (p. 129)

The spectrality of writing, then, emerges in the metafictional passages interwoven within the plot of *So I Am Glad*, reflecting literature's 'simulacral qualities'.[91] But there is another narrative strategy which is particularly noticeable in *So I Am Glad* and which reinforces the function of spectrality within the structure of the novel. In *Spectres of Marx* Derrida emphasises the disruptive temporality associated with ghosts: the apparition of a spectre 'de-synchronizes', Derrida argues, 'It recalls us to anachrony'.[92] The anachronism of spectres produces the perfect metaphors to represent the non-linearity of postmodernist fiction. Temporal disruption is a prominent aspect of this self-reflective strategy in *So I Am Glad*. The narrative begins in the present tense: 'I don't understand things sometimes' (p. 1), creating the impression of an absurd coincidence in story/narrative time:[93] the narrative progresses parallel to the development of the story events. Flashbacks ensure that some of the gaps in the narrator's story are filled, but the story unravels as if occurring simultaneously as the narrating time. The loosening of linear time is, of course, a convention in non-realist fiction of any kind; as it unnaturally travels forward and backward in time, the appearance of the ghost cannot but beg for a 'suspension of disbelief' in fantasies of the Gothic kind. Here, however, the frequent anachronisms facilitated by seventeenth-century revenant of Cyrano serve the purpose of undermining, at the same time, the conventions upon which the narrative is told; as Buse and Stott observe:

> In the figure of the ghost, we see that past and present cannot be neatly separated from one another, as any idea of the present is always constituted through the difference and deferral of the past, as well as anticipations of the future.[94]

At the same time, the narrator alerts the reader to her deliberate manipulation of narrative time. In other words, the lack of timely coherence, in the form of accelerations and deferrals, are all self-consciously deployed to lay the narrative structure bare: 'This chapter will roll its way forward in other times and places and, when I feel ambulant, I will abandon my room and go roaming about downstairs' (p. 68). As none of the chapters of *So I Am Glad* are actually numbered and the narrative moves back and forth in time, the plot seemingly fluctuates in a perpetually *anachronic* state, a timeless dimension, culminating with Savinien's return journey to Sannois, the place of his historical death. Retracing Savinien's death ultimately offers Kennedy the opportunity to reflect upon the 'death drive' and 'mourning' which belongs to (her) text: 'And maybe that was it – maybe we were simply too slow and the end of our story caught us up' (p. 268); the ending sustains the metaleptic quality of the novel, drawing the reader in the narrator's final reflection upon her story, and revealing, once again, the manipulative strategies in place:

> You'll have read, I suppose, the opening of this book, about all of that calmness I no longer have. Sometimes the best beginning is a lie. But I hope you'll accept my apology for it now.

> What do I have instead of the calm. A voice. I remember everything of
> one man's voice, not a part of it fades. (p. 280)

Having found the voice she was missing at the beginning of her story, significantly, the last scene shows a dialogue between Jennifer and her flatmate
Arthur, who admits, 'It'll be odd, not having you *disappear* at all hours'(p.
280; my emphasis), implying that Jennifer has been, after all, the absent/
present ghost of this story. As the novel draws to its end, hauntingly, her voice
bids her revenant and her readers a nostalgic farewell: 'I will miss this and I
will miss Savinien and I will be glad' (p. 280).

UNCANNY VOIDS: ALI SMITH'S *HOTEL WORLD*

In Smith's second novel, *Hotel World*, spectrality unravels as a postmodern
reflection on the uncanny voids of the 'real': the ghost disintegrates the subject's unity, blurring the boundaries between the semiotic and the symbolic
and compromising, with its inherent anachrony, linear time. Within the self-
reflective discourse on the vacuums of spectrality, the haunted narratives of
Hotel World reflect also on the problematic representation of lesbian desire.

The novel opens as a ghost story told from the point of view of the ghost;
the spirit of Sara Wilby, accidentally killed at the hotel where she used to
work as a maid, hauntingly links the parallel stories of *Hotel World*. Sara's
journey into the void 'starts at the end'.[95] Looking back on her last day before
her death, which resulted from a fall down a lift shaft at the Global Hotel,
she recalls feeling *invisible*, after falling in love with the girl at the watch
shop: 'Falling for her had made me invisible' (p. 23). As with Janet in *O
Caledonia* and Jennifer in *So I Am Glad*, Sara's spectral status paradoxically
precedes death; the specific quality of her desire is what makes Sara 'invisible': 'The kiss that doesn't happen, the kiss that can't happen, because one of
the women has become a ghost (or else is directly haunted by ghosts)', Terry
Castle argues, is an important metaphor in lesbian writing.[96] While the lesbian's confinement to the spectral condition is the symptomatic manifestation
of (latent) textual homophobia, articulated through the 'unrepresentability'
of lesbian sex,[97] in *Hotel World* the trope subverts this censored portrayal of
the lesbian ghost-lover; ironically, it is only as a ghost that Sarah attempts
to establish contact with the girl she loves: 'I passed through her. I couldn't
resist it. I felt nothing. I hope it was the right shop. I hope it was the right
girl' (p. 29). Sara's demise is, therefore, a *petite mort*, the climactic end of
her corporeal life that coincides with the recognition of her spectral desire.
Such subversive use of the lesbian ghost endorses Castle's argument that
'Used imaginatively – repossessed, so to speak – the very trope that evapo-
rated can also solidify. In the strangest turn of all, perhaps, the lesbian body
itself returns'.[98] Though Sara 'disappears' when she falls in love, her ghostly

existence is embraced with the strong awareness of her sexuality, which she attempts to fulfil by haunting, and ultimately 'penetrating' the object of her desire.

In ontological terms Sara's pre-mortal spectral position is a cogent manifestation of the simulative veneer of 'reality' in *Hotel World*. The Global is the postmodernist re-visitation of the haunted castle: like the fortress, the hotel symbolises the legitimisation of established power; here the reference to the hotel's 'global' status signifies both its affiliation to the anonymous power of multinational conglomerates and, simultaneously, the allegorical stage of a postmodern Everyman's story, as the title of the novel suggests. The Global hotel mirrors thus Marc Augé's definition of the 'non-places' of globalised postmodernity: 'A world where people are born in the clinic and die in hospital, where transit points and temporary abodes are proliferating under luxurious or inhuman conditions'.[99] In *Hotel World* the postmodern urban/suburban space becomes, as in Martin Amis's *London Fields* (1989), a 'necropolis': Sara's body crashes against the foundations of the hotel, after speeding down the lift shaft: the dumb-waiter becomes a coffin. The hotel is a crypt.[100] That spectrality is a 'global' condition is also underpinned by the loose setting of the novel, recognisable as contemporary Britain, but vague enough to underpin the indeterminacy of postmodern ghosts, as conveyed by the last section of the novel, 'Present', in which a seemingly omniscient voice (Sara's spirit?) pans over the country, starting from the 'cold-bound Highlands' (p. 226), travelling 'Down the country and over the border' (p. 227) and dwelling, along the way, on various ghosts, including an unknown Mrs M. Reid and the late Princess of Wales:

> historic and royal ghost, ghost of a rose, ghost in a million stammering living rooms, ghost again today on the pages of this morning's Daily Mail, still selling its copies by breathing her back to a life that's slightly more dated each time [. . .]. (p. 228)

Millennial Scotland/Britain, the novel seems to suggest, embodies the quintessentially postmodern condition; superimposed images, here crucially defined by the replicas of the 'ghost' of Princess Diana on 'teatowels and cups and trays and coasters' (p. 228) replace actual death and bereavement, reiterating, instead, 'the familiar rhetoric of grief and mourning' of contemporary culture.[101]

Against the capitalist economy of simulacra, the novel engages with problematic notions of immateriality. After her sister's death, Clare is concerned with the invisible traces left of Sara's existence:

> There are the dents left in the carpet they prove it was there if you put your hand down and feel you can feel the dips where the feet of the bed

were and there was all dust down the back of it that he hoovered up they told us in Biology that a lot of dust is made of human skin so if that is true then some of Sara is in the hoover. (p. 191)

A kind of telepathic link bridges the sisters' monologues: on the other side, suspended in limbo between the world of the living and an afterlife dimension, and in the desperate effort to escape the emptiness of afterlife, Sara's trapped soul holds on to similar images of waste matter: 'Beautiful dirt, grey and vintage, the grime left by life, sticking to the bony roof of a mouth and tasting of next to nothing, which is always better than nothing' (p. 5). The ghost's fear of annihilation informs the problematic sense of corporeality throughout the text: 'That's quite funny, the idea of fucking a nobody', Else, the homeless woman, notes, 'just a space there where a body might be, and yourself flailing backwards and forwards against the thin air' (p. 35): the playful notion of sexual intercourse with 'nobody' underpins the shallow spectrality of postmodernity: though alive, like the Streetpeople in *So I Am Glad*, Else is invisible – 'people don't see [her], or decide not' (p. 39). Nothingness is the starting point of the story and shared discourse of the novel's parallel stories.

The progressive temporal disintegration that follows Sara's death thrusts the notion of emptiness into anachrony. While, a few weeks before her death, time runs slower on Sara's watch, her name is suggestive of the ghost's permanent anachrony: a repetition of the French '*sera*' and English 'will be', Sara Wilby belongs in the unknown future. Preoccupations with time vacuums concern all the characters in *Hotel World*, as stressed by the grammatical tenses in the chapter headings – 'Past', 'Present Historic', 'Future Conditional', 'Perfect', 'Future in the Past', 'Present'. For Lise, whose last shift at the Global coincides with Sara's, time no longer has relevance: 'How many minutes were there in an hour? That's something she used to know, like people just know things' (p. 81). Like Sara's, Lise's existence is no longer controlled by time, which is only 'real' when she can visualise it as a simulated image on a computer screen (p. 101). Time exists only as past in the spectral realm of Lise's memory, as she realises that:

> Time is notoriously deceptive. [. . .] Because time seems to move in more or less simple linear chronology, from one moment, second, minute, hour, day, week, etc. to the next, [. . .] [the] linear sequence which itself translates into easily recognizable significance, or meaning. (p. 103)

Dyschrony is endemic in *Hotel World*: reminiscent of Homer's Penelope as she attempts to deceive time, Penny, the journalist, also reveals she cannot wear watches, as their mechanisms do not work properly around her wrist (p. 146); as Sara's monologue concludes with a suggestive appeal – 'I am hanging falling breaking between this word and the next. Time me, would you?' (p. 31) – the posthumous re-enactment of her death performed by Clare in Sara's uniform reveals that the fatal fall beat the demon of Sara's swimming training:

> Listen Sara even though you couldn't even though you couldn't move couldn't do anything about it listen to me you were fast you were really fast you were really really fast I know because I went there to see tonight I was there & you were so fast I still can't believe how fast you were less than four seconds just under four & a bit that's all you took I know I counted for you. (pp. 220–1)

The paradoxical speed record beaten by Sara at the moment of her death emphasises the novel's obsessive relationship with time. There is an understated irony and poignancy in this. There is a tragic recognition of death as fact, but also an almost comic, darkly absurd quality to Clare's urgent address to Sara. Spectrality disrupts time, which no longer stands as a linear chain of events, but shifts to accommodate a divine coalescence of past, present and future: the anachrony that the revenant (and its ghosted text) inhabits. Against the liminal threshold of the recent *fin de siècle* – 'all anyone is talking about at school is the millennium' (p. 208) – the time capsules mentioned in 'Future in the Past' (p. 212) reinforce the tension between the unchangeable past and the unknown eternity lying ahead of Sara's spirit. The novel's anachrony is embedded in its disrupted chronological structure, as the apparently parallel stories converge through cross-references and anticipations reminiscent of Spark's narrative technique: all the characters are linked to Sara's death, their predicaments anticipated in Sara's monologue (p. 30); Lise appears in Else's and Clare's story ('Future in the Past'); both Clare and Else reappear in Penny's story ('Perfect'), while the girl from the watch shop, mentioned at the beginning by Sara, reappears in the final chapter (pp. 233–4): evocative of the text's pervasive death-drives, these repetitions simultaneously push the parallel narratives beyond the logic of linear progression.

Like time, the increasing loss of symbolic coherence runs throughout the stories of *Hotel World*. Such deconstructive discourses are intimately linked with the spectral body of the story, as becomes apparent in Smith's self-conscious defamiliarising strategies, when Sara crosses the threshold of afterlife. It is in the unfamiliar and anarchic space of afterlife that the foundations of a solid signified/signifier relationship collapse. Despite the ghost's desperate attempt to fix meanings and recuperate lost words – 'I want to ask her the name again for the things we see with. I want to ask her the name for heated-up bread' (p. 26) – the clumsy syntax of her sentences and the restless search for words may signify the death of language. The metafictional passage also suggests that her disembodied voice is all the ghost is made of: 'Now that I'm silent forever, haha, it's all words words words with me' (pp. 5–6). Though broken, language is all that remains: words are all that connect her to the world. In fact, words *are* her world. To be out of words is, literally, to be out of the world, as expressed by the intense suggestiveness in the last passage of her story, marking a desperate, poignant appeal to the reader:

> I will miss the, the. What's the word? Lost, I've, the word. The word for. You know. I don't mean a house. I don't mean a room. I mean the way of the   . Dead to the   . Out of this   . Word. (p. 30)

The ghost's loss of life is reflected in the slow, inexorable disintegration of her language, progressively reduced to small, disjointed fragments, as highlighted by the typographic distance between words; this is mirrored, later, in the unpunctuated syntax of Clare's telepathic monologue: following Sara's gradual loss of language is the 'global' linguistic crisis that affects all characters, each narrative representing a different aspect of the inadequacy of language: an example of this is Penny's argument that poor people are spoilt by money based on the spurious notion that 'it was no accident that the words poor and pure were so similar' (p. 178); both Penny's review of the Global chain (pp. 180–1) for *The World* paper and Deirdre's poem 'Hotel World' (p. 93) reveal a self-conscious interrogation of the reliability of language and authenticity of writing; and while Lise's breakdown means that she cannot remember words – 'Shelfily. Was that a real word?' (p. 83) – she struggles filling the blank space with her personal description: 'I am a ( ) person' (p. 85); to the most marginal of the novel's characters, Else, language is reduced to the decaying fragments of short-hand:

> She imagines the pavement littered with the letters that fall out of the half-words she uses (she doesn't need the whole words). She imagines explaining to the police, or to council road-sweepers, or to angry passers-by. I'll clear up after me, she tells them in her head. It's just letters. Anyway, they are biodegradable. They rot like leaves do. (p. 47)

Residues of words can 'rot' and disintegrate in an imaginary landfill. Else has mutilated her words, maybe because people have cut off her ability to communicate and trust. The letters she imagines scattered across the road are the broken form of the only language that remains.[102]

It would be reductive to read spectrality in *Hotel World* as a manifestation of irreversible nihilism. As with her subversive use of the ghost-metaphor to represent lesbian desire, Smith consciously deconstructs other conventional assumptions about spectrality, inverting, in doing so, conventional readings of time and language. A glance at the textual body of the novel illustrates in fact how the text brings to the fore, rather than the rational foundations of logic categories, the irrational uncertainties and illogical empty spaces of our existence. The paratext, defined by Genette as 'threshold' or 'vestibule' to the main text,[103] occupies a liminal space, and significantly it is here that Smith subverts her own discourse, suggesting that voids are, just like the margins of her novel, full. This is endorsed, for instance, by the epigraphic quotations: Charles Jencks's *The Architecture of the Jumping Universe* (1995) – 'the cosmos is much more dynamic than either a pre-designed world or a dead machine. . . each jump is a great mystery' – reads as a celebration of the universe's anarchic entropy and the irrational gaps between each known phase or part of it; likewise, Edwin Muir's poem 'The Child Dying' highlights Smith's concerns with mortality and eternity and introduces the main motif of the story, that is what lies beyond the limits of mortality. Ultimately, it is Spark's epigraph – 'Remember you must die' – that plays a crucial function at both thresholds of *Hotel World*: at the end of the novel, Spark's epigraph reappears, a transtextual revenant returned to haunt the text beyond its limits. That the apparent death of language opens it to the limitless scope of the imagination is underlined by the plagiarised postscript that refashions Spark's epigraph and inverts its semantic resonance:

> remember
> you
> must
> live
> remember
> you
> most
> love
> remainder
> you
> mist
> leaf

The replacement of 'die' with 'life' and 'love' – or even 'leaf' – signals a hope of life after death, albeit faint, like the decreasing typeface used in the postscript. Sara's spirit might survive, after all, the oblivion of death: the void is filled, as the text stretches beyond its conventional limit, with the ghost's 'woohoo' printed on a blank sheet after the main text's closure: her voice can still be heard. Equally, time is no longer constrained, but stretched endlessly into eternity as the story is openly suspended into afterlife. Smith deliberately disarranges the ontological order of things as a range of voids – (lesbian) desire, death, anachrony and semiotic disruption – subverts the hierarchical order of heteronormative desire, linear time and the symbolic order.

Words may have *literally* gone missing, but Smith's dissemination of blank spaces reflectively enhances the gaps produced by spectrality in *Hotel World*. In the end, the void becomes the focus of the story: its irrational mystery is laid bare in its limitless potential.

An integral component of the Scottish uncanny, in the postmodern context ghosts represent the deferred embodiment of the 'other': occupying the transitory afterlife dimension beyond the threshold of death, spectres epitomise the grey areas between presence and absence, pleasure and self-annihilation, reality and dream. As in *Hotel World*, *O Caledonia* and *Pharos* deploy the spectre motif to question the patriarchal structures that constrain the female bodies. The revenants of Janet, Lucia and Sara purport the alienated female body/mind dichotomy and, in *Hotel World*, the 'invisibility' of lesbian desire. Alienated desire is also central to *So I Am Glad*; here Jennifer's encounter with the ghost of Cyrano de Bergerac also forces a reflection on contemporary Scottish/British culture, and an eminently postmodern sense of the simulated real. Similar issues are raised by the ghosted narratives of *Hotel World*: here deconstructive stances on the real, language and time, are evocatively rendered through Smith's playful deconstruction of literary conventions.

NOTES

1. Margaret Oliphant, 'The Open Door', in Ian Murray (ed.), *The New Penguin Book of Scottish Short Stories* (Harmondsworth: Penguin, 1983), pp. 56–96 (p. 64).
2. Avery F. Gordon, *Ghostly Matters: Haunting and the Sociological Imagination* (Minneapolis and London: University of Minnesota Press, 1997), p. 63.
3. Ralph Noyes, The Other Side of Plato's Wall', in Peter Buse and Andrew Stott (eds), *Ghosts: Deconstruction, Psychoanalysis, History* (Basingstoke: Macmillan, 1999), pp. 244–62.
4. Paul Barber, *Vampires, Burial and Death: Folklore and Reality* (New Haven and London: Yale University Press, 1988), p. 3.
5. Nina Auerbach, *Our Vampires, Ourselves* (Chicago and London: University of Chicago Press, 1995), p. 5.
6. The undead feature as characters and spectral narrators in popular television programmes both sides of the millennial threshold. They include Joss Whedon's *Buffy the Vampire Slayer* (1997–2003), Alan Ball's *Six Feet Under* (2001–5) and *True Blood* (2008–10), Marc Cherry's *Desperate Housewives* (2004–), John Gray's *The Ghost-Whisperer* (2005–), Toby Whithouse's *Being Human* (2008–), and David Winning's *Blood Ties* (2007–). Besides the recent success of the Catherine Hardwickle's and Chris Weitz's *Twilight* films, based on the novels by Stephenie Meyer, recent films include Tobe Hooper's *Poltergeist* (1982), Jerry Zucker's *Ghost* (1990), Tim Burton's *Sleepy Hollow* (1999), M. Knight Shyamalan's *The Sixth Sense* (1999), Sam Mendes's *American Beauty* (1999), Alejandro Amenabar's *The Others* (2001), Pedro Almodovar's *Volver* (2006), Mark Steven Johnson's *Ghost-Rider* (2007).
7. Buse and Stott, *Ghosts*, p. 3.
8. Catherine Belsey, *Desire: Love Stories in Western Culture* (Oxford: Blackwell, 1994), p. 174.
9. Gordon, *Ghostly Matters*, p. 53.
10. See Ronald Hutton, *The Pagan Religions of the Ancient British Isles* (Oxford: Blackwell, 1991), p. 184. See also Anne Ross, *The Folklore of the Highlands* (London: Batsford, 1976), pp. 12–13.

11. For a further discussion on Celtic Britain and the evolution of folk tradition in Scotland see Ross, *Folklore of the Highlands*, and *Pagan Celtic Britain* (London: Routledge and Kegan Paul, 1967).
12. John Berger, *Keeping a Rendezvous* [1991] (New York: Vintage International, 1992), pp. 68–9.
13. The Ettrick Shepherd, 'The Shepherd's Calendar. Class IX. Fairies, Brownies and Witches', first published in *Blackwood's Edinburgh Magazine*, XXIII: CXXXV (1828), republished in James Hogg, *The Shepherd's Calendar* [1829], ed. Douglas S. Mack (Edinburgh: Edinburgh University Press, 1995), pp. 200–22 (p. 200). Further references to Hogg's tales from this edition are given after quotations in text.
14. Manlove, *Scottish Fantasy Literature*, p. 2.
15. George Mackay Brown, 'Andrina', in Douglas Dunn (ed.), *The Oxford Book of Scottish Short Stories* (Oxford: Oxford University Press, 1995), pp. 326–33 (p. 326).
16. Nicholas Royle, *The Uncanny* (Manchester: Manchester University Press, 2003), pp. 108–11.
17. Royle, *The Uncanny*, p. 12.
18. Royle, *The Uncanny*, p. 6.
19. See David Ratmoko, *On Spectrality: Fantasies of Redemption in the Western Canon* (New York: Peter Lang, 2006), p. 1.
20. See Elizabeth Ferguson Ellis, *The Contested Castle: Gothic Novels and the Subversion of Domestic Ideology* (Urbana and Chicago: University of Illinois Press, 1989), p. 220.
21. Ruth Parkin-Gounelas, 'Anachrony and Anatopia: Spectres of Marx, Derrida and Gothic Fiction', in Buse and Stott, *Ghosts*, pp. 127–43 (p. 131).
22. See Elizabeth Ferguson Ellis, *The Contested Castle*, and Norman N. Holland and Leona F. Sherman, 'Gothic Possibilities', *New Literary History: A Journal of Theory and Interpretation* 8: 2 (1977), pp. 279–94.
23. Jodey Castricano, *Cryptomimesis: The Gothic and Jacques Derrida's Ghost Writing* (Montreal: McGill University Press, 2001), p. 9.
24. Castricano, *Cryptomimesis*, p. 9.
25. Nicholas Royle discusses the notion of imprisonment and the significance of doors as reading effects encrypted in *Wuthering Heights*. See Nicholas Royle, *Telepathy and Literature: Essays on the Reading Mind* (Oxford: Blackwell, 1991), pp. 34–62.
26. See Emily Brontë, *Wuthering Heights* [1847] (New York: Norton, 1990), p. 20.
27. David Punter, *Gothic Pathologies: The Text, The Body and The Law* (Basingstoke: Macmillan, 1998), p. 17.
28. Jacques Derrida, *Specters of Marx: The State of the Debt, the Work of the Mourning, and the New International* [1993], trans. Peggy Kamuf (New York: Routledge, 1994), pp. 6–7.
29. Victor Sage and Allan Lloyd Smith (eds), *Modern Gothic: A Reader* (Manchester: Manchester University Press, 1996), p. 7.
30. Gilles Deleuze, *The Logic of Sense* [1969], trans. Mark Lester, ed. Constantin V. Boundas (London: Continuum, 2004).
31. Baudrillard, *Simulacra and Simulation*, p. 1.
32. Baudrillard, *Simulacra and Simulation*, p. 3.
33. Walter Scott, *Letters on Demonology and Witchcraft* [1829–47] (London: Folklore Society, 2001), p. 11.
34. Sigmund Freud, *Totem and Taboo* [1913], *SE*, vol. 13, p. 61.
35. Nicholas Abraham, 'Notes on the Phantom: A Complement to Freud's Metapsychology' [1975], in Nicholas Abraham and Maria Torok, *The Shell and*

the Kernel: Renewals of Psychoanalysis, ed. and trans. Nicholas T. Rand, 2 vols (Chicago: University of Chicago Press, 1994), vol. 1, pp. 171–6 (p. 171).

36. See Lucie Armitt, Contemporary Women's Fiction and the Fantastic (Basingstoke: Macmillan, 2000), p. 102.

37. For an extensive discussion of the revenant motif in James Hogg's fiction, see also Monica Germanà, 'The Ghost and the Brownie: Scottish Influences on Emily Brontë', Women's Writing, Special Issue: Revisiting the Brontës, 14:1 (May 2007), pp. 91–116.

38. Belsey, Desire, p. 177.

39. Freud, 'Beyond the Pleasure Principle' [1920], SE, vol. 18, pp. 7–64 (p. 36).

40. Freud, 'Beyond the Pleasure Principle', p. 63.

41. Belsey, Desire, p. 57.

42. Jacques Lacan, Écrits: A Selection, trans. Alan Sheridan (London: Tavistock Publications, 1977), p. 265.

43. Belsey, Desire, p. 60.

44. Punter, Gothic Pathologies, p. 2.

45. Elisabeth Bronfen, Over Her Dead Body: Death, Femininity and the Aesthetic (Manchester: Manchester University Press, 1992), p. 349.

46. Buse and Stott, Ghosts, p. 8.

47. See Carol Anderson, 'Emma Tennant, Elspeth Barker, Alice Thompson: Gothic Revisited', in Aileen Christianson and Alison Lumsden (eds), Contemporary Scottish Women Writers (Edinburgh: Edinburgh University Press, 2000), pp. 117–30 (p. 125).

48. Julian Wolfreys, Victorian Hauntings: Spectrality, Gothic, the Uncanny and Literature (Basingstoke: Palgrave, 2002), p. xiii.

49. Derrida, Specters of Marx, p. xviii.

50. Buse and Stott, Ghosts, pp. 10–11.

51. See Hélène Cixous, 'Fiction and its Phantoms: A Reading of Freud's Das Unheimliche ('The Uncanny'), New Literary History 7 (1976), pp. 525–48 (p. 543).

52. Cixous, 'Fiction and its Phantoms', p. 548.

53. Andre Green, 'The Double and the Absent', in Alan Roland (ed.), Psychoanalysis, Creativity and Literature: A French-American Inquiry (New York: Columbia University Press, 1978), pp. 271–92 (p. 283).

54. Belsey, Desire, p. 19.

55. See McHale, Postmodernist Fiction, pp. 222–4.

56. Elspeth Barker, O Caledonia (Harmondsworth: Penguin, 1991), p. 61. Further references to this edition are given after quotations in the text.

57. Anderson, 'Emma Tennant, Elspeth Barker, Alice Thompson: Gothic Revisited', p. 125.

58. Douglas Gifford, 'Contemporary Fiction I: Tradition and Continuity', in Douglas Gifford and Dorothy McMillan (eds), A History of Scottish Women's Writing (Edinburgh: Edinburgh University Press, 1997), pp. 579–603 (p. 586).

59. Dorothy McMillan, 'Constructed out of Bewilderment: Stories of Scotland', in Ian A. Bell (ed.), Peripheral Visions: Images of Nationhood in Contemporary British Fiction (Cardiff: University of Wales Press, 1995), pp. 80–99 (p. 93); Elisabeth Bronfen, Over Her Dead Body: Death, Femininity and the Aesthetic (Manchester: Manchester University Press, 1992).

60. McMillan 'Constructed out of Bewilderment', p. 94.

61. Bronfen, Over Her Dead Body, p. 352.

62. Punter, Gothic Pathologies, p. 6.

63. McMillan, 'Constructed out of Bewilderment', p. 94.

64. See Anderson, 'Emma Tennant, Elspeth Barker, Alice Thompson: Gothic Revisited', p. 126.
65. See Anderson, 'Emma Tennant, Elspeth Barker, Alice Thompson: Gothic Revisited', p. 127.
66. Isobel Montgomery, '*Pharos*', *The Guardian*, Review Section, 21 December 2002, p. 30.
67. Roz Kaveney, 'Alice Thompson, *Pharos*', *Times Literary Supplement*, 2 August 2002, p. 20.
68. See Louise Rimmer, 'To the Lighthouse', *Scotland on Sunday*, Review, 9 June 2002, p. 4.
69. David Robinson, 'Through a Glass Darkly', *The Scotsman*, 8 June 2002, p. 6.
70. Walter Scott, *The Voyage of the Pharos* [1814] (Edinburgh: Scottish Library Association, 1998), p. 3.
71. Scott, *The Voyage of the Pharos*, p. 4.
72. Alice Thompson, *Pharos: A Ghost Story* (London: Virago, 2002), p. 5. Further references to this edition are given after quotations in the main text.
73. See Ellis, *The Contested Castle*, p. ix.
74. Norman N. Holland and Leona F. Sherman, 'Gothic Possibilities', *New Literary History: A Journal of Theory and Interpretation* 8: 2 (1977), pp. 279–94 (p. 286).
75. Castricano, *Cryptomimesis*, p. 9. See also Nicholas Abraham and Maria Torok, *The Wolf Man's Magic Word: A Cryptonymy*, trans. Nicholas Rand (Minneapolis: University of Minnesota Press, 1986), p. xxxvi.
76. See Baudrillard, *Simulacra and Simulation*, pp. 1–6.
77. Laurence Wareing, 'Magical Mystery Tour Wanders Into a Dream-Like Allegory', *The Glasgow Herald*, Weekend Living, 15 June 2002, p. 13.
78. See Rimmer, 'To the Lighthouse'.
79. See Montgomery, '*Pharos*' and Wareing, 'Magical Mystery Tour'.
80. Gifford, 'Contemporary Fiction II: Seven Writers in Scotland', in Gifford and MacMillan (eds), *A History of Scottish Women's Writing*, pp. 604–29 (p. 620).
81. Gifford, 'Contemporary Fiction II', p. 620.
82. A. L. Kennedy, *So I Am Glad* (London: Jonathan Cape, 1995), p. 280. Further references to this edition are given after quotations in the main text.
83. Christie L. March, *Rewriting Scotland: Welsh, McLean, Warner, Banks, Galloway and Kennedy* (Manchester: Manchester University Press, 2002), p. 148.
84. David Punter, 'Heart Lands: Contemporary Scottish Gothic', *Gothic Studies* 1: 1 (1999), pp. 101–18 (p. 105).
85. Sarah M. Dunnigan, 'A. L. Kennedy's Longer Fiction: Articulate Grace', in Aileen Christianson and Alison Lumsden (eds), *Contemporary Scottish Women Writers*, pp. 144–55 (p. 147).
86. Dunnigan, 'A. L. Kennedy's Longer Fiction', p. 148.
87. Dunnigan, 'A. L. Kennedy's Longer Fiction', p. 148.
88. Dunnigan, 'A. L. Kennedy's Longer Fiction', p. 146.
89. McHale, *Postmodernist Fiction*, p. 226.
90. McHale, *Postmodernist Fiction*, p. 222.
91. Buse and Stott, *Ghosts*, p. 8.
92. Derrida, *Specters of Marx*, pp. 6–7.
93. '[. . .] a kind of zero degree that would be a condition of perfect temporal correspondence between time and story': see Gérard Genette, *Narrative Discourse*, trans. Jane E. Lewin (Oxford: Blackwell, 1980), pp. 35–6.
94. Buse and Stott, *Ghosts*, pp. 10–11.

95. Ali Smith, *Hotel World* (London: Penguin, 2001), p. 3. Further references to this edition are given after quotations in the text.
96. Terry Castle, *The Apparitional Lesbian: Female Homosexuality and Modern Culture* (New York: Columbia University Press, 1993), p. 30.
97. Castle, *The Apparitional Lesbian*, p. 60.
98. Castle, *The Apparitional Lesbian*, pp. 46–7.
99. Marc Augé, *Non-Places: Introduction to an Anthropology of Supermodernity* [1992], trans. John Howe (London: Verso, 1995), p. 77.
100. Paulina Palmer has argued that 'the Global Hotel signifies both haunted house and crypt. The hotel is haunted by Sara's ghost. It enshrines, despite the manager's attempts to conceal it, the narrow cavity of the lift shaft, where Sara died, that signifies her grave. It represents both tomb and womb since it was here that she was spiritually reborn in order to make the crossing from the material world to the spectral'; Paulina Palmer 'Demonic and Spectral Doubles in Ellen Galford's *The Dyke and the Dybbuck*, Sarah Waters' *Affinity* and Ali Smith's *Hotel World*', unpublished conference paper, presented at Lesbian Lives XI Conference, University College Dublin, Ireland, 13–15 February 2004.
101. Alexandra Warwick, 'Feeling Gothicky?', *Gothic Studies* 9: 1 (2007), pp. 5–15 (p. 11).
102. See Germanà, unpublished interview with Ali Smith, in 'Re-working the Magic', pp. 367–73.
103. Genette, *Paratexts*, p. 2.

Chapter 6

THE DEATH OF THE OTHER?

What happens to the marginal 'other' when the boundaries that separate it from the hegemonic centre dissolve? Can the subversion of established hierarchies cause the death of the 'other'? This book began with an introduction to the three contexts of otherness (nation, gender, genre) that concern its scope. The discussion of the four thematic areas (quests and other worlds, witches, doubles and ghosts) in the light of their roots in the Scottish cultural canon has also led to the interrogation of the binary oppositions that underpin categorical readings of identity and ontology. As the examined texts have exposed, in different ways, the fragility of rigid parameters of thinking, the question that remains unanswered is whether it makes sense, in the so-called post-feminist, globalised, hyperreal age that, following postmodernism, still remains nameless, to engage with nation, gender and genre as valid critical paradigms.

The current political climate, dominated by a shift to the right in politics across Europe, and haunted by the spectres of globalised terrorism and xenophobia, foresees the disturbing return to nationalist conservativism. What repercussions this may have on the smaller nations is perhaps difficult to predict. Discussing the Scottish literary production up to the achievement of political devolution, in 1996 Richard Todd suggested that 'when the Union finally disintegrates [. . .], this problem of self-definition will be the most pressing facing Scottish nationalism'.[1] Rather than sheer optimism, post-devolution writing by Irvine Welsh, James Kelman and Alan Warner seems to suggest that little has changed with the advent of devolution, but for a more intense interrogation of national culture 'exposing the false mythology of Scotland as a single comprehensible entity',[2] as Richard Bradford notes of Warner's *The Sopranos* (1998). Bradford questions the Scottish identification of works by Michel Faber (*Under the Skin*, 2000) and even Kennedy and Smith, (erroneously) suggesting that 'Scotland [. . .] is completely absent from *Hotel World* (2001) and *The Accidental* (2005)', and the belonging of these authors in a 'tradition of writing where nationality is as much the animus as the framework of the text', epitomised, according to Bradford, by the works of Gray, Kelman and Welsh.[3] As Elphinstone proposes, however, 'a book by a Scottish writer does not have to be about Scotland':[4] the question at stake would seem to make national identity a reductive discourse: must Scottish writing *always* focus on national identity? By the same currency, then, one could dispute that *Hamlet* is an English play, as its setting is not obviously English. Or is this argument only viable for the cultures on the margins, whose claims to autonomy and legitimacy must inform their entire output? 'Scottish novels by Scottish novelists for Scottish readers about Scottish stuff is a kind of abyss':[5] the insularity of this position takes the (self-constructed) notion of national distinctiveness to a critical dead-end; moreover, from the point of view of the marginal culture, one of the risks implicit in this type of discourse is, as Michael Gardiner has provocatively put it, the over-reliance on self-fabricated, essentialist notions of national identity: 'the idea that Scots have always been the same people is an ethnocentric nonsense used to sell shortbread'.[6] Bradford concludes his overview of contemporary Scottish fiction, however, admitting that:

> The most conspicuous, pervasive feature of the Scottish renaissance [. . .] is a tendency to present Scotland and Scottishness in terms of their dynamic relationship with the Anglocentric behemoth that some would argue has variously inhibited, obscured and dominated Scottish culture for three centuries.[7]

The literature produced in Scotland over the last ten years appears, on one hand, to be concerned with the self-conscious creation of a specific kind of Scottish (working-class, white, male) identity (Gray, Kelman, Welsh), and, on the other, to interrogate the authenticity of monolithic, homogeneous parameters of modern identity that often exceeds the territorial boundaries of a nation: 'as the hybridity of nations becomes more complex and more explicitly recognized', Dominic Head argues, 'new kinds of narration may become necessary, capable of linking different perceptions of belonging – different territories, even – by means of mongrelized narrative forms'.[8] Contemporary Scottish literature is exploring various routes between the local Gothic mode, seen in the return to spectral motif in Thompson's most recent novel, *The Falconer* (2008), and Ali Smith's first published play, *The Seer* (2007), and wider explorations of the alienating effects of contemporary culture: works such as Welsh's *The Bedroom Secrets of the Master Chefs* (2006) and Kennedy's short-story collection *What Becomes* (2009) may have moved away from specific, localised questions of national identity, but still point to the broken selves and dark secrets of alienated psyches within a wider, global context.

Whilst advocating a literary future in the name of hybrid national identities, commenting on the references to the death of Princess Diana in Sheena Mackay's 'post-feminist' *The Artist's Widow* (1998), Head posits that androgynous models of gender emerge in contemporary readings of feminine subjectivity:

> What is required is an explanation of the collective empathy, a realization that the 'contradictions of gender' have been generally internalized, producing something that approaches an androgynous populace, with individuals hailing each other in a fleeting moment of recognition.[9]

Sexual ambivalence has been the prominent subject of much fiction from the late twentieth century, including, among others, Angela Carter's *Passion of New Eve* (1977) and, in the Scottish context, Iain Banks's *The Wasp Factory* (1984) and, more recently, Jackie Kay's *Trumpet* (1998) and Ali Smith's rewriting of Ovid's *Metamorphoses, Girl Meets Boy* (2007). What these texts, in different ways, expose is the lingering interest in the slippage between biological sex and an individual's gender identity, which encompasses the adherence/resistance to the complex cultural and social norms of patriarchal heteronormativity as well as one's sexuality and sexual habits. If the consensus is that foundations of sex/gender resist definition, the question that remains is what parameters, if any, should be used to discuss the elusive category of women's writing. Should this area of studies, which arguably still marginalises writing by women from the 'mainstream' literature of men, be made redundant to accommodate a more integrated approach to literary and gender studies?

This would, perhaps, be the desired solution, in a utopian world that does not respond to difference with diffidence and discrimination. While fiction still interrogates the ways in which we read, perform and censor gender, contemporary culture appears less inclined to do so. The progressive gendering of children's clothing and toys, for instance, speaks of certain radicalised views of conservative gender roles, whereby little girls are fashioned to be 'princesses' or 'angels', and boys are invited to identify with builders or professional fighters of all kinds.[10] What seems to have changed, perhaps, since the second-wave feminism of the 1960s and 1970s is the attitude of women towards the politics of gender: flattered by the economy that praises her for her looks, a young, educated, middle-class woman grows reluctant to engage with feminist discourse, preferring to advocate, instead, notions of femininity to recuperate the lost 'balance' between the sexes, for which she feels earlier generations of women have been responsible. What she does not realise, however, is that, although much has been achieved, prejudice and marginalisation still exist in the Western world, as in developing countries. As Rachel Cusk put it, commenting on the sixtieth anniversary of the publication of Beauvoir's *The Second Sex*, 'Hers is still the second sex, but she has earned the right to dissociate herself from it'.[11]

Having said that, that the works of contemporary Scottish women writers including Louise Welsh, Denise Mina and the later work of Kennedy may not overtly disclose a gender subtext, one could argue, may be the signal of a coming of age, the result of a newly acquired confidence that the work of Scottish female writing does not need justifying in terms of either national or gender identity. And while critics may feel that contemporary women's writing looks at questions of feminine subjectivity 'with a mixture of circumspection, disinterestedness and [. . .] deference',[12] contemporary feminist thought is still aware of the difficulties it faces: 'Until the last trace of oppression is removed', Catherine Belsey writes, 'we cannot afford relaxation and passivity';[13] a more decisive return to strong feminist politics is foreshadowed in new theoretical work such as Natasha Walter's forthcoming *Living Dolls: The Return of Sexism* (2010).

If gender appears to be still a contentious issue, the twenty-first century also reveals a problematic relationship with the real. After a slow start, James Cameron's mega-budget new film *Avatar* (2009) is a blockbuster, following a trend that has seen the adaptations of *The Lord of the Rings* trilogy (2001, 2002, 2003) and *Harry Potter* films (2001–) topping the profit charts of the noughties.[14] In response to the late twentieth-century strong fascination for vampires, ghosts, and (dark) magic, indicated by the best-selling works of J. K. Rowling, Dan Brown and Philip Pullman, fantasies of the Gothic kind have underpinned millennial anxieties, economic recession-led escapism and the consumerist lust for new taboos that characterises the current economic and cultural age: 'We all need a bit of magic in our lives', writes Jeanette Winterson, adding 'that's why adults took to Harry Potter'.[15] The popularity of the novels and film adaptations, which to various degrees have diluted the subversive supernatural darkness inherent in Gothic fantasy, has defined the cultural tastes of the early twenty-first century; the relentless repetition of stock motifs such as the 'journey to the north, realm of occult knowledge and dark forces', Scottish or otherwise, as featured in the *Harry Potter* series and *The Da Vinci Code*,[16] may be the symptom of millennial preoccupations with the world beyond, though these exceed the 'apocalyptic' anxieties which, cyclically, return to haunt epochal endings; as Catherine Spooner rightly notes, 'Gothic has now [. . .] become supremely commercialized, be it mainstream or niche-marketed'.[17] The Gothic revival Spooner refers to, however, has also signalled what Botting had already identified as the 'death' of the genre in relation to the romanticised adaptation of Francis Ford Coppola's *Dracula* (1992).[18] The 'vegetarian' vampires of Stephenie Meyer's *Twilight* (2005) are the most recent product of the commodification of what Botting defines as 'Candy Gothic', and the renewed enactment of the social conservativism of older Gothic texts:[19] rather than eroding the foundations of repressive regimes and social structures, these narratives draw attention to the horror implicit in transgression to provoke temporary pleasure and ultimately resume the status quo.

It cannot be denied that the end of the twentieth century and the first decade of the twenty-first century have signalled an ambivalent approach to the real. If television is anything to go by as an indicator of popular trends, the advent of reality TV shows, launched with the first UK edition of Big Brother in 2000, followed by endless variations of virtual prisons with or without the participation of celebrities, exposes the crucial role of voyeurism in the confounding of real with fantasy worlds; in a similar way, the addictive proliferation of videogames and widespread social networking sites such as Facebook and Twitter, and the compulsive behaviour they induce, reveal the mediation paradox of contemporary culture: your success is measured against the ability to lead your character to the positive completion of their virtual quest; the quality of your life must be endorsed by pictures and status updates; you take part in an experience only if you can somehow relate it to the community of voyeuristic friends who take pleasure in seeing what you are up to on their screens. The paradox of these self-authenticating tools is that they in fact dislocate the authenticity of the real experience: the statement 'M is writing her book' is a lie, because at the time of its enunciation, M is in fact deferring the real aim in favour of the virtual. The blurring of the real/fictional boundaries is simultaneously highlighted and concealed with the complicity of authors/performers and readers/spectators of the virtual community. The central position occupied by cultural products (TV programmes, websites, videogames) that, in one way or another, deal with fantasy worlds may have a 'dissolving' effect on the subversive function of fantasy: ceasing to be 'other', fantasy has in fact replaced the real. Alexandra Warwick reaches similar conclusions in relation to contemporary Gothic: 'Normality is Gothic and Gothic is normal',[20] in the 'rhetoric of grief and mourning' of a culture that revolves around 'the desire *for* trauma'.[21] Yet what the lucrative consumption of (Gothic) fantasies, virtual realities and avatars suggests is the constant deferral of desire, on one hand, and the dislocation of repressed anxieties, on the other.

To go back to a Scottish example, one could argue that Hyde performs exactly this dual function: on one level, it displaces the realisation of Jekyll's desire, on the other, it diffuses the taboo of (his) transgression, pointing to a pervasive notion of corruption. The most recent British TV adaptation of Stevenson's story, *Jekyll* (BBC 2007), moves the discourse of self and desire into a contemporary, global dimension. When the 'good' Jackman is haunted by the unwanted visits of Hyde, his stronger, smarter, and better-looking alter ego, he attempts to control his double through technology that records, surveys and mediates between the two sides of his psyche. Behind Jackman/Hyde's personal lives is the Utterson and Klein Medical Research company, an international corporation that has been after the 'perfect' genetic match of Jackman's body to the original Hyde since the death of the 'historical' Dr Jekyll, who, in this version, lives in Edinburgh rather than London; in this contemporary story of unknown origins and scientific hubris, the boundaries between human and inhuman are broken down through the erasure of the distinctions between original and clone, nature and technology, real and simulated; the safety of home, and, significantly, family history are also thrown into question: leading the conspiracy that wants his death, is, in fact, Jackman's estranged mother. Far from stylising woman as bad (m)other, the twenty-first-century Jekyll/ Hyde dichotomy exposes a range of unstable sexualities and complex gender roles: Miranda, the lesbian detective who helps solve the conspiracy, and Claire, Jackman's wife, are powerful examples of the complex range of women characters that subvert the all-male narrative of Stevenson's text.

If *Jekyll* registers a legitimate account of wider contemporary social and cultural questions, it also deliberately returns to the Scottish roots of the story, to subvert them. In this sense, the future of Scottish Gothic fantasy is likely to reflect the paradoxical concern of the contemporary Scottish psyche: to embrace an international level of recognition and to preserve a distinctive edge against the threat of global cultural dilution. In the current political climate of (hyperreal) terror and growing intolerance towards the other and re-entrenchment of gender categories, the main currency of cultural discourse is not likely to steer away from the perpetually deferred and dislocated fears and desires of Gothic fantasies.

NOTES

1. Richard Todd, *Consuming Fictions: The Booker Prize and Fiction in Britain Today* (London: Bloomsbury, 1996), p. 163.
2. Richard Bradford, *The Novel Now: Contemporary British Fiction* (Oxford: Blackwell, 2007), p. 169.
3. Bradford, *The Novel Now*, p. 172.
4. Germanà, 'Re-working the Magic', p. 324.
5. Stuart Kelly, 'Wha's Like Us?', *The Guardian*, Review Section, 17 May 2008, p. 3.
6. Michael Gardiner, *From Trocchi To Transpotting: Scottish Critical Theory Since 1960* (Edinburgh: Edinburgh University Press, 2006), p. 179.
7. Bradford, *The Novel Now*, p. 176.
8. Dominic Head, *The Cambridge Introduction to Modern British Fiction, 1950–2000* (Cambridge: Cambridge University Press, 2002), p. 155.
9. Head, *The Cambridge Introduction to Modern British Fiction*, p. 113.
10. See John Henley, 'The Power of Pink', *The Guardian*, 12 December 2009. Available at: http://www.guardian.co.uk/theguardian/2009/dec/12/pinkstinks-the-power-of-pink (accessed 14 December 2009).

11. Rachel Cusk, 'Shakespeare's Daughters', *The Guardian*, Review Section, 12 December 2009. Available at: http://www.guardian.co.uk/books/2009/dec/12/rachel-cusk-women-writing-review (accessed 14 December 2009).
12. Bradford, *The Novel Now*, p. 140.
13. Catherine Belsey, 'Writing as a Feminist', *Signs* 25: 4 (Summer 2000), pp. 1157–60 (p. 1157).
14. See Katie Allen, 'Coming to a Cinema Near You – The £1bn Blockbuster Tale of a Booming Business', *The Guardian*, 12 December 2009, p. 41.
15. Jeanette Winterson, 'Author Author', *The Guardian*, Review Section, 19 December 2009, p. 15.
16. John Dugdale, 'Vampires, Blockbusters and the Occasional Gem', *The Guardian*, Review Section, 2 January 2010, pp. 14–15 (p. 15).
17. Catherine Spooner, *Contemporary Gothic* (London: Reaktion, 2006), p. 23.
18. Fred Botting, *Gothic* [1996] (London and New York: Routledge, 2004), p. 180.
19. Fred Botting, 'CandyGothic', in Fred Botting (ed.), *The Gothic* (Cambridge: D. S. Brewer, 2001), pp. 133–52 (pp. 134, 136).
20. Alexandra Warwick, 'Feeling Gothicky?', *Gothic Studies* 9: 1 (2007), pp. 5–15 (p. 14).
21. Warwick, 'Feeling Gothicky?', p. 11.

APPENDIX: GENEALOGIES IN SIAN HAYTON'S TRILOGY

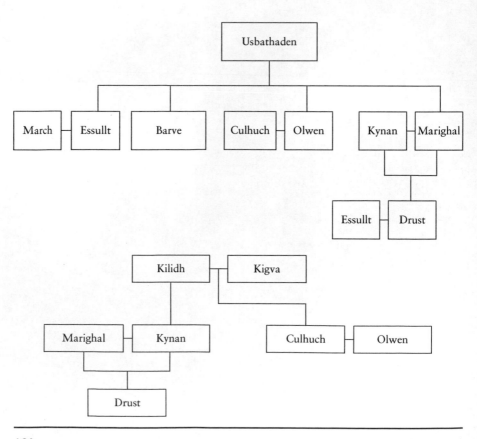

BIBLIOGRAPHY

PRIMARY TEXTS

Atkinson, Kate, *Behind the Scenes at the Museum* (London: Black Swan, 1995).

Barker, Elspeth, *O Caledonia* (Harmondsworth: Penguin, 1991).

Elphinstone, Margaret, *The Incomer* (London: Women's Press, 1987).

Elphinstone, Margaret, *A Sparrow's Flight: A novel of a future* (Edinburgh: Polygon, 1989).

Elphinstone, Margaret, *The Sea Road* (Edinburgh: Canongate, 2000).

Fell, Alison, *The Bad Box* (London: Virago, 1987).

Fell, Alison, *The Mistress of Lilliput* (London: Doubleday, 1999).

Galford, Ellen, *Queendom Come* (London: Virago, 1990).

Galford, Ellen, *The Fires of Bride* [1986] (London: Women's Press, 1994).

Hayton, Sian, *Cells of Knowledge* (Edinburgh: Polygon, 1989).

Hayton, Sian, *Hidden Daughters* (Edinburgh: Polygon, 1992).

Hayton, Sian, *The Governors* (Nairn: Balnain Books, 1992).

Hayton, Sian, *The Last Flight* (Edinburgh: Polygon, 1993).

Kennedy, A. L., *So I Am Glad* (London: Jonathan Cape, 1995).

Smith, Ali, *Hotel World* (London: Penguin, 2001).

Smith, Ali, *The Accidental* (London: Hamish Hamilton, 2005).

Spark, Muriel, *The Ballad of Peckham Rye* (Harmondsworth: Penguin, 1963).

Spark, Muriel, *The Prime of Miss Jean Brodie* [1961] (London: Penguin, 2000).

Spark, Muriel, *Symposium* [1990] (London: Virago, 2006).

Tennant, Emma, *The Bad Sister* [1978], in *The Bad Sister: An Emma Tennant Omnibus* (Edinburgh: Canongate, 2000).

Tennant, Emma, *Wild Nights* [1979], in *The Bad Sister: An Emma Tennant Omnibus* (Edinburgh: Canongate, 2000).

Tennant, Emma, *Two Women of London: The Strange Case of Ms Jekyll and Mrs Hyde* [1989], in *The Bad Sister: An Emma Tennant Omnibus* (Edinburgh: Canongate, 2000).

Thompson, Alice, *Justine* (Edinburgh: Canongate, 1996).

Thompson, Alice, *Pandora's Box* (London: Little Brown and Company, 1998).

Thompson, Alice, *Pharos* (London: Virago, 2002).

REFERENCE, CRITICISM, THEORY AND OTHER WORKS

Anon., 'Some stories about witches', *Celtic Magazine* XIII (December 1887), pp. 92–4.

Aarne, Antti, *The Types of the Folktale: A Classification and Bibliography*, trans. Stith Thompson (Helsinki: Academia Scientiarium Fennica, 1964).

Abel, Elizabeth (ed.), *Writing and Sexual Difference* (Brighton: Harvester Press, 1982).

Abraham, Nicholas and Maria Torok, *The Wolf Man's Magic Word: A Cryptonymy*, trans. Nicholas Rand (Minneapolis: University of Minnesota Press, 1986).

Abraham, Nicholas and Maria Torok, *The Shell and the Kernel: Renewals of Psychoanalysis*, ed. and trans. Nicholas T. Rand, 2 vols (Chicago: University of Chicago Press, 1994).

Acton, William, *The Functions and Disorders of the Reproductive Organs* [1857] (Philadelphia: Lindsay and Blakiston, 1867).

Aitken, Hannah, *A Forgotten Heritage: Original Folk tales of Lowland Scotland* (Edinburgh: Scottish Academic Press, 1973).

Alexander, Flora, 'Contemporary Fiction III: The Anglo-Scots', in Douglas Gifford and Dorothy McMillan (eds), *A History of Scottish Women's Writing* (Edinburgh: Edinburgh University Press, 1997), pp. 630–40.

Allan, Graham, *Intertextuality* (London and New York: Routledge, 2000).

Allen, Katie, 'Coming to a Cinema Near You – the £1bn Blockbuster Tale of a Booming Business', *The Guardian*, 12 December 2009, p. 41.

Anderson, Benedict, *Imagined Communities: Reflections on the Origin and Spread of Nationalism* [1983] (London: Verso: 1991).

Anderson, Carol, 'Listening to the Women Talk', in Gavin Wallace and Randall Stevenson (eds), *The Scottish Novel Since The Seventies* (Edinburgh: Edinburgh University Press, 1993), pp. 170–86.

Anderson, Carol, 'Emma Tennant, Elspeth Barker, Alice Thompson: Gothic Revisited', in Aileen Christianson and Alison Lumsden (eds), *Contemporary Scottish Women Writers* (Edinburgh: Edinburgh University Press, 2000), pp. 117–30.

Anderson, Carol and Christianson, Aileen (eds), *Scottish Women's Fiction, 1920s to 1960s: Journeys Into Being* (East Linton: Tuckwell Press, 2000).

Apter, T. E., *Fantasy Literature. An Approach to Reality* (London and Basingstoke: Macmillan, 1982).

Armitt, Lucie, *Where No Man Has Gone Before: Women and Science Fiction* (London and New York: Routledge, 1991).

Armitt, Lucie, *Theorising the Fantastic* (London: Arnold, 1996).

Armitt, Lucie, 'Space, Time and Female Genealogies: A Kristevan Reading of Feminist Science Fiction', in Sarah Sceats and Gail Cunningham (eds), *Image and Power: Women in Fiction in the Twentieth Century* (London: Longman, 1996), pp. 51–61.

Armitt, Lucie, *Contemporary Women's Fiction and the Fantastic* (Basingstoke: Macmillan, 2000).

Atwood, Margaret, *Negotiating with the Dead: A Writer on Writing* (Cambridge: Cambridge University Press, 2002).

Auerbach, Erich, *Mimesis. The Representation of Reality in Western Literature* [1946], trans. Willard R. Trask (Princeton: Princeton University Press, 1973).

Auerbach, Nina, *Our Vampires, Ourselves* (Chicago and London: University of Chicago Press, 1995).

Augé, Marc, *Non-Places: Introduction to an Anthropology of Supermodernity* [1992], trans. John Howe (London: Verso, 1995).

Barber, Paul, *Vampires, Burial and Death: Folklore and Reality* (New Haven and London: Yale University Press, 1988).

Barrie, J. M., *Peter Pan in Kensington Gardens and Peter Pan and Wendy*, ed. Peter Hollindale (Oxford: Oxford University Press, 2008).

Baudrillard, Jean, *Simulacra and Simulation* [1981], trans. Sheila Faria Glaser (Ann Arbor: University of Michigan Press, 2006).

Beauvoir, Simone de, *The Second Sex* [1949], trans. and ed. H. M. Parshley (Harmondsworth: Penguin, 1972).

Beauvoir, Simone de, 'Must we Burn Sade?', trans. Annette Michelson, in Marquis de Sade, *The 120 Days of Sodom and Other Writings*, comp. and trans. Austryn Wainhouse and Richard Seaver (London: Arrow Books, 1991), pp. 3–64.

Bell, Ian A. (ed.), *Peripheral Visions: Images of Nationhood in Contemporary British Fiction* (Cardiff: University of Cardiff Press, 1995).

Belsey, Catherine, *Desire: Love Stories in Western Culture* (Oxford: Blackwell, 1994).

Belsey, Catherine, 'Writing as a Feminist', *Signs* 25: 4 (Summer 2000), pp. 1157–60.

Bennett, Margaret, *Scottish Customs from the Cradle to the Grave* [1992] (Edinburgh: Polygon, 2004).

Berger, John, *Ways of Seeing* (London: Viking, 1972).

Berger, John, *Keeping a Rendezvous* [1991] (New York: Vintage International, 1992).

Bettelheim, Bruno, *The Uses of Enchantment: The Meaning and Importance of Fairytales* (London: Penguin, 1991).

Beville, Maria, *Gothic-Postmodernism: Voicing the Terrors of Postmodernity* (Amsterdam: Rodopi, 2009).

Bhabha, Homi K., *The Location of Culture* (London and New York: Routledge, 1994).

Botting, Fred (ed.), *The Gothic* (Cambridge: D. S. Brewer, 2001).

Botting, Fred, *Gothic* [1996] (London and New York: Routledge, 2004).

Botting, Fred, *Gothic Romanced: Consumption, Gender and Technology in Contemporary Fictions* (London and New York: Routledge, 2008).

Brackett, Virginia, *Classic Love and Romance Literature: An Encyclopaedia of Works, Characters, Authors and Themes* (Santa Barbara, CA: ABC-CLIO, 1999).

Bradford, Richard, *The Novel Now: Contemporary British Fiction* (Oxford: Blackwell, 2007).

Braidotti, Rosi, *Nomadic Subjects: Embodiment and Sexual Difference in Contemporary Feminist Theory* (New York: Columbia University Press, 1994).

Brewster, Scott, 'Madness, Mimicry and Scottish Gothic', *Gothic Studies* 7: 1 (2005), pp. 79–86.

Bromwich, Rachel and D. Simon Evans (eds), *Culhwuch and Olwen: An Edition and Study of the Oldest Arthurian Tale* (Cardiff: University of Wales Press, 1992).

Bronfen, Elisabeth, *Over Her Dead Body: Death, Femininity and the Aesthetic* (Manchester: Manchester University Press, 1992).

Brontë, Emily, *Wuthering Heights* [1847] (New York: Norton, 1990).

Brown, George Mackay, 'Andrina', in Douglas Dunn (ed.), *The Oxford Book of Scottish Short Stories* (Oxford: Oxford University Press, 1995), pp. 326–33.

Bruce, Susan, 'The Flying Island and Female Anatomy: Gynaecology and Power in *Gulliver's Travels*', *Genders* 2 (1988), pp. 60–76.

Bruford, A. J. and D. A. MacDonald (eds), *Scottish Traditional Tales* (Edinburgh: Polygon, 1994).

Brunel, Pierre (ed.), *A Companion to Literary Myths, Heroes and Archetypes* (London: Routledge, 1988).

Burger, Patrick R., *The Political Unconscious of the Fantasy Sub-genre of Romance* (Lewiston: Edwin Mellen Press, 2001).

Buse, Peter and Andrew Stott (eds), *Ghosts: Deconstruction, Psychoanalysis, History* (Basingstoke: Macmillan, 1999).

Butler, Judith, *Bodies That Matter: On the Discursive Limits of Sex* (New York: Routledge, 1993).

Butler, Judith, *Gender Trouble: Feminism and the Subversion of Identity* [1990] (New York and London: Routledge, 1999).

Butler, Judith and Joan W. Scott (eds), *Feminists Theorize the Political* (New York and London: Routledge, 1992).

Campbell, J. F. (ed.), *Popular Tales of the West Highlands*, 2 vols (London: Alexander Gardner, 1890).

Campbell, Joseph, *The Masks of God: Primitive Mythology* (Harmondsworth: Penguin, 1976).

Carroll, Lewis, *The Complete Illustrated Lewis Carroll* (Ware: Wordsworth Classics, 1997).

Carter, Angela, *The Sadeian Woman: An Exercise in Cultural History* [1979] (London: Virago, 1982).

Carter, Angela, *Collected Short Stories* (London: Vintage, 1996).

Castle, Terry, *The Apparitional Lesbian: Female Homosexuality and Modern Culture* (New York: Columbia University Press, 1993).

Castricano, Jodey, *Cryptomimesis: The Gothic and Jacques Derrida's Ghost Writing* (Montreal: McGill University Press, 2001).

Cavendish, Richard, *The Tarot* (London: Michael Joseph, 1975).

Chanady, Amaryll Beatrice, *Magical Realism and the Fantastic: Resolved versus Unresolved Antinomy* (London: Garland Publishing, 1985).

Child, F. J. (ed.), *English and Scottish Popular Ballads*, 5 vols (Boston and New York: Houghton, Mifflin and Company, 1882–9).

Christianson, Aileen, 'Imagined Corners to Debatable Land: Passable Boundaries', *Scottish Affairs* 17 (1996), pp. 120–34.

Christianson, Aileen and Alison Lumsden (eds), *Contemporary Scottish Women Writers* (Edinburgh: Edinburgh University Press, 2000).

Cixous, Hélène, 'Fiction and its Phantoms: A Reading of Freud's *Das Unheimliche* ('The Uncanny')', *New Literary History* 7 (1976), 525–48.

Cixous, Hélène, 'The Laugh of the Medusa', trans. Keith Cohen and Paula Cohen, *Signs* 1: 4 (Summer 1976), pp. 875–93.

Cixous, Hélène and Catherine Clément, *The Newly Born Woman* [1975] (London: I. B. Tauris, 1996).

Clute, John and John Grant, *The Encyclopaedia of Fantasy* (London: Orbit, 1997).

Coates, Paul, *The Double and The Other* (London: Macmillan, 1988).

Connor, Steven, *The English Novel in History: 1950–1995* (London: Routledge and Kegan Paul, 1996).

Connor, Steven, *Postmodernist Culture*, 2nd edn (Oxford: Blackwell, 1997).

Cornwell, Neil, *The Literary Fantastic* (London: Harvester Wheatsheaf, 1990).

Craig, Cairns, *The Modern Scottish Novel: Narrative and the National Imagination* (Edinburgh: Edinburgh University Press, 1999).

Creed, Barbara, *The Monstrous Feminine: Film, Feminism, Psychoanalysis* (London: Routledge, 1993).

Crownfield, David (ed.), *Body/Text in Julia Kristeva: Religion: Women and Psychoanalysis* (Albany: State University of New York Press, 1992).

Culler, Jonathan, *On Deconstruction: Theory and Criticism after Structuralism* (London: Routledge and Kegan Paul, 1983).

Cusk, Rachel, 'Shakespeare's Daughters', *The Guardian*, Review Section, 12 December 2009,. Available at: http://www.guardian.co.uk/books/2009/dec/12/rachel-cusk-women-writing-review/ (accessed 14 December 2009).

Deleuze, Gilles, *The Logic of Sense* [1969], trans. Mark Lester, ed. Constantin V. Boundas (London: Continuum, 2004).

Deleuze, Gilles and Féliz Guattari, *A Thousand Plateaus* [1980] (London: Continuum, 2004).

Derrida, Jacques, *Speech and Phenomena and Other Essays on Husserl's Theory of Signs*, trans. David B. Allison (Evanston: Northwestern University Press, 1973).

Derrida, Jacques, *Specters of Marx: The State of the Debt, the Work of the Mourning, and the New International* [1993], trans. Peggy Kamuf (New York: Routledge, 1994).

Devine, Tom and Paddy Logue (eds), *Being Scottish: Personal Reflections on Scottish Identity Today* (Edinburgh: Polygon, 2002).

Dobyns, Ann, *The Voices of Romance: Studies in Dialogue and Character* (Newark: University of Delaware Press, 1989).

Donald, Ann, 'Like for Like', *The List*, 11–24 July 1997, p. 74.

Duff, David (ed.), *Modern Genre Theory* (Harlow: Pearson Education, 2001).

Dugdale, John, 'Vampires, Blockbusters and the Occasional Gem', *The Guardian*, Review Section, 2 January 2010, pp. 14–15.

Dunn, Douglas (ed.), *The Oxford Book of Scottish Short Stories* (Oxford: Oxford University Press, 1995).

Dunnigan, Sarah M., 'A. L. Kennedy's Longer Fiction: Articulate Grace', in Aileen Christianson and Alison Lumsden (eds), *Contemporary Scottish Women Writers* (Edinburgh: Edinburgh University Press, 2000), pp. 144–55.

Eagleton, Mary 'Genre and Gender', in David Duff (ed.), *Modern Genre Theory* (Harlow: Pearson Education, 2001), pp. 250–62.

Eliot, T. S., *The Complete Poems and Plays of T. S. Eliot* (London: Faber and Faber, 1969).

Ellis, Elizabeth Ferguson, *The Contested Castle: Gothic Novels and the Subversion of Domestic Ideology* (Urbana and Chicago: University of Illinois Press, 1989).

Ellis, Havelock, *Sexual Inversion* [1897] (Basingstoke: Macmillan, 2007).

Ellis, Peter Berresford, *Dictionary of Celtic Mythology* (London: Constable, 1992).

Elphinstone, Margaret, 'Contemporary Feminist Fantasy in the Scottish Literary Tradition', in Caroline Gonda (ed.), *Tea and Leg-Irons: New Feminist Readings From Scotland* (London: Open Letters, 1992), pp. 45–59.

Elphinstone, Margaret, 'The Quest: Two Contemporary Adventures', in Christopher Whyte (ed.), *Gendering The Nation: Studies in Modern Scottish Literature* (Edinburgh: Edinburgh University Press, 1995), pp. 107–36.

Elphinstone, Margaret, 'Scottish Fantasy Today', *Ecloga* 1 (2000–1), pp. 15–25.

Elphinstone, Margaret, 'Waylaid by Islands', *The Bottle Imp* 2 (November 2007). Available at: http://www.arts.gla.ac.uk/ScotLit/ASLS/SWE/TBI/TBIIssue2/Waylaid.html (accessed 3 September 2009).

Felman, Shoshana, 'Women and Madness: The Critical Fallacy', *Diacritics* 5: 4 (Winter 1975), pp. 2–10.

Foucault, Michel, *Discipline and Punish: The Birth of the Prison*, trans. Alan Sheridan (Harmondsworth: Penguin, 1977).

Foucault, Michel, 'Of Other Spaces', trans. Jay Miskowiec, *Diacritics* 16: 1 (Spring 1986), pp. 22–7.

Fox, Christopher and Brenda Tooley (eds), *Walking Naboth's Vineyard: New Studies on Swift* (Notre Dame, IN: University of Notre Dame Press, 1995).

France, Louise, 'Life Stories', *The Observer*, 22 May 2005. Available at: http://www.guardian.co.uk/books/2005/may/22/fiction.bookerprize2005 (accessed 10 December 2009).

Frazer, J. G., *The Golden Bough* (London: Oxford University Press, 1994).

Freeman, Alan, 'A Bit of the Other: *Symposium*, Futility and Scotland', in Martin McQuillan (ed.), *Theorizing Muriel Spark: Gender, Race and Deconstruction* (Basingstoke: Macmillan, 2002), pp. 127–38.

French, Claire, *The Celtic Goddess: Great Queen or Demon Witch?* (Edinburgh: Floris Books, 2001).

Freud, Sigmund, *The Standard Edition of the Complete Psychological Works of Sigmund Freud*, 24 vols, trans. James Strachey (London: Hogarth Press, 1953–74).

Frye, Northrop, *Anatomy of Criticism: Four Essays* (Princeton: Princeton University Press, 1957).

Frye, Northrop, *The Secular Scripture: A Study of the Structure of Romance* (Cambridge, MA: Harvard University Press, 1976).

Gaborit, Lydia, Yveline Gusdon and Myriam Boutrolle-Caporal, 'Witches', in Pierre Brunel (ed.), *A Companion to Literary Myths, Heroes and Archetypes* (London: Routledge, 1988), pp. 1163–78.

Gantz, Timothy, *Early Greek Myth* (Baltimore and London: Johns Hopkins University Press, 1993).

Gardiner, Michael, *From Trocchi to Trainspotting: Scottish Critical Theory Since 1960* (Edinburgh: Edinburgh University Press, 2006).

Genette, Gérard, *Narrative Discourse*, trans Jane E. Lewin (Oxford: Blackwell, 1980).

Genette, Gérard, *Palimpsests* [1982], trans. Channa Newman and Claude Doubinsky (Lincoln: University of Nebraska Press, 1997).

Genette, Gérard, *Paratexts: Thresholds of Interpretation* [1987], trans. Jane E. Lewin (Cambridge: Cambridge University Press, 1997).

Germanà, Monica, 'Re-Working the Magic: A Parallel Study of Six Women Writers of the Late Twentieth Century', unpublished doctoral thesis (Glasgow: University of Glasgow, 2004).

Germanà, Monica, 'The Ghost and the Brownie: Scottish Influences on Emily Brontë', *Women's Writing*, Special Issue: *Revisiting the Brontës,* 14:1 (May 2007), pp. 91–116.

Germanà, Monica, 'Re-writing Female Monstrosity: Schizoid Misogyny in Alison Fell's *The Mistress of Lilliput* and Emma Tennant's *Two Women of London*', in Adalgisa Giorgio and Julia Waters (eds), *Women's Writing in Western Europe: Gender, Generation and Legacy* (Newcastle: Cambridge Scholars, 2007), pp. 102–17.

Germanà, Monica, 'Crossing Dream Boundaries: Decoding Nonsense and Fantastic Ambiguities in Naomi Mitchison's *Beyond this Limit*', in Pauline McPherson, Christopher Murray, Gordon Spark and Kevin Corstorphine (eds), *Sub-versions: Cultural Status, Genre and Critique* (Newcastle: Cambridge Scholars, 2008), pp. 135–48.

Gifford, Douglas, *James Hogg* (Edinburgh: Ramsay Head Press, 1976).

Gifford, Douglas, 'A New Diversity', *Books in Scotland* 26 (Winter 1987), p. 11.

Gifford, Douglas, 'Inventing Solace and Despair', *Books in Scotland* 55 (1995), pp. 6–11.

Gifford, Douglas, 'Imagining Scotlands: The Return to Mythology in Modern Scottish Fiction', in Susanne Hageman (ed.), *Studies in Scottish Fiction: 1945 to the Present* (Frankfurt am Main: Peter Lang, 1996), pp. 17–49.

Gifford, Douglas, 'Autumn Fiction: Clever Books and Sad People', *Books in Scotland* 59 (Autumn 1996), pp. 1–8.

Gifford, Douglas, 'Contemporary Fiction I: Tradition and Continuity', in Douglas Gifford and Dorothy McMillan (eds), *A History of Scottish Women's Writing* (Edinburgh: Edinburgh University Press, 1997), pp. 579–603.

Gifford, Douglas, 'Contemporary Fiction II: Seven Writers in Scotland', in Douglas Gifford and Dorothy McMillan (eds), *A History of Scottish Women's Writing* (Edinburgh: Edinburgh University Press, 1997), pp. 604–29.

Gifford, Douglas, 'Scottish Fiction and Millennial Uncertainty', *In Scotland* 1: 1 (Autumn 1999), pp. 23–39.

Gifford, Douglas and Dorothy McMillan (eds), *A History of Scottish Women's Writing* (Edinburgh: Edinburgh University Press, 1997).

Gilbert, Sandra M. and Susan Gubar, *The Madwoman in the Attic: The Woman Writer and the Nineteenth-Century Literary Imagination* (New Haven and New York: Yale University Press, 1979).

Giorgio, Adalgisa (ed.), *Writing Mothers and Daughters: Renegotiating the Mother in Western European Narratives by Women* (New York: Bergharn Books, 2002).

Giorgio, Adalgisa and Julia Waters (eds), *Women's Writing in Western Europe: Gender, Generation and Legacy* (Newcastle: Cambridge Scholars, 2007).

Glücklich, Ariel, *The End of Magic* (New York and Oxford: Oxford University Press, 1997).

Goodare, Julian, Lauren Martin, Joyce Miller and Louise Yeoman, *The Survey of Scottish Witchcraft* (Edinburgh: University of Edinburgh, 2003). Available at: http://www.shc.ed.ac.uk/Research/witches/index.html (accessed 13 January 2010).

Gonda, Caroline (ed.), *Tea and Leg Irons: New Feminist Readings From Scotland* (London: Open Letters, 1992).

Gordon, Avery F., *Ghostly Matters: Haunting and the Sociological Imagination* (Minneapolis and London: University of Minnesota Press, 1997).

Green, Andre, 'The Double and the Absent', in Alan Roland (ed.), *Psychoanalysis, Creativity and Literature: A French-American Inquiry* (New York: Columbia University Press, 1978), pp. 271–92.

Green, Miranda Jane, *Celtic Myths* (London: British Museum Press, 1993).

Greer, Germaine, *The Female Eunuch* [1970] (London: Flamingo, 1993).

Haffenden, John, *Novelists in Interview* (London: Methuen, 1985).

Haraway, Donna, *Simians, Cyborgs and Women: The Reinvention of Nature* (New York: Routledge, 1991).

Harris, J. Rendel, *Boanerges* (Cambridge: Cambridge University Press, 1913).

Hartland, E. Sidney, 'Twins', in James Hastings (ed.), *Encyclopaedia of*

Religion and Ethics, 26 vols (Edinburgh: T. and T. Clark, 1911–58), vol. 12, pp. 491–500.

Hastings, James (ed.), *Encyclopaedia of Religion and Ethics*, 26 vols (Edinburgh: T. and T. Clark, 1911–58).

Hawthorn, Jeremy, *Multiple Personality and the Disintegration of Literary Character* (New York: St Martin's Press, 1983).

Head, Dominic, *The Cambridge Introduction to Modern British Fiction, 1950–2000* (Cambridge: Cambridge University Press, 2002).

Hearn, Jonathan, *Claiming Scotland: National Identity and Liberal Culture* (Edinburgh: Polygon, 2000).

Heller, Dana A., *The Feminization of Quest-Romance: Radical Departures* (Austin: University of Texas Press, 1990).

Heller, Reinhold, 'Some Observations Concerning Grim Ladies, Dominating Women, and Frightened Men Around 1900', in *The Earthly Chimera and the Femme Fatale: Fear of Woman in Nineteenth-Century Art* (Chicago: University of Chicago, Congress Printing Company, 1981), pp. 7–13.

Henderson, Lizanne, 'The Survival of Witchcraft Prosecutions and Witch Belief in South-West Scotland', *Scottish Historical Review* LXXXV, 1: no. 219 (April 2006), pp. 52–74.

Henderson, Lizanne and Edward J. Cowan, *Scottish Fairy Belief: A History* (East Linton: Tuckwell Press, 2001).

Henley, John, 'The Power of Pink', *The Guardian*, 12 December 2009. Available at: http://www.guardian.co.uk/theguardian/2009/dec/12/pinkstinks-the-power-of-pink (accessed 14 December 2009).

Herdman, John, *The Double In Nineteenth-Century Fiction* (London: Macmillan, 1990).

Hogg, James, *The Private Memoirs and Confessions of a Justified Sinner* [1824] (Edinburgh: Canongate, 1994).

Hogg, James, *The Shepherd's Calendar* [1829], ed. Douglas S. Mack (Edinburgh: Edinburgh University Press, 1995).

Hogle, Jerrold (ed.), *The Cambridge Companion to Gothic Fiction* (Cambridge: Cambridge University Press, 2002).

Holland, Norman N. and Leona F. Sherman, 'Gothic Possibilities', *New Literary History: A Journal of Theory and Interpretation* 8: 2 (1977), pp. 279–94.

Homer, Sean, *Jacques Lacan* (New York: Routledge, 2005).

Hughes-Hallett, Lucy, 'Fiction: *The Accidental* by Ali Smith', *The Times*, 22 May 2005. Available at: http://entertainment.timesonline.co.uk/tol/arts_and_entertainment/books/article523700.ece (accessed 10 December 2009).

Hutcheon, Linda, *The Politics of Postmodernism* (London: Routledge, 1989).

Hutcheon, Linda, *A Poetics of Postmodernism: History, Theory, Fiction* (London: Routledge, 1990).

Hutton, Ronald, *The Pagan Religions of the Ancient British Isles* (Oxford: Blackwell, 1991).

Hynes, Joseph (ed.), *Critical Essays On Muriel Spark* (New York: J. K. Hall and Co., 1992).

Irigaray, Luce, *This Sex Which is Not One* [1977] (Ithaca: Cornell University Press, 1985).

Jackson, Rosemary, *Fantasy: The Literature of Subversion* (London: Routledge, 1981).

James, Edward and Farah Mendlesohn (eds), *The Cambridge Companion to Science Fiction* (Cambridge: Cambridge University Press, 2003).

Jencks, Charles, *The Architecture of the Jumping Universe* (London: Academy Editions, 1995).

Jones, Ernest, *On The Nightmare* (London: Hogarth Press, 1931).

Jones, Gwyn (ed.), *Eirik the Red and Other Icelandic Sagas* (Oxford: Oxford University Press, 1980).

Jones, Gwyn and Thomas Jones (eds and trans.), *The Mabinogion* (London: Everyman, 1994).

Jung, C. G., *The Collected Works of C.G. Jung*, 20 vols, ed. Herbert Read, Michael Fordham and Gerard Adler (London: Routledge and Kegan Paul, 1953–79).

Kenyon, Olga, *Women Writers Talk* (Oxford: Lennard Publishing, 1989).

Kaveney, Roz, 'Alice Thompson, Pharos', *Times Literary Supplement*, 2 August 2002, p. 20.

Kelly, Stuart, 'Wha's Like Us?', *The Guardian*, Review Section, 17 May 2008, p. 3.

Keppler, C. F., *The Literature of The Second Self* (Tucson: University of Arizona, 1972).

Kramer, Heinrich and James Sprenger, *Malleus Maleficarum* [1486], trans. Montague Summers [1928] (New York: Dover Publications, 1971).

Kristeva, Julia, *Desire in Language: A Semiotic approach to Literature and Art* [1980], ed. Leon S. Roudiez, trans. Thomas Gora, Alice Jardine and Leon S. Roudiez (Oxford: Basil Blackwell, 1980).

Kristeva, Julia, *Revolution in Poetic Language* [1974] trans. Leon S. Roudiez (New York: Columbia University Press, 1984).

Kristeva, Julia, *The Kristeva Reader*, ed. Toril Moi (Oxford: Blackwell, 1986).

Kristeva, Julia, *New Maladies of the Soul* (New York: Columbia University Press, 1995).

Kristeva, Julia, *Julia Kristeva Interviews*, ed. Ross Gubermann (New York: Columbia University Press, 1996).

Lacan, Jacques, *Écrits: A Selection*, trans. Alan Sheridan (London: Tavistock Publications, 1977).

Lacan, Jacques, *The Four Fundamental Concepts of Psychoanalysis*, trans. Alan Sheridan (London: Penguin, 1977).

Lacan, Jacques, *The Seminar of Jacques Lacan, Book VII: The Ethics of Psychoanalysis 1959–1960* [1986], ed. J. A. Miller, trans. D. Porter (London: Routledge, 1992).

Larner, Christina, *Enemies of God: The Witch Hunt in Scotland* [1981] (Edinburgh: John Donald Publisher, 2000).

Larner, Christina, C. H. Lee and H. V. MacLachlan, *A Sourcebook of Scottish Witchcraft* (Glasgow: University of Glasgow, 1977).

Lawrance, Robert, 'The Legend of Lianachan, or a story of "the Grey Hag"', *Celtic Monthly* XI (1902–3; July 1903), pp. 196–7 (p. 196).

Levack, Brian P., *The Witch-Hunt in Early-Modern Europe*, 2nd edn (London: Longman, 1995).

Lodge, David, *The Novelists at the Crossroads And Other Essays on Fiction and Criticism* (London: Routledge and Kegan Paul, 1971).

Luckhurst, Roger and Peter Marks (eds), *Literature and the Contemporary: Fictions and Theories of the Present* (Harlow: Longman, 1999).

Lyle, E. B., 'The Ballad of "Tam Lin" and Traditional Tales of Recovery from the Fairy Troop', *Studies in Scottish Literature* 6 (1968–9), pp. 175–85.

Lyle, Emily (ed.), *Scottish Ballads* (Edinburgh: Canongate, 1994).

McAfee, Noëlle, *Julia Kristeva* (New York and London: Routledge, 2004).

McDermott, Sinead, 'Kate Atkinson's Family Romance: Missing Mothers and Hidden Histories in *Behind the Scenes at the Museum*', *Critical Survey* 18: 2 (2006), pp. 67–78.

MacDiarmid, Hugh, 'The Plea for Synthetic Scots', *Scots Observer* 6: 310 (1932), p. 10.

MacDiarmid, Hugh, *Aesthetics in Scotland* (Edinburgh: Mainstream Publishing, 1984).

MacDonald, George, *Phantastes* [1858] (Grand Rapids: Eerdmans Publishing, 2000).

MacDonald, Stuart, *The Witches of Fife: Witch-Hunting in a Scottish Shire, 1560– 1710* (East Linton: Tuckwell Press, 2002).

MacDougall, Donald, 'Maccodrum's Seal Wife' [1968], in A. J. Bruford and D. A. MacDonald (eds), *Scottish Traditional Tales* (Edinburgh: Polygon, 1994), pp. 365–7.

McGillivray, Alan, 'Interview with Margaret Elphinstone', *Laverock* 1 (1995), pp. 29–38.

McHale, Brian, *Postmodernist Fiction* (London: Routledge, 1987).

Maclain, 'A Long Island Witch', *Celtic Magazine* X: CXVII (July 1885), pp. 433–4.

MacKay, John (ed. and trans.), *More West Highland Tales*, 2 vols (Edinburgh and London: Oliver and Boyd, 1940).

MacKenzie, Donald A., 'A Highland Goddess', *Celtic Review* VII (1911–12), pp. 336–45.

McMillan, Dorothy, 'Constructed out of Bewilderment: Stories of Scotland', in Ian A. Bell (ed.), *Peripheral Visions: Images of Nationhood in Contemporary British Fiction* (Cardiff: University of Wales Press, 1995), pp. 80–99.

McNeill, F. Marian, *The Silver Bough* [1957–68], 4 vols (Edinburgh: Canongate, 1989).

McQuillan, Martin (ed.), *Theorizing Muriel Spark: Gender, Race and Deconstruction* (Basingstoke: Macmillan, 2002).

Madsen, Deborah L. (ed.), *Post-Colonial Literatures: Expanding the Canon* (London: Pluto Press, 1999).

Manlove, Colin, *Modern Fantasy: Five Studies* (Cambridge: Cambridge University Press, 1975).

Manlove, Colin, *The Impulse of Fantasy Literature* (London: Macmillan, 1983).

Manlove, Colin, *Scottish Fantasy Literature: A Critical Survey* (Edinburgh: Canongate Academic, 1994).

March, Christie L., *Rewriting Scotland: Welsh, McLean, Warner, Banks, Galloway and Kennedy* (Manchester: Manchester University Press, 2002).

March, Jenny, *Cassell's Dictionary of Classical Mythology* (London: Cassell & Co., 1999).

Mason, Michael York, 'The Three Burials in Hogg's *Justified Sinner*', *Studies in Scottish Literature* 13 (1978), pp. 15–23.

Miles, Robert, *Gothic Writing 1750–1820: A Genealogy* [1993], 2nd edn (Manchester: Manchester University Press, 2002).

Miller, Hugh, *Scenes and Legends of the North of Scotland or the Traditional History of Cromarty* (Edinburgh: Nimmo, Hay and Mitchell, 1889).

Miller, Karl (ed.), *Memoirs of a Modern Scotland* (London: Faber and Faber, 1970).

Miller, Karl, *Doubles: Studies in Literary History* (Oxford: Oxford University Press, 1985).

Montgomery, Isobel, '*Pharos*', *The Guardian*, Review Section, 21 December 2002, p. 30.

Morrison, George, 'The Witch of Cnoc-Na-Moine', *Celtic Monthly* VI (May 1898), pp. 159–60.

Muir, Edwin, *Scott and Scotland: The Predicament of the Scottish Writer* (London: Routledge, 1936).

Muir, Edwin, *The Story and The Fable* (London: George G. Harrap, 1940).

Mulvey, Laura, 'Visual Pleasure and Narrative Cinema', *Screen* 16: 3 (Autumn 1975), pp. 6–18.

Murray, Ian (ed.), *The New Penguin Book of Scottish Short Stories* (Harmondsworth: Penguin, 1983).

Murray, Margaret, *The Witch-Cult in Western Europe* (Oxford: Clarendon Press, 1921).

Murray, Margaret, *The God of the Witches* (London: Sampson Low, Marston, 1933).

Murray, Margaret, *The Divine King of England* (London: Faber and Faber, 1954).

Mussel, Kay, *Fantasy and Reconciliation: Contemporary Formulas of Women's Romance Fiction* (Westport, CT: Greenwood Press, 1984).

Newall, Venetia (ed.), *The Witch Figure* (London: Routledge and Kegan Paul, 1973).

Niles, John, '"Tam Lin": Form and Meaning in a Traditional Ballad', *Modern Language Quarterly* 38 (1977), pp. 336–47.

Noyes, Ralph, 'The Other Side of Plato's Wall', in Peter Buse and Andrew Stott (eds), *Ghosts: Deconstruction, Psychoanalysis, History* (Basingstoke: Macmillan, 1999), pp. 244–62.

Nussbaum, Felicity A., 'Gulliver's Malice: Gender and the Satiric Stance', in Jonathan Swift, *Gulliver's Travels* [1726] (Boston: Bedford Books at St Martin's Press, 1995), pp. 318–34.

Okri, Ben, *An African Elegy* (London: Jonathan Cape, 1992).

Oliphant, Margaret, 'The Open Door', in Ian Murray (ed.), *The New Penguin Book of Scottish Short Stories* (Harmondsworth: Penguin, 1983), pp. 56–96.

Orbach, Susie, *Fat is a Feminist Issue* (London: Arrow, 1988).

Page, Norman, *Muriel Spark* (Basingstoke: Macmillan, 1990).

Palmer, Paulina, *Contemporary Lesbian Writing: Dreams, Desire, Difference* (Buckingham: Open University Press, 1993).

Palmer, Paulina, 'Demonic and Spectral Doubles in Ellen Galford's *The Dyke and the Dybbuck*, Sarah Waters' *Affinity* and Ali Smith's *Hotel World*', unpublished conference paper, presented at Lesbian Lives XI Conference, University College Dublin, Ireland, 13–15 February 2004.

Palmer, Paulina, 'Ellen Galford's "Ghost Writings": Dykes, Dybbucks, and Doppelgängers', in Claire M. Tylee (ed.), *'In the Open': Jewish Women Writers and British Culture* (Newark: University of Delaware Press, 2006), pp. 65–78.

Parker, Emma, *Kate Atkinson's* Behind the Scenes at the Museum (New York: Continuum, 2002).

Parkin-Gounelas, Ruth, 'Anachrony and Anatopia: Spectres of Marx, Derrida and Gothic Fiction', in Peter Buse and Andrew Stott (eds), *Ghosts:*

Deconstruction, Psychoanalysis, History (Basingstoke: Macmillan, 1999), pp. 127–43.

Patmore, Coventry, *Angel in The House* [1854] (London and Cambridge: Macmillan, 1863).

Philip, N. (ed.), *The Penguin Book of Scottish Folk-Tales* (London: Penguin, 1995).

Phillips, John, *How to Read Sade* (London: Granta, 2005).

Plato, *Symposium*, trans. and ed. Seth Bernardete and Allan Bloom (Chicago: University of Chicago Press, 2001).

Pope, Alexander, *The Works of Alexander Pope*, 10 vols, ed. Whitwell Elwin and William John Curthope (London: John Murray, 1871–89).

Punter, David, *The Literature of Terror* [1980], 2 vols (Harlow: Longman, 1996).

Punter, David, *Gothic Pathologies: The Text, the Body and the Law* (Basingstoke: Macmillan, 1998).

Punter, David, 'Heart Lands: Contemporary Scottish Gothic', *Gothic Studies* 1: 1 (1999), pp. 101–18.

Punter, David (ed.), *A Companion to the Gothic* (Oxford: Blackwell, 2001).

Radcliffe, Allan, 'Super Ali', *The List*, 15–29 March 2001, p. 18.

Ratcliffe, Sophie, 'Life in Sonnet Form', *Times Literary Supplement*, 20 May 2005, p. 19.

Ratmoko, David, *On Spectrality: Fantasies of Redemption in the Western Canon* (New York: Peter Lang, 2006).

Rank, Otto, *Beyond Psychology* (New York: Dover Publications, 1941).

Rank, Otto, *Psychology and The Soul* (New York: A. S. Barnes & Company, 1961).

Ratmoko, David, *On Spectrality: Fantasies of Redemption in the Western Canon* (New York: Peter Lang, 2006).

Rendel Harris, J., *Boanerges* (Cambridge: Cambridge University Press, 1912).

Riach, Alan, *First and Last Songs* (Edinburgh: Chapman, 1995).

Rice, Philip and Patricia Waugh (eds), *Modern Literary Theory* [1989], 4th edn (London: Arnold, 2001).

Rimmer, Louise, 'To the Lighthouse', *Scotland on Sunday*, Review, 9 June 2002, p. 4.

Robinson, David, 'Through a Glass Darkly', *The Scotsman*, 8 June 2002, p. 6.

Roland, Alan (ed.), *Psychoanalysis, Creativity and Literature: A French-American Inquiry* (New York: Columbia University Press, 1978).

Rose, Jacqueline, *The Case of Peter Pan or the Impossibility of Children's Fiction* (Basingstoke: Macmillan, 1994).

Ross, Anne, *Pagan Celtic Britain* (London: Routledge and Kegan Paul, 1967).

Ross, Anne, 'The Divine Hags of the Pagan Celts', in Venetia Newall (ed.), *The Witch Figure* (London: Routledge and Kegan Paul, 1973), pp. 139–64.

Ross, Anne, *The Folklore of the Highlands* (London: Batsford, 1976).

Royle, Nicholas, *Telepathy and Literature: Essays on the Reading Mind* (Oxford: Blackwell, 1991).

Royle, Nicholas, *The Uncanny* (Manchester: Manchester University Press, 2003).

Rushdie, Salman, *Imaginary Homelands* (London: Granta, 1991).

Sade, Marquis de, *Justine, Philosophy in the Bedroom and Other Writings*, comp. and trans. Austryn Wainhouse and Richard Seaver (New York: Grove Press, 1965).

Sade, Marquis de, *The 120 Days of Sodom and Other Writings*, comp. and trans. Austryn Wainhouse and Richard Seaver (London: Arrow Books, 1991).

Sage, Lorna, 'Seeing Things from the End' [1990], reprinted in Joseph Hynes (ed.), *Critical Essays on Muriel Spark* (New York: J. K. Hall, 1992), pp. 275–8.

Sage, Victor and Allan Smith Lloyd (eds), *Modern Gothic: A Reader* (Manchester: Manchester University Press, 1996).

Sceats, Sarah and Gail Cunningham (eds), *Image and Power: Women in Fiction in the Twentieth Century* (London: Longman, 1996).

Scott, Walter, *Minstrelsy of the Scottish Border*, 4 vols, ed. Thomas Finlayson Henderson (Edinburgh and London: William Blackwood and Sons, 1902).

Scott, Walter, *The Voyage of the Pharos* [1814] (Edinburgh: Scottish Library Association, 1998).

Scott, Walter, *Letters on Demonology and Witchcraft* [1829–47] (London: Folklore Society, 2001).

Sedgwick, Eve Kosofsky, *The Coherence of Gothic Conventions* (New York: Methuen, 1986).

Sellers, Susan, *Myth and Fairy Tale in Contemporary Women's Fiction* (Basingstoke: Palgrave, 2001).

Sims, Robin, 'Facing the Thing: The Green Man, Psychoanalysis and Kingsley Amis', *Critical Survey* 19: 2 (2007), pp. 82–100.

Smith, Ali, 'Wave your Hankie', *The Guardian*, 20 March 2004, Review Section, p. 27.

Smith, Frederick N. (ed.), *The Genres of* Gulliver's Travels (Cranbury, NJ, and London: Associated University Presses, 1990).

Smith, G. Gregory, *Scottish Literature: Character and Influence* (London: Macmillan, 1919).

Soyinka, Wole, *Myth, Literature and the African World* (Cambridge: Cambridge University Press, 1976).

Splendore, Paola, 'Bad Daughters and Unmotherly Mothers: The New Family Plot in the Contemporary English Novel', in Adalgisa Giorgio (ed.), *Writing Mothers and Daughters: Renegotiating the Mother in Western European Narratives by Women* (New York: Bergharn Books, 2002), pp. 185–214.

Spooner, Catherine, *Fashioning Gothic Bodies* (Manchester: Manchester University Press, 2004).

Spooner, Catherine, *Contemporary Gothic* (London: Reaktion, 2006).

Sproxton, Judy, *The Women of Muriel Spark* (London: Constable, 1992).

Stephens, Walter, *Demon Lovers: Witchcraft, Sex and the Crisis of Belief* (Chicago: University of Chicago Press, 2002).

Stevenson, Robert Louis, *Strange Case of Dr Jekyll and Mr Hyde* [1886], in *Dr Jekyll and Mr Hyde and Other Stories*, ed. Jenni Calder (Harmondsworth: Penguin, 1979).

Stringfellow, Frank, *The Meaning of Irony: A Psychoanalytic Investigation* (Albany: State University of New York Press, 1994).

Swift, Jonathan, *Gulliver's Travels* [1726], ed. Robert A. Greenberg (New York: Norton and Company, 1970).

Swinfen, Ann, *In Defence of Fantasy: A Study of the Genre in English and American Literature since 1945* (London: Routledge and Kegan Paul, 1984).

Tennant, Emma, 'Intrinsically Scottish', *Times Literary Supplement*, August 2001, p. 15.

Tew, Philip, *The Contemporary British Novel*, 2nd edn (London: Continuum, 2007).

'Thomas The Rhymer', in Emily Lyle (ed.), *Scottish Ballads* (Edinburgh: Canongate, 1994), pp. 132–4.

Thompson, David, *The People of the Sea: Celtic Tales of the Seal-Folk* (Edinburgh: Canongate, 2000).

Thompson, Stith, *The Folktale* (New York: Holt, Rinehart and Winston, 1946).

Thorpe, Adam, 'Love in the Mesolithic Era', *The Guardian*, Review Section, 25 July 2009, p. 8.

Todd, Richard, *Consuming Fictions: The Booker Prize and Fiction in Britain Today* (London: Bloomsbury, 1996).

Todorov, Tzvetan, *The Fantastic: A Structural Approach To A Literary Genre* [1970] (Ithaca: Cornell University Press, 1975).

Tolkien, J. R. R., *Tree and Leaf* [1964] (London: Harper Collins, 2001).

Turner, Victor W., *The Ritual Process: Structure and Anti-Structure* (London: Routledge and Kegan Paul, 1969).

Van Gennep, Arnold, *The Rites of Passage* (Chicago: Chicago University Press, 1960).

Wallace, Gavin and Randall Stevenson (eds), *The Scottish Novel Since The Seventies* (Edinburgh: Edinburgh University Press, 1993).

Wang, Robert, *An Introduction to the Golden Dawn Tarot* [1996] (Hammersmith: Thorsons, 2001).

Wareing, Laurence, 'Magical Mystery Tour Wanders into a Dream-Like Allegory', *The Glasgow Herald*, Weekend Living, 15 June 2002, p. 13.

Warhol, Robyn R. and Diane Price Herndl (eds), *Feminisms: An Anthology of Theory and Criticism* (New Brunswick: Rutgers University Press, 1993).

Warner, Marina, *Monuments and Maidens: The Allegory of the Female Form* [1985] (London: Vintage, 1996).

Warner, Marina, *Fantastic Metamorphoses, Other Worlds: Ways of Telling the Self* (Oxford: Oxford University Press, 2002).

Warwick, Alexandra, 'Feeling Gothicky?', *Gothic Studies* 9: 1 (2007), pp. 5–15.

Watson, E. C., 'Highland Mythology', *Celtic Review* V (July 1908), pp. 48–70 (p. 65).

Waugh, Patricia, *Feminine Fictions: Revisiting the Postmodern* (London and New York: Methuen, 1984).

Webster, Graham, *The British Celts and their Gods under Rome* (London: B. T. Batsford, 1986).

Weston, Jessie L., *The Legend of Sir Perceval: Studies upon its Origin, Development and Position in the Arthurian Cycle*, 2 vols (London: David Nutt, 1906–9).

Weston, Jessie L., *The Quest for the Holy Grail* (London: G. Bell and Sons, 1913).

Weston, Jessie L., *From Ritual To Romance* [1920] (Garden City: Doubleday and Company, 1957).

Whyte, Christopher (ed.), *Gendering the Nation: Studies in Modern Scottish Literature* (Edinburgh: Edinburgh University Press, 1995).

Whyte, Christopher, 'Postmodernism, Gender and Belief in Recent Scottish Fiction', *Scottish Literary Journal* 23: 1 (1996), pp. 50–64.

Whyte, Christopher, *Modern Scottish Poetry* (Edinburgh: Edinburgh University Press, 2004).

Widdowson, John, 'The Witch as a Frightening and Threatening Figure', in Venetia Newall (ed.), *The Witch Figure* (London: Routledge and Kegan Paul, 1973), pp. 200–20.

Wimberly, Charles, *Folklore in English and Scottish Ballads* (Chicago: University of Illinois Press, 1928).

Winterson, Jeanette, 'Introduction', in Jonathan Swift, *Gulliver's Travels* (Oxford: Oxford University Press, 1999), pp. v–xii.

Winterson, Jeanette, 'Author Author', *The Guardian*, Review Section, 19 December 2009, p. 15.

Wittgenstein, Ludwig, *Tractatus Logico-Philosophicus* [1921], trans. D. F. Pears and B. F. McGuinness (London: Routledge and Kegan Paul, 1977).

Wolfreys, Julian, *Victorian Hauntings: Spectrality, Gothic, the Uncanny and Literature* (Basingstoke: Palgrave, 2002).

Wollstonecraft, Mary, *A Vindication of the Rights of Woman* [1792] (London: Penguin, 1992).

Woolf, Virginia, *Selected Essays*, ed. David Bradshaw (Oxford: Oxford University Press, 2008).

Žižek, Slavoj, *The Žižek Reader*, ed. Elizabeth Wright and Edmond Wright (Oxford: Blackwell, 1999).

INDEX